U.S. Politics
and
Elections

AMERICAN GOVERNMENT AND HISTORY INFORMATION GUIDE SERIES

Series Editor: Harold Shill, Chief Circulation Librarian, Adjunct Assistant Professor of Political Science, West Virginia University, Morgantown

Also in this series:

AMERICAN EDUCATIONAL HISTORY—*Edited by Timothy Walsh and Michael W. Sedlak**

HISTORICAL SOURCES ON U.S. CULTURAL HISTORY—*Edited by Philip I. Mitterling**

HISTORICAL SOURCES ON U.S. RELIGION AND CHURCH HISTORY—*Edited by Garth Rosell**

IMMIGRATION AND ETHNICITY—*Edited by John D. Buenker and Nicholas C. Burckel*

PROGRESSIVISM—*Edited by John D. Buenker and Nicholas C. Burckel**

PUBLIC ADMINISTRATION—*Edited by John E. Rouse, Jr.**

PUBLIC POLICY—*Edited by William J. Murin, Gerald Michael Greenfield, and John D. Buenker**

SOCIAL HISTORY OF THE UNITED STATES—*Edited by Donald F. Tingley*

U.S. CONSTITUTION—*Edited by Earlean McCarrick**

U.S. FOREIGN RELATIONS—*Edited by Elmer Plischke**

U.S. WARS AND MILITARY HISTORY—*Edited by Jack Lane**

URBAN HISTORY AND URBANIZATION—*Edited by John D. Buenker, Gerald Michael Greenfield, and William J. Murin**

*in preparation

The above series is part of the

GALE INFORMATION GUIDE LIBRARY

The Library consists of a number of separate series of guides covering major areas in the social sciences, humanities, and current affairs.

General Editor: Paul Wasserman, Professor and former Dean, School of Library and Information Services, University of Maryland

Managing Editor: Denise Allard Adzigian, Gale Research Company

U.S. Politics
and
Elections

A GUIDE TO INFORMATION SOURCES

Volume 2 in the American Government and History Information Guide Series

David J. Maurer

Professor of History
Eastern Illinois University
Charleston

Gale Research Company
Book Tower, Detroit, Michigan 48226

Library of Congress Cataloging in Publication Data

Maurer, David J
   U.S. politics and elections.

   (American Government and history information guide
series ; v. 2)
   Includes indexes.
   1. United States—Politics and government—Bibliography. 2. Elections—United States—Bibliography.
3. Political parties—United States—Bibliography.
I. Title. II. Series.
Z1236.M39   [E183]   016.3209'73   78-13669
ISBN 0-8103-1367-7

VITA

David J. Maurer is currently professor of history at Eastern Illinois University at Charleston. He received his B.A. degree from Beloit College and his M.A. and Ph.D. degrees from Ohio State University.

Maurer's essays have appeared in John Braeman et al., THE NEW DEAL; Donald Tingley, ed., ESSAYS IN ILLINOIS HISTORY; Donald Tingley, ed., THE EMERGING UNIVERSITY; and Robert Sutton, ed., THE PRAIRIE STATE: A DOCUMENTARY HISTORY OF ILLINOIS. He is presently at work on the research for an essay on the "Black Legion: A Paramilitary-Fascist Organization in the Midwest During the 1930's."

CONTENTS

Contents

ACKNOWLEDGMENTS

During the preparation of this bibliography I have incurred numerous obligations. I should like specifically to thank Mrs. Leta Ridgeway, reference librarian at Eastern Illinois University; my daughter, Elizabeth June Maurer, for assistance in helping me collect entries; and my wife, Ellen Joyce Maurer, for assistance in typing and editing the manuscript.

PREFACE

The serious study of American political history began almost before the American colonies were securely established. The special conditions of colonial settlement in all of the colonies created interest in our political processes. From that time to this, change in our political theories and methods has remained constant. Americans have had an abiding interest in politics and this has resulted in a voluminous literature on the subject. For this reason, this volume includes only the most recent secondary works and reference materials, or older works that have not been superseded by more recent scholarship.

This bibliography is intended for the student of American political history. Although the titles selected for this volume are only a fraction of the reference materials and monographs available for the subject, those included are generally available in many libraries and, in some cases, are paperback editions. If the student uses the bibliographies furnished in most of the secondary works included in this volume, he will be able to track down other valuable sources on the topic he is pursuing.

Periodical literature on the subject is not included in this guide; serious researchers should consult periodical reference works like AMERICA: HISTORY AND LIFE, SOCIAL SCIENCES INDEX, HISTORICAL ABSTRACTS, and others listed in this guide under reference works (chapter XI, section 1). For additional material on their topics, researchers are advised to examine scholarly journals such as the AMERICAN HISTORICAL REVIEW, the JOURNAL OF AMERICAN HISTORY (formerly the MISSISSIPPI VALLEY HISTORICAL REVIEW), the JOURNAL OF SOUTHERN HISTORY, the JOURNAL OF NEGRO HISTORY, the JOURNAL OF POLITICS, and other historical journals, including the publications of state historical societies, and political science journals.

Some of the nation's publishers have provided the student of American political history with some excellent series dealing with American politics. Many of their monographs are included in the appropriate category in this volume. However, the user should check with librarians, BOOKS IN PRINT, and PAPER-BOUND BOOKS IN PRINT, to see if new titles are available. Of particular note are the series indicated below: The New American Nation Series published by Harper and Row, New York; The American Presidency Series published

by The Regents Press of Kansas, Lawrence; The Library of American Biography published by Little, Brown and Company, Boston; The Making of America Series
published by Hill and Wang, New York; and The Urban Life in America Series
published by Oxford University Press, New York.

Another source that the student should explore is the continually expanding series
of collections of public and private papers by major political figures from the
American Revolution to the present.

The user of this bibliography should note that some of the entries are designated
as paperback (pap.). This does not necessarily mean that only a paperback version is available, but means that the paperback edition is often readily at hand.
Many of the other entries are available in paperback, but libraries prefer to
acquire hardback editions. If the researcher is interested in a paperback copy,
he should check PAPERBOUND BOOKS IN PRINT to see if the work is in print.

Another instruction to the user of this bibliography is the admonition to note
that the categorization of the entries is not always exact. For example, biographies often cross the chronological division used, and a good many of the
entries listed in the General sections often contain information about specific
persons and/or events. The compiler has tried to place entries in the grouping
that seems to be appropriate to the needs of most researchers, but a good many
users may find excellent leads to their topics in other categories.

Chapter I
THE THIRTEEN COLONIES, 1607-1763

Section 1. GENERAL

Andrews, Charles M. THE COLONIAL PERIOD OF AMERICAN HISTORY. 4
vols. New Haven, Conn.: Yale University Press, 1934-38.

> Andrews's classic study examines the maze of imperial administra-
> tion and colonial politics. This is an excellent introduction, al-
> though a lengthy one, to the study of the period.

Bailyn, Bernard. THE ORIGINS OF AMERICAN POLITICS. New York: Alfred
A. Knopf, 1968. xi, 161 p.

> A laudable examination of American politics, but not American
> government, before the Revolution. Bailyn is interested in how
> political power was obtained, not how it was used or who had it.

Barck, Oscar T., and Lefler, Hugh T. COLONIAL AMERICA. 2d ed. New
York: Macmillan Co., 1968. ix, 753 p. Maps, illus.

> An excellent survey of the period from discovery to the Constitu-
> tion. The authors also include a detailed bibliography for each
> chapter.

Bishop, Cortlandt F. HISTORY OF ELECTIONS IN THE AMERICAN COLONIES.
1893. Reprint. New York: Burt Franklin, 1968. v, 297 p. Appendixes.

> This study provides useful information on the technical aspects of
> elections prior to the Revolution.

Craven, Wesley F. THE COLONIES IN TRANSITION, 1660-1713. New York:
Harper and Row, 1968. xii, 363 p. Illus.

> Craven incorporates more recent research on the political, social,
> and economic development of the Restoration colonies.

Greene, Evarts Boutell. THE PROVINCIAL GOVERNOR IN THE ENGLISH COLONIES OF NORTH AMERICA. 1898. Reprint. New York: Russell and Russell, 1966. x, 292 p. Appendixes.

A classic study of the subject.

Kammen, Michael. DEPUTYES AND LIBERTYES: THE ORIGINS OF REPRE-SENTATIVE GOVERNMENT IN COLONIAL AMERICA. New York: Alfred A. Knopf, 1969. xiv, 212, iv p.

An essay on the development of representative government in the colonies and a collection of documents.

_____. EMPIRE AND INTEREST: THE AMERICAN COLONIES AND THE POLITICS OF MERCANTILISM. Philadelphia: J.B. Lippincott Co., 1970. x, 186 p.

Somewhat revisionist, the author explores the political effect of elements in colonial society ignored by earlier historians. Their competition with traditional political powers created conditions that Parliament and government representatives found difficult to deal with.

Larabee, Leonard Woods. ROYAL GOVERNMENT IN AMERICA: A STUDY OF THE BRITISH COLONIAL SYSTEM BEFORE 1783. 1930. Reprint. New York: Frederick Ungar Publishing Co., 1958. xii, 491 p.

The author is concerned with the great contest between the assemblies and the crown over the royal prerogative, which is the central theme of the constitutional history of the colonies.

Leder, Lawrence H. LIBERTY AND AUTHORITY: EARLY AMERICAN POLITI-CAL IDEOLOGY, 1689-1763. Chicago: Quadrangle Books, 1968. 167 p.

An examination of the political theory that supported the demands made by the American colonists to Great Britain. The author believes that the American Revolution was an ideological revolution; hence it is important to understand the theories that shaped the thinking of the revolutionists.

Lovejoy, David S. THE GLORIOUS REVOLUTION IN AMERICA. New York: Harper and Row, 1972. xvi, 396 p.

An analysis of the effect of the Glorious Revolution of 1688 in England and its effects on the American colonies and how the colonists exploited that revolution for their own political ends.

McKinley, Albert E. THE SUFFRAGE FRANCHISE IN THE THIRTEEN ENGLISH COLONIES IN AMERICA. 1905. Reprint. New York: Burt Franklin, 1969. v, 518 p.

A voluminous work with specific references to sources.

Olson, Alison G., and Brown, Richard M., eds. ANGLO-AMERICAN POLITI-
CAL RELATIONS, 1675-1775. New Brunswick, N.J.: Rutgers University Press,
1970. x, 283 p.

> Traces the effect of party politics on colonial administration in a
> series of essays by some of the recent historians of the colonial
> period.

Rossiter, Clinton. SEEDTIME OF THE REPUBLIC: THE ORIGIN OF THE AMERI-
CAN TRADITION OF POLITICAL LIBERTY. New York: Harcourt, Brace and
Co., 1953. xiv, 558 p.

> Rossiter examines the institutions that shaped the political process
> in the colonies, several of the political leaders, and the colonial
> experience.

Ver Steeg, Clarence L. THE FORMATIVE YEARS, 1607-1763. New York:
Hill and Wang, 1964. vi, 342 p.

> Chapter 11, "The Structure of Provincial Politics," is particularly
> useful.

Zemsky, Robert. MERCHANTS, FARMERS, AND RIVER GODS: AN ESSAY ON
EIGHTEENTH CENTURY AMERICAN POLITICS. Boston: Gambit, 1971. xiii,
361 p. Illus.

> A solid treatment of the distribution of political power in Massa-
> chusetts.

Section 2. INDIVIDUAL COLONIES AND REGIONS

Abbot, William W. THE ROYAL GOVERNORS OF GEORGIA, 1754-1775.
Chapel Hill: University of North Carolina Press, for the Institute of Early
American History and Culture at Williamsburg, Va., 1959. vii, 192 p.

Adams, James T. REVOLUTIONARY NEW ENGLAND, 1691-1776. Boston:
Atlantic Monthly Press, 1923. xiv, 469 p. Illus.

> The author's anti-Puritan bias in places mars his otherwise brilliant
> perspective on the political changes and demands in New England.
> Over half of the work is concerned with the period before 1763.

Barnes, Viola F. THE DOMINION OF NEW ENGLAND: A STUDY IN BRITISH
COLONIAL POLICY. 1923. Reprint. New York: Frederick Ungar Publishing
Co., 1960. 303 p.

> This work remains an important analysis--the establishment of
> the short-lived Dominion and the far-reaching effects on
> subsequent relations between New England and the mother
> country.

Bonomi, Patricia U. A FACTIOUS PEOPLE: POLITICS AND SOCIETY IN
COLONIAL NEW YORK. New York: Columbia University Press, 1971. xiii,
342 p. Appendixes.

Carl Becker's study (HISTORY OF POLITICAL PARTIES IN THE
PROVINCE OF NEW YORK, 1909. See chapter II, section 1),
although valuable, suffers from major deficiencies. Bonomi has
reviewed the documents, recent geographies, doctoral dissertations,
and other studies, and has come up with a survey of the colony--
within which New York politics evolved.

Breen, Timothy H. THE CHARACTER OF THE GOOD RULER: A STUDY OF
PURITAN POLITICAL IDEAS IN NEW ENGLAND, 1630-1730. New Haven,
Conn.: Yale University Press, 1970. xx, 301 p.

A thorough study of the development of Puritan political thought.
The author examines the effect of imported ideas on the wilderness
experience during the first century of settlement.

Brown, Robert E[ldon]., and Brown, Katherine. VIRGINIA, 1705-1786: DEMOC-
RACY OR ARISTOCRACY? East Lansing: Michigan State University Press, 1964.
333 p.

The authors conclude that Virginia was far more democratic than
earlier scholars have led us to believe.

Carr, Lois G., and Jordan, David W. MARYLAND'S REVOLUTION OF
GOVERNMENT, 1689-1692. Ithaca, N.Y.: Cornell University Press, 1974.
xviii, 321 p. Tables, appendixes.

Craven, Wesley F. NEW JERSEY AND THE ENGLISH COLONIZATION OF
NORTH AMERICA. Princeton, N.J.: D. Van Nostrand Co., 1964. xiii,
114 p. Illus.

A very useful study of New Jersey's early and tangled political
history.

_____. THE SOUTHERN COLONIES IN THE SEVENTEENTH CENTURY, 1607-
1689. Baton Rouge: Louisiana State University Press, 1949. xv, 451 p. Illus.

A well-written examination of southern society with a fair amount
of information on the politics of the period.

Greene, Jack P. THE QUEST FOR POWER: THE LOWER HOUSES OF ASSEM-
BLY IN THE SOUTHERN ROYAL COLONIES, 1689-1776. Chapel Hill: Uni-
versity of North Carolina Press, for the Institute of Early American History and
Culture at Williamsburg, Va., 1963. xi, 528 p. Tables.

Traces the rising power of the lower houses of assembly in the
southern colonies.

Griffith, Lucille B. VIRGINIA HOUSE OF BURGESSES, 1750-1774. Northport, Ala.: Colonial Press, 1963. xi, 245 p.

An analysis of the structure of politics in the colony. The author is interested in how elections worked, who voted, and how the controversies of the period effected government. The rivalry between the burgesses and the governor and council created some of the best democratic institutions.

Haskins, George L. LAW AND AUTHORITY IN EARLY MASSACHUSETTS: A STUDY IN TRADITION AND DESIGN. 1960. Reprint. Hamden, Conn.: Archon Books, 1968. xvi, 298 p.

Describes political and social as well as legal institutions in a broader fashion than the title indicates.

Hoffman, Ronald. A SPIRIT OF DISSENSION: ECONOMICS, POLITICS, AND THE REVOLUTION IN MARYLAND. Baltimore: Johns Hopkins Press, 1973. xiv, 280 p. Map.

A good examination of the impact of economic conditions on politics of the colonial and revolutionary period.

Hutson, James H. PENNSYLVANIA POLITICS, 1746-1770: THE MOVEMENT FOR ROYAL GOVERNMENT AND ITS CONSEQUENCES. Princeton, N.J.: Princeton University Press, 1972. viii, 264 p.

An account of efforts to establish royal government in the colony. Limited discussion of internal politics and colonial views concerning George III and his governments.

Katz, Stanley N. NEWCASTLE'S NEW YORK: ANGLO-AMERICAN POLITICS, 1732-1753. Cambridge, Mass.: Harvard University Press, 1968. xi, 285 p. Appendixes.

Examines the importance of British "connections" in the competition for political power and wealth in the colony.

Lefler, Hugh T., and Newsome, Albert R. NORTH CAROLINA: THE HISTORY OF A SOUTHERN STATE. 3d ed. Chapel Hill: University of North Carolina Press, 1973. xiii, 807 p. Appendixes, illus.

The first twelve chapters deal with the colonial period. Chapters 10 and 11 are particularly interesting to those looking for the political history of the colony.

Lockridge, Kenneth A. A NEW ENGLAND TOWN: THE FIRST HUNDRED YEARS, DEDHAM, MASSACHUSETTS, 1636-1736. New York: W.W. Norton and Co., 1970. xv, 208 p. Pap.

The author revises the traditional views regarding the political role played by the New England town in our early history. He carefully examines what was and what was not "American" in Dedham.

McCain, Paul M. THE COUNTY COURT IN NORTH CAROLINA BEFORE 1750.
Durham, N.C.: Duke University Press, 1954. vi, 163 p. Pap.

Useful in unraveling the connection between political authority and
the courts.

Morison, Samuel E[liot]. BUILDERS OF THE BAY COLONY. 1930. Reprint.
Boston: Houghton Mifflin Co., 1976. xiv, 365 p. Illus.

An excellent introduction to the history of New England. Morison
goes beyond piety and politics to explain the remarkable institutions
and courageous actions of Americans in the wilderness.

Nash, Gary B. QUAKERS AND POLITICS: PENNSYLVANIA, 1681-1726.
Princeton, N.J.: Princeton University Press, 1968. xii, 362 p.

An in-depth examination of the political problems facing the Quakers with the Penn family, the English government, and later settlers
in the colony.

Pomfret, John E. THE NEW JERSEY PROPRIETORS AND THEIR LANDS. Princeton, N.J.: D. Van Nostrand Co., 1964. xvii, 135 p. Illus.

Porter, Albert O. COUNTY GOVERNMENT IN VIRGINIA: A LEGISLATIVE
HISTORY, 1607-1904. New York: Columbia University Press, 1947. Reprint.
New York: AMS Press, 1966. 356 p.

The first two chapters are useful for the political history of the
colony.

Sirmans, M. Eugene. COLONIAL SOUTH CAROLINA: A POLITICAL HISTORY,
1663-1763. Chapel Hill: University of North Carolina Press, for the Institute
of Early American History and Culture at Williamsburg, Va., 1966. xiii, 394 p.

The author's research challenges traditional views of the colony's
political history, particularly in the period before 1712 and after
1743. He is particularly impressed by the compromising ability of
those governors who solved problems rather than initiated them.

Sosin, Jack M. WHITEHALL AND THE WILDERNESS: THE MIDDLE WEST IN
BRITISH COLONIAL POLICY, 1760-1775. Lincoln: University of Nebraska
Press, 1961. xi, 307 p. Appendix, maps.

Recent scholarship has altered traditional views of the political
problems created by acquisition of the Mississippi Valley by Great
Britain. The author's research and that of others that he acknowl-
edges develops a new understanding of British colonial politics.

Sydnor, Charles S. GENTLEMEN FREEHOLDERS: POLITICAL PRACTICES IN
WASHINGTON'S VIRGINIA. Chapel Hill: University of North Carolina Press,

for the Institute of Early American History and Culture at Williamsburg, Va., 1952. ix, 180 p. Appendixes.

> Considered by most historians a definitive study of the sources and uses of political power in the late colonial period.

Thayer, Theodore. PENNSYLVANIA POLITICS AND THE GROWTH OF DEMOC-RACY, 1740-1776. Harrisburg: Pennsylvania Historical and Museum Commission, 1953. x, 234 p. Appendixes, illus.

> By examining the struggle for political power in the colony, the author explains how Pennsylvania came to have the most liberal and democratic constitution adopted in America during the revolutionary period.

Wall, Robert Emmet. MASSACHUSETTS BAY: THE CRUCIAL DECADE, 1640-1650. New Haven, Conn.: Yale University Press, 1972. x, 292 p. Appendix.

> A useful examination of the early politics of the colony. The author is particularly concerned with the rivalry between the magistrates and deputies.

Washburn, Wilcomb E. THE GOVERNOR AND THE REBEL: A HISTORY OF BACON'S REBELLION IN VIRGINIA. Chapel Hill: University of North Carolina Press, for the Institute of Early American History and Culture at Williamsburg, Va., 1957. xv, 248 p. Illus.

> The author is mainly concerned with Bacon's Rebellion and a defense of Governor Berkeley.

Wertenbaker, Thomas J. THE FOUNDING OF AMERICAN CIVILIZATION: THE MIDDLE COLONIES. New York: Charles Scribner's Sons, 1938. Reprint. New York: Cooper Square Publishers, 1963. xiii, 367 p. Illus.

> Although the author is concerned with cultural, economic, and social developments, his graceful and scholarly study makes the political events worth extracting.

_____. GIVE ME LIBERTY: THE STRUGGLE FOR SELF-GOVERNMENT IN VIRGINIA. Philadelphia: American Philosophical Society, 1958. ix, 275 p. Illus.

> The author tells the story of the weakening of the king's prerogative, the decline of the governor's authority, and the emergence of the political power of the assembly.

_____. THE OLD SOUTH: THE FOUNDING OF AMERICAN CIVILIZATION. New York: Charles Scribner's Sons, 1942. Reprint. New York: Cooper Square Publishers, 1963. xiv, 364 p. Illus.

One of the best introductions to the history of the southern colonies,
although the author purposely neglects political history.

_____. THE PURITAN OLIGARCHY: THE FOUNDING OF AMERICAN CIVI-
LIZATION. New York: Charles Scribner's Sons, 1947. ix, 359 p. Illus.

This volume examines the close relationship between the church and
government in Massachusetts. The author is careful to develop his
thesis that the Bible state was a unique and interesting experiment.

Section 3. BIOGRAPHY

Alden, John R. ROBERT DINWIDDIE: SERVANT OF THE CROWN. Williamsburg, Va.: Colonial Williamsburg Foundation, 1973. x, 126 p. Illus. Distributed by the University Press of Virginia, Charlottesville.

Dillon, Dorothy R. NEW YORK TRIUMVIRATE: A STUDY OF LEGAL AND
POLITICAL CAREERS OF WILLIAM LIVINGSTON, JOHN MORIN SCOTT, WIL-
LIAM SMITH, JR. New York: Columbia University Press, 1949. Reprint.
New York: AMS Press, 1968. 217 p.

This is a useful study of colonial New York politics before the
American Revolution.

Dunn, Mary Maples. WILLIAM PENN: POLITICS AND CONSCIENCE. Princeton, N.J.: Princeton University Press, 1967. x, 206 p.

The author seeks to explain the twists and turn of Penn's political
career in the complex period between 1660 and 1689. Penn's emphasis on liberty of conscience was often threatened by his own
needs and that of political leaders in England.

Dunn, Richard S. PURITANS AND YANKEES: THE WINTHROP DYNASTY OF
NEW ENGLAND, 1630-1717. Rev. ed. Princeton, N.J.: Princeton University
Press, 1971. xi, 379 p.

Hall, Michael G. EDWARD RANDOLPH AND THE AMERICAN COLONIES,
1676-1703. Chapel Hill: University of North Carolina Press, for the Institute
of Early American History and Culture at Williamsburg, Va., 1960. xi, 241 p.

The author examines the turmoil, political and economic, after the
establishment of the Navigation Acts. Randolph is seen as one of
the figures who shaped the English empire in America.

Hedges, J. B. THE BROWNS OF PROVIDENCE PLANTATIONS. 2 vols.
Cambridge, Mass.: Harvard University Press, 1952-68. Illus.

The author illustrates the connection between politics and economics
in his history of the Brown family. The first volume is concerned
with the colonial period.

Illick, Joseph E. WILLIAM PENN THE POLITICIAN: HIS RELATIONS WITH THE ENGLISH GOVERNMENT. Ithaca, N.Y.: Cornell University Press, 1965. x, 267 p.

The author is mainly concerned with Penn's relations with the English government.

Knollenberg, Bernhard. GEORGE WASHINGTON: THE VIRGINIA PERIOD, 1732-1775. Durham, N.C.: Duke University Press, 1964. x, 238 p. Appendixes.

An excellent source for information on Washington's early political career, including his opposition to British policies. There is also considerable description of colonial politics.

Leder, Lawrence H. ROBERT LIVINGSTON, 1654-1728, AND THE POLITICS OF COLONIAL NEW YORK. Chapel Hill: University of North Carolina Press, for the Institute of Early American History and Culture at Williamsburg, Va., 1961. xii, 306 p. Illus.

Leisler's rebellion, its causes and consequences, and the role of the Livingstons in New York's politics are effectively told.

Morgan, Edmund S. PURITAN DILEMMA: THE STORY OF JOHN WINTHROP. Boston: Little, Brown and Co., 1958. xii, 224 p.

The story of Winthrop is also the story of politics that forced the Puritans from England and the story of the politics of the new colony in Massachusetts.

Murdock, Kenneth Ballard. INCREASE MATHER, THE FOREMOST AMERICAN PURITAN. 1953. Reprint. New York: Russell and Russell, 1966. xv, 442 p. Illus., appendixes.

Peare, Catherine O. WILLIAM PENN: A BIOGRAPHY. 1957. Reprint. Ann Arbor: University of Michigan Press, 1966. 448 p.

Most authorities agree that Penn lacks a first-rate scholarly biography but this volume, aimed at the nonprofessional, is worthwhile and does explore some of the Pennsylvania founder's major political problems.

Wertenbaker, Thomas J. TORCHBEARER OF REVOLUTION: THE STORY OF BACON'S REBELLION AND ITS LEADER. Princeton, N.J.: Princeton University Press, 1940. vi, 237 p.

An excellent account of politics in colonial Virginia although the author glorifies Bacon more than some other historians do.

Wildes, Harry E. WILLIAM PENN. New York: Macmillan Co., 1974. ix, 469 p. Appendixes.

A well-written biography based on Penn's correspondence, recent studies of the colony, and observations on some of Penn's contemporaries.

Winslow, Ola E. MASTER ROGER WILLIAMS: A BIOGRAPHY. 1957. Reprint. New York: Octagon Books, 1973. xi, 328 p. Illus.

The author includes a good description of the political events that surrounded the life of Williams and early Rhode Island.

Chapter II

THE AMERICAN REVOLUTION, 1763-83

Section 1. BEFORE THE REVOLUTION

Abbott, Wilbur C. NEW YORK IN THE AMERICAN REVOLUTION. 1929.
Reprint. New York: Charles Scribner's Sons, 1973. xiii, 302 p. Illus.

> New York was often at the center of the conflict with the British.
> The first five chapters deal with the period between 1763 and 1775.

Adams, R. G. POLITICAL IDEAS OF THE AMERICAN REVOLUTION: BRITAN-
NIC-AMERICAN CONTRIBUTIONS TO THE PROBLEM OF IMPERIAL ORGANI-
ZATION, 1765-1775. New York: Facsimile Library, 1939. 207 p.

> Tells the story of how the colonies struggled to become self-
> governing institutions.

Ammerman, David. IN THE COMMON CAUSE: AMERICAN RESPONSE TO
THE COERCIVE ACTS OF 1774. Charlottesville: University Press of Virginia,
1974. xii, 170 p.

> The author analyzes the American response to the Coercive Acts.

Bailyn, Bernard. THE IDEOLOGICAL ORIGINS OF THE AMERICAN REVOLU-
TION. Cambridge, Mass.: Belknap Press of Harvard University Press, 1967.
xiii, 335 p.

> A strong affirmation of the thesis that the American Revolution was
> a political rather than a social or economic event.

Becker, Carl. THE HISTORY OF POLITICAL PARTIES IN THE PROVINCE OF
NEW YORK, 1760-1766. 1909. Reprint. Madison: University of Wisconsin
Press, 1960. v, 319 p.

> Becker argues that in New York the Revolution involved not only
> a quarrel with the British about home rule but also a quarrel over
> "who should rule at home."

Boyd, Julian. ANGLO-AMERICAN UNION: JOSEPH GALLOWAY'S PLANS
TO PRESERVE THE BRITISH EMPIRE, 1774-1783. Philadelphia: University of
Pennsylvania Press, 1941. x, 185 p. Appendixes.

> Boyd argues that the conservatives failed to appreciate that human
> rights were as important to many of the colonists as property rights.
> As a consequence, any plan to maintain union would founder if
> freedom were not explicitly protected.

Brown, Richard D. REVOLUTIONARY POLITICS IN MASSACHUSETTS: THE
BOSTON COMMITTEE OF CORRESPONDENCE AND THE TOWNS, 1772-1774.
Cambridge, Mass.: Harvard University Press, 1970. xiv, 282 p. Illus.

> An important analysis of the connection of the local political
> leaders and the better-known leaders in Boston and in other colonies.

Brown, Robert Eldon. MIDDLE-CLASS DEMOCRACY AND THE REVOLUTION
IN MASSACHUSETTS, 1691-1780. Ithaca, N.Y.: Cornell University Press for
the American Historical Association, 1955. ix, 458 p.

> Brown's classic examines the relationship between economic and
> political power in Massachusetts.

Daniell, Jere R. EXPERIMENT IN REPUBLICANISM: NEW HAMPSHIRE POLI-
TICS AND THE AMERICAN REVOLUTION, 1741-1794. Cambridge, Mass.:
Harvard University Press, 1970. xiv, 261 p. Illus.

Dickerson, Oliver M. THE NAVIGATION ACTS AND THE AMERICAN REV-
OLUTION. Philadelphia: University of Pennsylvania Press, 1951. Reprint.
New York: Octagon Books, 1974. xv, 344 p. Tables.

> The author argues that the Navigation Acts were not really an im-
> portant factor in creating the Revolution.

Donoughue, Bernard. BRITISH POLITICS AND THE AMERICAN REVOLUTION:
THE PATH TO WAR, 1773-75. New York: St. Martin's Press, 1965. x,
323 p.

> Examines the failure of the British government to acknowledge the
> maturation of the colonies, and the effect of the Peace of Paris
> in 1763.

Egerton, Hugh E. THE CAUSES AND CHARACTER OF THE AMERICAN REVO-
LUTION. London: Oxford University Press, 1923. vi, 207 p.

> A traditional survey of the causes of the Revolution, somewhat
> superseded by more recent studies.

Ernst, Joseph A. MONEY AND POLITICS IN AMERICA, 1755-1775: A STUDY
IN THE CURRENCY ACT OF 1764 AND THE POLITICAL ECONOMY OF REV-

OLUTION. Chapel Hill: University of North Carolina Press, for the Institute of Early American History and Culture at Williamsburg, Va., 1973. xix, 403 p. Illus.

Explains the political effects of the Currency Act of 1764 in particular and British fiscal policy in general.

Gipson, Lawrence H. THE COMING OF THE REVOLUTION, 1763-1775. New York: Harper and Row, 1954. xiii, 287 p. Illus.

The author argues that the British economic demands on the colonists were just, but the colonies were correct in their opposition to the infringement of their self-government. He also notes that the king failed to provide the necessary leadership to hold the colonies.

Hooker, Richard J., ed. THE CAROLINA BACKCOUNTRY ON THE EVE OF THE REVOLUTION: THE JOURNAL AND OTHER WRITINGS OF CHARLES WOODMASON, ANGLICAN ITINERANT. Chapel Hill: University of North Carolina Press, for the Institute of Early American History and Culture at Williamsburg, Va., 1953. xxxix, 305 p.

Although the bulk of this volume is from Woodmason's journal, the commentary by the editor is useful in unraveling the political divisions in North Carolina prior to the Revolution.

Jensen, Merrill. THE FOUNDING OF A NATION: A HISTORY OF THE AMERICAN REVOLUTION, 1763-1776. New York: Oxford University Press, 1968. xiii, 735 p.

A classic political history that focuses on the action of men in the political arena on both sides of the Atlantic, and on those American leaders on both sides of the question of independence.

Kammen, Michael. A ROPE OF SAND: THE COLONIAL AGENTS, BRITISH POLITICS AND THE AMERICAN REVOLUTION. Ithaca, N.Y.: Cornell University Press, 1968. xviii, 349 p. Illus.

Knollenberg, Bernhard. ORIGIN OF THE AMERICAN REVOLUTION, 1759-1766. Rev. ed. New York: Free Press, 1960. 350 p.

American and British politics are analyzed. Knollenberg examines the British political, trade, and religious activities that created (in his view) the revolutionary situation.

Labaree, Benjamin W. THE BOSTON TEA PARTY. New York: Oxford University Press, 1964. viii, 347 p.

Shows how the tensions surrounding the event created the revolutionary crisis.

Lovejoy, David S. RHODE ISLAND POLITICS AND THE AMERICAN REVO-
LUTION, 1760-1776. Providence, R.I.: Brown University Press, 1958. 256 p.

Traces the political conflicts and illustrates how almost all factions
were united against the English.

Maier, Pauline. FROM RESISTANCE TO REVOLUTION: COLONIAL RADI-
CALS AND THE DEVELOPMENT OF AMERICAN OPPOSITION TO BRITAIN,
1765-1776. New York: Alfred A. Knopf, 1972. xviii, 318, xxvi p. Appendix.

A well-written interpretation of the radical position in the colonies.
The author is interested in the question, "When and Why did the
colonists reshape their views of the Mother Country?"

Martin, James Kirby. MEN IN REBELLION: HIGHER GOVERNMENTAL
LEADERS AND THE COMING OF THE AMERICAN REVOLUTION. New Brunswick, N.J.: Rutgers University Press, 1973. xiii, 263 p. Appendixes, tables.

A significant study of the provincial elite. Indicates that the Revolution was in part a struggle within the ruling class for political
power.

Miller, John C. ORIGINS OF THE AMERICAN REVOLUTION. Boston: Little,
Brown and Co., 1943. xiv, 519 p.

A comprehensive treatment of the variety of causes that raised the
hostility of the colonists to the point of revolution.

Morgan, Edmund S., and Morgan, Helen M. THE STAMP ACT CRISIS: PRO-
LOGUE TO REVOLUTION. Chapel Hill: University of North Carolina Press,
for the Institute of Early American History and Culture at Williamsburg, Va.,
1953. x, 310 p.

Pares, Richard. KING GEORGE III AND THE POLITICIANS. London: Oxford University Press, 1954. 214 p.

A very important book for the student of the causes of the American Revolution. Pares pulls recent scholarship together in order
to explain the political conditions in England which created tension between the colonies and the mother country.

Pole, J. R. POLITICAL REPRESENTATION IN ENGLAND AND THE ORIGINS
OF THE AMERICAN REPUBLIC. New York: St. Martin's Press, 1966. xvii,
606 p. Appendixes.

Examines the rise of representative government in America. Particularly effective in the analysis of English institutions and their
relationship to the colonial experience.

Schlesinger, Arthur Meier. THE COLONIAL MERCHANTS AND THE AMERICAN REVOLUTION, 1763-1776. New York: Facsimile Library, 1939. 647 p. Appendix. Distributed by Barnes and Noble, New York.

> The thesis is that the merchant class initially were the prime movers in the quarrel with England but they became wary as their own position was threatened by the growing demands of other classes in the colonies.

Sosin, Jack M. AGENTS AND MERCHANTS: BRITISH COLONIAL POLICY AND THE ORIGINS OF THE AMERICAN REVOLUTION, 1763-1775. Lincoln: University of Nebraska Press, 1965. xvi, 267 p. Illus.

> Evaluates the role of colonial agents and British merchants in imperial administration. Factionalism in Parliament and in the provincial assemblies often hindered a resolution of political problems.

Ubbelohde, Carl. THE VICE-ADMIRALTY COURTS AND THE AMERICAN REVOLUTION. Chapel Hill: University of North Carolina Press, for the Institute of Early American History and Culture at Williamsburg, Va., 1960. 242 p.

> The author argues that the courts themselves were not particularly unpopular, but the laws they enforced created considerable political turmoil.

Walsh, Richard. CHARLESTON'S SONS OF LIBERTY: A STUDY OF THE ARTISANS, 1763-1789. Columbia: University of South Carolina Press, 1959. xii, 166 p. Illus.

Zeichner, Oscar. CONNECTICUT'S YEARS OF CONTROVERSY, 1750-1776. Chapel Hill: University of North Carolina Press, for the Institute of Early American History and Culture at Williamsburg, Va., 1949. xiv, 404 p. Illus.

> Explores the internal political divisions in the colony before independence. Especially valuable because the history of the origins of the Revolution has usually been written in terms of the experiences of the larger colonies.

Section 2. DURING AND AFTER THE REVOLUTION

Aptheker, Herbert. THE AMERICAN REVOLUTION, 1763-1783: A HISTORY OF THE AMERICAN PEOPLE, AN INTERPRETATION. New York: International Publishers, 1960. 304 p.

> A Marxist interpretation by a respected scholar.

Bakeless, John E. TURNCOATS, TRAITORS AND HEROES. Philadelphia: J. B. Lippincott Co., 1959. 406 p.

> Focuses on the American Revolution.

Benton, William A. WHIG-LOYALISM: AN ASPECT OF POLITICAL IDEOLOGY IN THE AMERICAN REVOLUTION. Rutherford, N.J.: Fairleigh Dickinson University Press, 1969. 231 p.

> Whig-Loyalist refers to those colonists that were classed as patriots prior to the American Revolution or just after it began and subsequently reestablished their loyalty to the crown. The author seeks to determine why they switched their allegiance.

Brunhouse, Robert L. THE COUNTER-REVOLUTION IN PENNSYLVANIA, 1776-1790. Harrisburg: Pennsylvania Historical Commission, 1942. Reprint. New York: Octagon Books, 1971. viii, 368 p. Appendixes.

> A survey of the political changes that took place in Pennsylvania. The author argues that the conservatives played a larger role than generally acknowledged.

Burnett, Edmund C. THE CONTINENTAL CONGRESS. New York: Macmillan Co., 1941. Reprint. New York: W.W. Norton and Co., 1964. xii, 757 p. Pap.

> The author begins the narrative in 1774 and ends it with the sitting of the U.S. Congress in 1789. Burnett believes that the history of the Congress cannot be divided between the Continental Congress and the Congress of Confederation.

Calhoon, Robert M. THE LOYALISTS IN REVOLUTIONARY AMERICA, 1760-1781. New York: Harcourt Brace Jovanovich, 1965. xviii, 580 p.

> A comprehensive account of the background and activities of the Loyalists.

Coleman, Kenneth. THE AMERICAN REVOLUTION IN GEORGIA, 1763-1789. Athens: University of Georgia Press, 1958. viii, 352 p.

> An interesting perspective on the causes of the Revolution from the vantage point of the youngest and weakest of the southern colonies.

DeMond, Robert O. THE LOYALISTS IN NORTH CAROLINA DURING THE REVOLUTION. Durham, N.C.: Duke University Press, 1940. Reprint. Hamden, Conn.: Archon Books, 1964. viii, 286 p. Appendixes.

> North Carolina had a sizable Loyalist population. The story of how they failed to overcome the patriots is told in this volume.

Douglass, Elisha P. REBELS AND DEMOCRATS. THE STRUGGLE FOR EQUAL POLITICAL RIGHTS AND MAJORITY RULE DURING THE REVOLUTION. Chapel Hill: University of North Carolina Press, 1955. xiv, 368 p.

> According to the author, farmers and mechanics saw the Revolution as not only a break with England but as an opportunity to obtain greater political power for themselves and greater economic opportunity for their children.

Ferguson, Elmer J. THE POWER OF THE PURSE: A HISTORY OF AMERICAN PUBLIC FINANCE, 1776-1790. Chapel Hill: University of North Carolina Press, for the Institute of Early American History and Culture at Williamsburg, Va., 1961. viii, 358 p. Tables.

A useful examination of the connection between economics and politics. This volume is particularly good on the problem of financing the Revolution.

Granger, Bruce I. POLITICAL SATIRE IN THE AMERICAN REVOLUTION, 1763-1783. Ithaca, N.Y.: Cornell University Press, 1960. xi, 314 p.

Hancock, Harold B. THE DELAWARE LOYALISTS. Wilmington: Historical Society of Delaware, 1940. Reprint. Boston: Gregg Press, 1972. x, 76 p.

Henderson, Herbert James. PARTY POLITICS IN THE CONTINENTAL CONGRESS. New York: McGraw-Hill Book Co., 1974. xvii, 475 p.

A computer analysis of voting patterns in the Continental Congress demonstrates the existence of legislative parties on a national level.

McDonald, Forrest. THE FORMATION OF THE AMERICAN REPUBLIC, 1776-1790. Baltimore: Penguin Books, 1965. xv, 326 p. Pap.

A well-written account that traces events and reveals the motives of those involved with founding the nation. The sweep is broad so it is useful to a discussion of the Philadelphia Convention.

Main, Jackson Turner. THE SOVEREIGN STATES, 1775-1783. New York: Franklin Watts, 1973. vii, 502 p.

An in-depth study of American states during the Revolution.

_____. THE UPPER HOUSE IN REVOLUTIONARY AMERICA, 1763-1788. Madison: University of Wisconsin Press, 1967. xii, 311 p.

The author develops the thesis that the Revolution had a democratizing effect on this legislative branch in most colonial governments.

Miller, John D. TRIUMPH OF FREEDOM, 1775-1783. Boston: Little, Brown and Co., 1948. xviii, 718 p.

The author explores the politics of the American Revolution in an even-handed way.

Montross, Lynn. THE RELUCTANT REBELS: THE STORY OF THE CONTINENTAL CONGRESS, 1774-1789. New York: Harper and Brothers, 1950. viii, 467 p. Illus.

A well-written account of the issues and personalities that shaped the country from independence to the completion of the Constitution.

Nelson, William H. THE AMERICAN TORY. London: Oxford University Press, 1961. vi, 194 p.

> Briefly relates the political failure of the Loyalists.

Nevins, Allan. THE AMERICAN STATES DURING AND AFTER THE REVOLUTION, 1775-1789. New York: Macmillan Co., 1924. xviii, 728 p.

Patterson, Stephen E. POLITICAL PARTIES IN REVOLUTIONARY MASSACHUSETTS. Madison: University of Wisconsin Press, 1973. ix, 299 p. Appendixes.

> Examines the internal political conflicts in the colony that created tensions within the political leadership.

Robson, Eric. THE AMERICAN REVOLUTION, IN ITS POLITICAL AND MILITARY ASPECTS, 1763-1783. New York: W.W. Norton and Co., 1966. vi, 250 p.

Rossman, Kenneth R. THOMAS MIFFLIN AND THE POLITICS OF THE AMERICAN REVOLUTION. Chapel Hill: University of North Carolina Press, 1952. xii, 344 p. Illus.

> Although Mifflin was a secondary figure, the politics of the American Revolution are further told in this biography.

Taylor, R. J. WESTERN MASSACHUSETTS IN THE REVOLUTION. Providence, R.I.: Brown University Press, 1954. viii, 227 p.

> Explores the nature of internal class conflict in the colony before the Revolution.

Van Tyne, Claude H. THE LOYALISTS IN THE AMERICAN REVOLUTION. New York: Macmillan Co., 1902. Reprint. Gloucester, Mass.: Peter Smith, 1959. xii, 360 p. Appendixes.

> A scholarly examination of the role played by the Tories. The author concludes that they were articulate, often reasonable, and much maligned.

Wright, Esmond. FABRIC OF FREEDOM, 1763-1800. New York: Hill and Wang, 1961. xiii, 298 p.

> A useful survey of the politics of the period.

Young, Alfred F. THE DEMOCRATIC REPUBLICANS OF NEW YORK: THE ORIGINS, 1763-1797. Chapel Hill: University of North Carolina Press, for the Institute of Early American History and Culture at Williamsburg, Va., 1967. xv, 636 p. Tables, appendix.

Section 3. BIOGRAPHY

Aldridge, Alfred O. MAN OF REASON: THE LIFE OF THOMAS PAINE. Philadelphia: J.B. Lippincott Co., 1959. 348 p. Illus.

> Considered to be one of the most balanced biographies of this controversial political figure who was both an idealist and agitator.

Allan, Herbert S. JOHN HANCOCK: PATRIOT IN PURPLE. New York: Macmillan Co., 1949. xvi, 422 p. Illus.

> A useful biography of a major political figure.

Bailyn, Bernard. THE ORDEAL OF THOMAS HUTCHINSON. Cambridge, Mass.: Harvard University Press, 1974. xx, 423 p. Illus.

> An excellent biography of one of the most prominent Tories in the colonies. Bailyn's thesis is that the success of the Revolution cannot be fully understood unless the student comprehends what the issues were to the losing side.

Beeman, Richard R. PATRICK HENRY: A BIOGRAPHY. New York: McGraw-Hill Book Co., 1974. xvi, 229 p. Illus.

> Richard Beeman concentrates on Henry's public life, particularly during the revolutionary era.

Berkin, Carol. JONATHAN SEWALL: ODYSSEY OF AN AMERICAN LOYALIST. New York: Columbia University Press, 1974. xi, 200 p.

> A good brief examination of one of the prominent Loyalists and of Loyalist politics.

Bowen, Catherine D. JOHN ADAMS AND THE AMERICAN REVOLUTION. Boston: Little, Brown and Co., 1950. xvii, 699 p. Illus.

> One of the best one-volume biographies of the second president.

Cary, John. JOSEPH WARREN: PHYSICIAN, POLITICIAN, PATRIOT. Urbana: University of Illinois Press, 1961. ix, 260 p.

> According to the author, Joseph Warren ranks with Samuel Adams as one of the most important leaders in the Massachusetts revolutionary movement.

Coleman, John M. THOMAS MCKEAN: FORGOTTEN LEADER OF THE REVOLUTION. Rockaway, N.J.: American Faculty Press, 1975. xi, 332 p.

> An important part of this biography is the author's analysis of Pennsylvania politics in the pre-Declaration of Independence period.

Conner, Paul W. POOR RICHARD'S POLITICKS: BENJAMIN FRANKLIN AND HIS NEW AMERICAN ORDER. New York: Oxford University Press, 1965. xiv, 285 p.

The author constructs an important reevaluation of Franklin's place in American political history.

Crane, Verner W. BENJAMIN FRANKLIN AND A RISING PEOPLE. Boston: Little, Brown and Co., 1954. x, 219 p.

A brief but well-written account of Franklin's political role in America's history.

Dangerfield, George. CHANCELLOR ROBERT R. LIVINGSTON OF NEW YORK, 1746-1813. New York: Harcourt, Brace and Co., 1960. viii, 532 p.

Explains why Livingston, a man of great talent, had an aversion to popular politics which made him politically unpopular.

Freeman, Douglas Southall. GEORGE WASHINGTON, A BIOGRAPHY. 7 vols. New York: Charles Scribner's Sons, 1948-57. Illus.

This multivolume study covers Washington's entire life. A good source for the political connection between Washington and the colony of Virginia, the independent states, and the nation.

Gipson, Lawrence H. AMERICAN LOYALIST: JARED INGERSOLL. New Haven, Conn.: Yale University Press, 1971. xxvi, 432 p.

Howe, John R., Jr. THE CHANGING POLITICAL THOUGHT OF JOHN ADAMS. Princeton, N.J.: Princeton University Press, 1966. xv, 259 p.

Adams's political views were shaped by the struggle with Great Britain even before independence. The author ties his activities with his thought.

Meade, Robert D. PATRICK HENRY. 2 vols. Philadelphia: J.B. Lippincott Co., 1957-69. Illus.

A well-written life and times, this work takes advantage of more recent scholarship and gives the reader a better perspective on Patrick Henry's role in American politics.

Mitchell, Broadus. ALEXANDER HAMILTON: YOUTH TO MATURITY, 1755-1788. New York: Macmillan Co., 1957. xvi, 675 p.

Nettels, Curtis P. GEORGE WASHINGTON AND AMERICAN INDEPENDENCE. Boston: Little, Brown and Co., 1951. 338 p. Illus.

Discusses the important role Washington played in the break with England and the politics surrounding his appointment as commander of the revolutionary army.

Newcomb, Benjamin H. FRANKLIN AND GALLOWAY: A POLITICAL PART-
NERSHIP. New Haven, Conn.: Yale University Press, 1972. 332 p.

Tyler, Moses Coit. PATRICK HENRY. Rev. ed. Boston: Houghton, Mifflin
and Co., 1887. x, 454 p. Illus.

> Although dated, this volume is worthwhile to the student examining
> Henry's political career. Later scholars have had material which
> has revised our interpretations of some of the events and personali-
> ties associated with Henry, but his story is largely unaffected.

Van Doren, Carl. BENJAMIN FRANKLIN. New York: Viking Press, 1938.
xix, 845 p.

> A well-written biography that is useful to the general student on
> Franklin's political views and activities.

Chapter III

FEDERAL AMERICA, 1783-1815

Section 1. GENERAL

Abernethy, Thomas P. THE SOUTH IN THE NEW NATION, 1789-1819. Baton Rouge: Louisiana State University Press, 1961. xvi, 529 p. Maps, charts.

> A major study of the South in the federal period. A must for the student initiating an examination of the politics of the region.

Borden, Morton. PARTIES AND POLITICS IN THE EARLY REPUBLIC, 1789-1815. New York: Thomas Y. Crowell Co., 1967. vii, 119 p. Pap.

> A short but useful survey of the period; capitalizes on recent scholarship.

Buel, Richard, Jr. SECURING THE REVOLUTION: IDEOLOGY IN AMERICAN POLITICS, 1789-1815. Ithaca, N.Y.: Cornell University Press, 1972. xii, 391 p.

> The focus is on both issues and ideology during the federal period.

Chambers, William N. POLITICAL PARTIES IN A NEW NATION: THE AMERICAN EXPERIENCE, 1776-1809. New York: Oxford University Press, 1963. 231 p.

> An excellent account of party battles and Republican party organization.

Chase, James S. EMERGENCE OF THE PRESIDENTIAL NOMINATING CONVENTION, 1789-1832. Urbana: University of Illinois Press, 1973. xvii, 332 p.

> Chase explores the origins of the convention system, the reasons for its establishment, and its strengths and weaknesses.

Cunliffe, Marcus. THE NATION TAKES SHAPE, 1789-1837. Chicago: University of Chicago Press, 1959. vii, 223 p.

In this brief survey, Cunliffe notes that in spite of divisions the American national character developed rapidly.

Darling, Arthur B. OUR RISING EMPIRE, 1763-1803. New Haven, Conn.: Yale University Press, 1940. 595 p. Appendix.

A good survey of the period.

Hofstadter, Richard. THE IDEA OF A PARTY SYSTEM: THE RISE OF LEGITIMATE OPPOSITION IN THE UNITED STATES, 1780-1840. Berkeley and Los Angeles: University of California Press, 1969. xiii, 280 p.

Hofstadter argues that a party system was virtually nonexistent in the 1790s.

Kass, Alvin. POLITICS IN NEW YORK, 1800-1830. Syracuse, N.Y.: Syracuse University Press, 1965. xii, 221 p.

Lynch, William O. FIFTY YEARS OF PARTY WARFARE, 1789-1837. Indianapolis: Bobbs-Merrill Co., 1931. viii, 506 p.

Main, Jackson Turner. POLITICAL PARTIES BEFORE THE CONSTITUTION. Chapel Hill: University of North Carolina Press, for the Institute of Early American History and Culture at Williamsburg, Va., 1973. xx, 481 p. Maps, tables, appendix.

A systematic study of the votes in state legislatures during the confederation period. Ignores conceptual and historical problems but provides a useful background to the study of Federalist and Anti-Federalist politics.

Miller, John C. THE YOUNG REPUBLIC, 1789-1815. New York: Free Press, 1970. ix, 308 p.

An even-handed survey of the period that incorporates a considerable amount of recent scholarship on the major political events and personalities.

Nettels, Curtis P. THE EMERGENCE OF A NATIONAL ECONOMY, 1775-1815. New York: Holt, Rinehart & Winston, 1962. xvi, 424 p. Appendixes, tables, illus.

An excellent economic history of the period, which also is concerned with political issues.

Pratt, Julius W. EXPANSIONISTS OF 1812. New York: Macmillan Co., 1925. Reprint. Gloucester, Mass.: Peter Smith, 1957. 309 p.

This is one of the very important studies of the politics of American imperialism.

Risjord, Norman K. THE OLD REPUBLICANS: SOUTHERN CONSERVATISM IN THE AGE OF JEFFERSON. New York: Columbia University Press, 1965. 340 p.

John Randolph and other conservative Republicans are studied.

Robinson, Donald L. SLAVERY IN THE STRUCTURE OF AMERICAN POLITICS, 1765-1820. New York: Harcourt Brace Jovanovich, 1971. xii, 564 p. Tables.

The question of slavery created political tension long before the Missouri Compromise. This volume explains the issues that preceded the compromise.

Watlington, Patricia. THE PARTISAN SPIRIT: KENTUCKY POLITICS, 1779-1792. New York: Atheneum, for the Institute of Early American History and Culture at Williamsburg, Va., 1972. viii, 276 p.

An excellent discussion of the personalities and issues that dominated the Old West and affected politics in the young Republic.

Wiltse, Charles M. THE NEW NATION, 1800-1845. New York: Hill and Wang, 1961. ix, 237 p.

A brief but excellent survey that focuses on the country's developing nationalism.

Section 2. CONFEDERATION AND CONSTITUTION

Beard, Charles A. AN ECONOMIC INTERPRETATION OF THE CONSTITUTION OF THE UNITED STATES. New York: Macmillan Co., 1913. vii, 330 p.

A classic study of the effect of economic interest. Beard's thesis has been vigorously refuted or modified by subsequent scholarship.

Brant, Irving. THE BILL OF RIGHTS: ITS ORIGIN AND MEANING. Indianapolis: Bobbs-Merrill Co., 1965. vi, 567 p.

Although at first glance the title does not point to politics, this work contains a generous amount of information on politics in the new nation.

Brown, Robert E[ldon]. REINTERPRETATION OF THE FORMATION OF THE AMERICAN CONSTITUTION. Boston: Boston University Press, 1963. 63 p.

Brown contends that the Constitution represented the interests of the middle class instead of the upper class. This slim volume refutes Charles Beard's writing on the Constitution (cited above, this section).

Cochran, Thomas C. NEW YORK IN THE CONFEDERATION. Philadelphia:

University of Pennsylvania Press, 1932. Reprint. Clifton, N.J.: Augustus M. Kelley, 1972. ix, 220 p. Appendixes.

> New York's importance to the Confederation made the state a principal military and political battleground. Cochran particularly emphasizes the economic considerations that affected political decisions.

De Pauw, Linda G. THE ELEVENTH PILLAR: NEW YORK STATE AND THE FEDERAL CONVENTION. Ithaca, N.Y.: Cornell University Press for the American Historical Association, 1966. xvi, 328 p. Appendixes, tables.

> The author argues that a study of New York State is necessary in order to understand the Federalist success on the national as well as on the local level in the early years of the Republic.

Farrand, Max. THE FRAMING OF THE CONSTITUTION OF THE UNITED STATES. 1913. Reprint. New Haven, Conn.: Yale University Press, 1967. ix, 281 p. Appendixes. Pap.

> This early classic has fortunately been reprinted in paperback. A vivid analysis of the conditions, the convictions, and the men who framed the Constitution.

Hall, Van Beck. POLITICS WITHOUT PARTIES: MASSACHUSETTS, 1780-1791. Pittsburgh: University of Pittsburgh Press, 1972. xvii, 375 p.

> Examines Massachusetts politics during the critical period.

Henderson, Herbert J[ames]. PARTY POLITICS IN THE CONTINENTAL CONGRESS. New York: McGraw-Hill Book Co., 1974. xvii, 475 p.

Jensen, Merrill. THE ARTICLES OF CONFEDERATION: AN INTERPRETATION OF THE SOCIAL-CONSTITUTIONAL HISTORY OF THE AMERICAN REVOLUTION. Madison: University of Wisconsin Press, 1966. xxiii, 284 p. Appendix. Pap.

> This work examines the decisions surrounding the writing of what we can consider the first constitution of the United States.

_____. THE NEW NATION: A HISTORY OF THE UNITED STATES DURING THE CONFEDERATION, 1781-1789. New York: Alfred A. Knopf, 1967. xvii, 433, xi p.

> A very good survey of the period. Cited by many scholars as the definitive study of the Confederation.

Levy, Leonard W. LEGACY OF SUPPRESSION: FREEDOM OF SPEECH AND PRESS IN EARLY AMERICAN HISTORY. Cambridge, Mass.: Harvard University Press, 1960. xiv, 353 p. Appendix.

An analysis of the First Amendment and the argument that it gave less protection to freedom of speech and press than we had believed.

McDonald, Forrest. WE THE PEOPLE: THE ECONOMIC ORIGINS OF THE CONSTITUTION. Chicago: University of Chicago Press, 1958. x, 436 p.

An attack on Charles A. Beard's economic interpretations (cited above, this section) of the Constitution.

Main, Jackson T[urner]. THE ANTIFEDERALISTS: CRITICS OF THE CONSTITUTION, 1781-1788. Chapel Hill: University of North Carolina Press, for the Institute of Early American History and Culture at Williamsburg, Va., 1961. xv, 308 p. Appendixes.

An examination of the personalities and issues of the anti-Federalist coalition before and after the Constitutional Convention.

Purcell, Richard J. CONNECTICUT IN TRANSITION, 1775-1800. Rev. ed. Middletown, Conn.: Wesleyan University Press, 1963. xvii, 305 p. Appendix, maps.

A standard work cited by many historians as important for the study of the Revolution and postrevolutionary period. Purcell explains the small states' concerns at the Constitutional Convention.

Rossiter, Clinton. 1787: THE GRAND CONVENTION. New York: Macmillan Co., 1966. 443 p. Appendixes, illus.

A well-written account that celebrates what the author argues was the most fateful year in our history.

Rutland, Robert A. THE BIRTH OF THE BILL OF RIGHTS, 1776-1791. Chapel Hill: University of North Carolina Press, for the Institute of Early American History and Culture at Williamsburg, Va., 1955. vi, 243 p. Appendixes.

No serious study of the writing of the Constitution is complete without an examination of the fight over the Bill of Rights. Rutland's study is considered to be one of the best recent histories.

_____. THE ORDEAL OF THE CONSTITUTION: THE ANTIFEDERALIST AND RATIFICATION STRUGGLE OF 1787-1788. Norman: University of Oklahoma Press, 1966. xiii, 329 p. Illus.

Rutland relates the intense story of the political battle to secure ratification. He brings his own first-rate scholarship together with other recent scholarship to provide a definitive account of this most important event in American history.

Spaulding, Ernest. NEW YORK IN THE CRITICAL PERIOD, 1783-1789. New York: Columbia University Press, 1932. Reprint. Port Washington, N.Y.: Ira J. Friedman, 1963. xiii, 334 p. Appendix, illus.

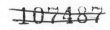

An excellent political history that ties New York's problems to the nation.

Van Doren, Carl. THE GREAT REHEARSAL: THE STORY OF THE MAKING AND RATIFYING OF THE CONSTITUTION OF THE UNITED STATES. New York: Viking Press, 1948. xii, 336 p. Appendixes, illus.

Van Doren's account is one of the most gracefully written of all the considerable number of histories on the subject.

Section 3. FEDERALISTS AND DEMOCRATIC-REPUBLICANS

Abernethy, Thomas P. THE BURR CONSPIRACY. New York: Oxford University Press, 1954. xi, 301 p.

The author examines some new materials relating to the conspiracy, and he avoids the partisanship that marred some of the earlier studies.

Baldwin, Leland D. THE WHISKEY REBELS: THE STORY OF A FRONTIER UPRISING. Rev. ed. Pittsburgh: University of Pittsburgh Press, 1968. 326 p.

An in-depth study of the economic conditions in western Pennsylvania that led to political turmoil there and created the threat of anarchy for George Washington's administration.

Banner, James M., Jr. TO THE HARTFORD CONVENTION: THE FEDERALISTS AND THE ORIGINS OF PARTY POLITICS IN MASSACHUSETTS, 1789-1815. New York: Alfred A. Knopf, 1970. xiv, 378, xii p. Appendixes.

Explores the Federalists' attachment to the republican principles of government. The author argues that the Hartford Convention cannot be fully understood without reference to the political community in Massachusetts.

Beard, Charles A. ECONOMIC ORIGINS OF JEFFERSONIAN DEMOCRACY. New York: Macmillan Co., 1915. ix, 474 p. Illus.

His thesis is that the rise of the Republican party was a result of the small farmer's hostility to the Constitution.

Bell, Rudolph M. PARTY AND FACTION IN AMERICAN POLITICS: THE HOUSE OF REPRESENTATIVES, 1789-1801. Westport, Conn.: Greenwood Press, 1973. xiii, 311 p.

A very important study of factions and the origins of political alignments.

Charles, Joseph. THE ORIGINS OF THE AMERICAN PARTY SYSTEM. Williamsburg, Va.: Institute of Early American History and Culture, 1956. 147 p.

The author refutes Charles Beard's contention that small-farmer hostility created the Republican party. (See Beard's study above, this section.)

Coles, Harry L. THE WAR OF 1812. Chicago: University of Chicago Press, 1965. vii, 298 p. Illus. Pap.

A brief, but one of the best, accounts of the war.

Cunningham, Noble E., Jr. THE JEFFERSONIAN REPUBLICANS: THE FORMATION OF PARTY ORGANIZATION, 1789-1801. Chapel Hill: University of North Carolina Press, for the Institute of Early American History and Culture at Williamsburg, Va., 1957. x, 279 p. Illus., appendix.

A good description of the political organizing activities of the Republican party. The section on the election of 1800 is particularly helpful.

_____. THE JEFFERSONIAN REPUBLICANS IN POWER: PARTY OPERATIONS, 1801-1809. Chapel Hill: University of North Carolina Press, for the Institute of Early American History and Culture at Williamsburg, Va., 1967. ix, 318 p. Illus.

Cited by many historians as one of the best studies of the development of party organization in the young Republic.

Dauer, Manning J. THE ADAMS FEDERALISTS. Baltimore: Johns Hopkins Press, 1953. xxiii, 381 p. Appendixes.

This study is very helpful in the unraveling of the actions of the Federalists and Republicans.

Fischer, David H. THE REVOLUTION OF AMERICAN CONSERVATISM: THE FEDERALIST PARTY IN THE ERA OF JEFFERSONIAN DEMOCRACY. New York: Harper and Row, 1965. xx, 455 p. Tables.

Goodman, Paul. THE DEMOCRATIC-REPUBLICANS OF MASSACHUSETTS: POLITICS IN A YOUNG REPUBLIC. Cambridge, Mass.: Harvard University Press, 1964. xiii, 281 p.

The author argues that the small farmer was not the source of hostility to the Constitution.

Kerber, Linda K. FEDERALISTS IN DISSENT: IMAGERY AND IDEOLOGY IN JEFFERSONIAN AMERICA. Ithaca, N.Y.: Cornell University Press, 1970. xii, 233 p.

A study of Federalist political and social thought. The author takes advantage of recent scholarship in order to give us a better balanced assessment of the Federalists.

Kurtz, Stephen G. THE PRESIDENCY OF JOHN ADAMS: THE COLLAPSE OF FEDERALISM, 1795-1800. Philadelphia: University of Pennsylvania Press, 1957. 448 p. Illus.

Link, Eugene Perry. DEMOCRATIC-REPUBLICAN SOCIETIES, 1790-1800. New York: Columbia University Press, 1942. Reprint. New York: Octagon Books, 1965. xii, 256 p.

    An analysis of the nature of political discontent during the 1790s.

McCaleb, Walter F. THE AARON BURR CONSPIRACY. 1903. Reprint. New York: Wilson-Erickson, 1966. xxiv, 318 p. Illus.

    A sympathetic portrait that is flawed by the author's obvious bias.

Magrath, C. Peter. YAZOO: LAW AND POLITICS IN THE NEW REPUBLIC, THE CASE OF FLETCHER V. PECK. New York: W. W. Norton and Co., 1967. ix, 235 p. Appendixes. Pap.

    A thorough exploration of the politics and scandals that surrounded the Yazoo claims during the administrations of Washington, Adams, Jefferson, and Madison.

Miller, John C. CRISIS IN FREEDOM: THE ALIEN AND SEDITION LAWS. Boston: Little, Brown and Co., 1951. 253 p.

    Miller sees the laws as a test of real "Americanism," concluding that freedom survived one of the severest attacks leveled against it.

_____. THE FEDERALIST ERA, 1789-1801. New York: Harper and Row, 1960. xiii, 304 p. Illus.

    A well-written survey of an intensely political period in American history. Miller explains in detail the reason for the quarrel between the Hamiltonians and Jeffersonians.

Munroe, John A. FEDERALIST DELAWARE, 1775-1815. New Brunswick, N.J.: Rutgers University Press, 1954. xiv, 286 p. Appendix.

    An excellent analysis of the Federalist position in one of the mid-Atlantic states.

Pasler, Rudolph J., and Pasler, Margaret C. THE NEW JERSEY FEDERALISTS. Rutherford, N.J.: Fairleigh Dickinson University Press, 1975. 256 p.

    The authors bring earlier material together but they do not challenge traditional views of the political origins of the Federalists.

Renzulli, L. Marx, Jr. MARYLAND: THE FEDERALIST YEARS. Rutherford, N.J.: Fairleigh Dickinson University Press, 1972. 354 p. Illus.

Very good on Maryland politics up to 1800, although the author continues his narrative up until the year 1818.

Rose, Lisle A. PROLOGUE TO DEMOCRACY: THE FEDERALISTS IN THE SOUTH, 1789-1800. Lexington: University of Kentucky Press, 1968. xvii, 326 p. Appendix.

An analysis of the appeal of the Federalist position to the southern states and of the quarrel with the Republican coalition.

Smelser, Marshall. THE DEMOCRATIC REPUBLIC, 1801-1815. New York: Harper and Row, 1968. xiv, 369 p. Illus.

A very good survey of the period. Smelser challenges some of the traditional views on Jefferson, Madison, and the causes of the War of 1812.

Smith, James M. FREEDOM'S FETTERS. Ithaca, N.Y.: Cornell University Press, 1956. xv, 464 p. Appendix.

A good account of the origins and effects of the Alien and Sedition Acts. The author attempts to assess their influence in shaping the political process of republicanism, with its dual goals of majority rule and individual rights.

Tinkcom, Harry M. THE REPUBLICANS AND FEDERALISTS IN PENNSYLVANIA, 1790-1801: A STUDY IN NATIONAL STIMULUS AND LOCAL RESPONSE. Harrisburg: Pennsylvania Historical and Museum Commission, 1950. viii, 354 p.

Very necessary to a thorough understanding of politics in the period.

Warren, Charles. JACOBIN AND JUNTO: OR EARLY AMERICAN POLITICS AS VIEWED IN THE DIARY OF DR. NATHANIEL AMES, 1758-1822. Cambridge, Mass.: Harvard University Press, 1931. Reprint. New York: AMS Press, 1970. 324 p.

The author examines the positions of Nathaniel and Fisher Ames, who took opposite attitudes upon every important political question of the 1790s.

Section 4. BIOGRAPHY

Bernhard, Winfred E. A. FISHER AMES, FEDERALIST AND STATESMAN, 1758-1808. Chapel Hill: University of North Carolina Press, for the Institute of Early American History and Culture at Williamsburg, Va., 1965. xiii, 372 p. Illus.

This is the only complete biography of this leading Federalist statesman. No study of the early national period would be complete without notice of this award-winning volume (Institute Manuscript Award by the College of William and Mary and Colonial Williamsburg).

Borden, Morton. THE FEDERALISM OF JAMES A. BAYARD. New York: Columbia University Press, 1955. 256 p.

Bayard played a decisive role in the choice of Thomas Jefferson for president over Aaron Burr.

Bowers, Claude G. JEFFERSON AND HAMILTON: THE STRUGGLE FOR DEMOCRACY IN AMERICA. Boston: Houghton, Mifflin and Co., 1925. xvii, 531 p. Illus.

Bowers is a partisan of Jefferson, but the account of the political activities of an infant nation is fascinating.

Boyd, George A. ELIAS BOUDINOT: PATRIOT AND STATESMAN, 1740-1821. Princeton, N.J.: Princeton University Press, 1952. xiii, 321 p. Illus.

A lesser-known figure, Boudinot's story is gracefully told in this volume. Boudinot's association with many of the young Republic's leaders provides the reader with an interesting perspective on federal-era politics.

Brant, Irving. JAMES MADISON. 6 vols. Indianapolis: Bobbs-Merrill Co., 1941-1961. Illus.

A well-researched and well-written life and times biography.

Destler, Chester M. JOSHUA COIT: AMERICAN FEDERALIST, 1758-1798. Middletown, Conn.: Wesleyan University Press, 1962. xiii, 191 p.

Although Coit's name is not well remembered, this study of his life is very useful in the understanding of Federalist politics.

Ernst, Robert. RUFUS KING: AMERICAN FEDERALIST. Chapel Hill: University of North Carolina Press, for the Institute of Early American History and Culture at Williamsburg, Va., 1968. xiii, 446 p. Illus.

Probably the most eloquent orator in the Constitutional Convention, King supported a vigorous central government.

Hacker, Louis M. ALEXANDER HAMILTON IN THE AMERICAN TRADITION. New York: McGraw-Hill Book Co., 1957. xi, 273 p.

Hanna, William S. BENJAMIN FRANKLIN AND PENNSYLVANIA POLITICS. Stanford, Calif.: Stanford University Press, 1964. x, 239 p.

Ketcham, Ralph. JAMES MADISON: A BIOGRAPHY. New York: Macmillan Co., 1971. xiv, 753 p. Illus.

A well-balanced and well-written biography.

Kirk, Russell, JOHN RANDOLPH OF ROANOKE: A STUDY IN AMERICAN POLITICS. Chicago: Henry Regnery Co., 1964. 485 p.

Initially an opponent of the Federalists, he later broke with Jefferson and Madison. A master parliamentarian, defender of personal liberty and states' rights.

Koch, Adrienne. JEFFERSON AND MADISON: THE GREAT COLLABORATION. New York: Oxford University Press, 1964. xiv, 294 p. Pap.

The author offers fresh insights into the political views and actions of Jefferson and Madison. She sees her subjects as committed to liberty but willing to accept some features of strong government.

Malone, Dumas. JEFFERSON THE PRESIDENT: SECOND TERM, 1805-1809. Boston: Little, Brown and Co., 1974. xxxi, 704 p.

_____. THOMAS JEFFERSON AS POLITICAL LEADER. Berkeley and Los Angeles: University of California Press, 1963. viii, 75 p.

Of the many books on the subject, this one should be examined first.

Miller, Helen Day [Hill]. GEORGE MASON, CONSTITUTIONALIST. Cambridge, Mass.: Harvard University Press, 1938. Reprint. Gloucester, Mass.: Peter Smith, 1966. xii, 300 p. Illus.

Mason played an important role in the revolutionary movement in Virginia as well as in the Constitutional Convention.

Monaghan, Frank. JOHN JAY: DEFENDER OF LIBERTY. Indianapolis: Bobbs-Merrill Co., 1935. xi, 407 p. Illus.

An excellent biography of an important political figure of the federal period. Jay's influence on the Constitution and in Federalist politics was considerable.

Morison, Samuel Eliot. THE LIFE AND LETTERS OF HARRISON GRAY OTIS, FEDERALIST, 1765-1848. 2 vols. Boston: Houghton, Mifflin and Co., 1913. Illus.

A leading Federalist politician from Massachusetts, Otis was a leading figure at the Hartford Convention. Opposed the abolitionist movement. Morison deals with a controversial figure with grace and fair-mindedness.

Peterson, Merrill D. THOMAS JEFFERSON AND THE NEW NATION: A BIOGRAPHY. New York: Oxford University Press, 1970. ix, 1,072 p. Illus.

A good one-volume biography that incorporates some of the best scholarship on Jefferson and his times.

Rutland, Robert A. GEORGE MASON: RELUCTANT STATESMAN. Charlottesville: University Press of Virginia, 1963. xvi, 123 p. Illus.

Schachner, Nathan. AARON BURR: A BIOGRAPHY. N.p.: Frederick A. Stokes Co., 1937. Reprint. New York: A.S. Barnes and Co., 1961. xii, 563 p. Illus. Pap.

An excellent study of the complicated politics that produced the Hamilton-Burr tragedy.

_____. ALEXANDER HAMILTON. New York: Appleton-Century Co., 1946. vi, 488 p.

One of the best one-volume biographies of Hamilton.

_____. THE FOUNDING FATHERS. New York: Capricorn Books, 1954. x, 630 p. Pap.

Smith, Page. JOHN ADAMS. 2 vols. Garden City, N.Y.: Doubleday and Co., 1962. Illus.

A classic biography.

Walters, Raymond, Jr. ALBERT GALLATIN: JEFFERSONIAN FINANCIER AND DIPLOMAT. New York: Macmillan Co., 1957. 461 p.

Gallatin began his political career as a radical member of the 1788 Harrisburg, Pennsylvania, conference considering revision of the U.S. Constitution. He served as a senator, representative, and secretary of the treasury in the Jefferson administration. Walters provides the reader with an insight into the complex political issues of the period from the vantage point of an important Republican party member.

Zahniser, Marvin R. CHARLES COTESWORTH PINCKNEY: FOUNDING FATHER. Chapel Hill: University of North Carolina Press, for the Institute of Early American History and Culture at Williamsburg, Va., 1967. ix, 295 p.

C. C. Pinckney served in the colonial and state legislatures of South Carolina. A lifelong Federalist, he was his party's nominee for vice-president in 1800, and for president in 1804 and 1808.

Chapter IV

EARLY NATIONAL, 1815-60

Section 1. GENERAL

Alexander, Thomas B. SECTIONAL STRESS AND PARTY STRENGTH: A STUDY OF ROLL-CALL VOTING PATTERNS IN THE UNITED STATES HOUSE OF REP-RESENTATIVES, 1836-1860. Nashville, Tenn.: Vanderbilt University Press, 1967. xvii, 284 p. Tables.

> A highly technical, quantitative analysis of voting patterns.

Ames, William E. A HISTORY OF THE NATIONAL INTELLIGENCER. Chapel Hill: University of North Carolina Press, 1972. xi, 376 p.

> The story of one of the most important political newspapers in the early national period.

Billington, Ray A. THE PROTESTANT CRUSADE, 1800-1860: A STUDY OF THE ORIGINS OF AMERICAN NATIVISM. Chicago: Quadrangle Books, 1964. viii, 514 p. Appendix, maps. Pap.

> This is a classic study of the politics of prejudice. Billington examines the origins of anti-Catholic prejudice and its apex in the pre-Civil War period.

Bowers, Claude G. PARTY BATTLES OF THE JACKSON PERIOD. Boston: Houghton, Mifflin and Co., 1922. xix, 506 p.

> Although recent scholars are much more accurate and penetrating in their analysis of the period, no one has produced a more readable political history.

Carroll, E. Malcom. ORIGINS OF THE WHIG PARTY. Durham, N.C.: Duke University Press, 1925. Reprint. Gloucester, Mass.: Peter Smith, 1964. viii, 260 p. Appendix.

> An examination of the events and personalities that influenced the development of the Whig party to 1840. The author cites John Quincy Adams's lack of skill as a politician as a factor in the weakness of the party.

Dangerfield, George. THE AWAKENING OF AMERICAN NATIONALISM, 1815-1828. New York: Harper and Row, 1965. x, 331 p. Illus. Pap.

The author brilliantly focuses on the central theme of the period-- the contest between the economic nationalism expounded by Henry Clay and John Quincy Adams, and the democratic nationalism of the partisans of Andrew Jackson.

_____. THE ERA OF GOOD FEELINGS. New York: Harcourt, Brace and Co., 1952. xiv, 525 p.

The author develops the story of political activity in a period sup- posedly without politics.

Gammon, Samuel R., Jr. THE PRESIDENTIAL CAMPAIGN OF 1832. Balti- more: Johns Hopkins Press, 1922. Reprint. Westport, Conn.: Greenwood Press, 1971. ix, 180 p. Appendixes.

Gunderson, Robert G. THE LOG-CABIN CAMPAIGN. Lexington: University of Kentucky Press, 1957. xi, 292 p. Illus.

The election of 1840 is famous because of its emphasis on emo- tional and demagogic appeal.

Haines, Charles G., and Sherwood, Foster H. THE ROLE OF THE SUPREME COURT IN GOVERNMENT AND POLITICS, 1835-1864. Berkeley and Los Angeles: University of California Press, 1957. x, 533 p. Tables.

The authors develop the thesis that Jackson's appointments to the Court did not significantly alter the political outlook of the Su- preme Court.

Hammond, Bray. BANKS AND POLITICS IN AMERICA FROM THE REVOLU- TION TO THE CIVIL WAR. Princeton, N.J.: Princeton University Press, 1957. xi, 771 p.

A classic study of the confluence of money and politics.

Livermore, Shaw, Jr. THE TWILIGHT OF FEDERALISM: THE DISINTEGRA- TION OF THE FEDERALIST PARTY, 1815-1830. Princeton, N.J.: Princeton University Press, 1962. x, 292 p.

This is an excellent study of the tragedy of the Federalist party.

McCormick, Richard P. THE SECOND AMERICAN PARTY SYSTEM: PARTY FORMATION IN THE JACKSONIAN ERA. Chapel Hill: University of North Carolina Press, 1966. x, 389 p.

The author argues that the first party system existed between 1800 and 1820 but a second developed in 1824 and was fully developed by 1840. He is particularly concerned with the factors that created a two-party system rather than the differences between the Whigs and Democrats.

Nichols, Roy F. THE DEMOCRATIC MACHINE, 1850-1854. New York: Columbia University, 1923. 248 p. Illus.

Paul, James C. N. RIFT IN THE DEMOCRACY. Philadelphia: University of Pennsylvania Press, 1951. xiv, 200 p.

Deals with the early 1840s.

Rayback, Joseph G. FREE SOIL: THE ELECTION OF 1848. Lexington: University of Kentucky Press, 1970. ix, 326 p.

The author observes that in James K. Polk's administration "many of the developments of the American past were completed . . . " and future movements were initiated, hence the importance of the election of 1848.

Remini, Robert V. THE ELECTION OF ANDREW JACKSON. Philadelphia: J. B. Lippincott Co., 1963. 224 p.

Profound changes in American politics in the 1820s, according to the author, did not just happen. He contends that the politicians intended to initiate a political revolution.

_____. THE REVOLUTIONARY AGE OF ANDREW JACKSON. New York: Harper and Row, 1976. x, 205 p.

Schlesinger, Arthur M., Jr. THE AGE OF JACKSON. Boston: Little, Brown and Co., 1945. xiv, 577 p. Appendix.

Includes a description and analysis of Jacksonian politics. The author argues that the general precepts of Jacksonian democracy were shaped by reasoned and systematic notions about society; his thesis therefore clashes with some of the earlier studies of the period.

Sharp, James Roger. THE JACKSONIANS VERSUS THE BANKS: POLITICS IN THE STATES AFTER THE PANIC OF 1837. New York: Columbia University Press, 1970. xii, 392 p. Illus.

Van Deusen, Glyndon G. THE JACKSONIAN ERA, 1828-1848. New York: Harper and Row, 1959. xii, 290 p. Illus. Pap.

An excellent survey by one of the best-known scholars of the period.

Weston, Florence. THE PRESIDENTIAL ELECTION OF 1828. Washington, D.C.: Ruddick Press, 1938. Reprint. Philadelphia: Porcupine Press, 1974. 217 p.

Section 2. ANTISLAVERY POLITICS

Barnes, Gilbert Hobbs. THE ANTISLAVERY IMPULSE, 1830-1844. New York: Appleton-Century, 1933. Reprint. New York: Harcourt, Brace and World, 1964. xxxv, 298 p. Pap.

> This book resulted in the major reinterpretation of the origins of the Civil War. Barnes's major points have been qualified by subsequent research, but his views remain. Essentially, he debunks the role of William Lloyd Garrison in the antislavery crusade, and substitutes Theodore Weld and others as legitimate crusading heroes.

Blue, Frederick J. THE FREE SOILERS: THIRD PARTY POLITICS, 1848-54. Urbana: University of Illinois Press, 1973. xii, 350 p. Appendixes.

> A comprehensive treatment of the Free Soil movement from its inception in 1848 to its absorption by the Republicans in 1854.

Dillon, Merton L. THE ABOLITIONISTS: THE GROWTH OF A DISSENTING MINORITY. De Kalb: Northern Illinois University Press, 1974. xiii, 298 p. Illus.

> An in-depth account of the abolition movement.

Dumond, Dwight L. ANTISLAVERY: THE CRUSADE FOR FREEDOM IN AMERICA. Ann Arbor: University of Michigan Press, 1961. x, 422 p. Illus.

> A classic account of antislavery movements and politics.

Filler, Louis. THE CRUSADE AGAINST SLAVERY, 1830-1860. New York: Harper and Row, 1960. xv, 318 p. Illus.

> The focus of this book is the case against slavery, rather than an analysis of the institution itself. It is the author's thesis that William Lloyd Garrison was the seminal figure in the antislavery movement.

Foner, Eric. FREE SOIL, FREE LABOR, FREE MEN: THE IDEOLOGY OF THE REPUBLICAN PARTY BEFORE THE CIVIL WAR. New York: Oxford University Press, 1970. xii, 353 p.

Morrison, Chaplain W. DEMOCRATIC POLITICS AND SECTIONALISM: THE WILMOT PROVISO CONTROVERSY. Chapel Hill: University of North Carolina Press, 1967. viii, 244 p.

> A very necessary study of the division that helped to create the conditions for the Civil War.

Nichols, Roy F. THE DISRUPTION OF AMERICAN DEMOCRACY. New York: Macmillan Co., 1948. xviii, 612 p. Illus.

> The author describes the disruption of political stability during the years 1856–61.

Potter, David M. THE IMPENDING CRISIS, 1848–1861. Completed and edited by Don E. Fehrenbacher. New York: Harper and Row, 1976. xv, 638 p.

> An examination of American politics by one of the greatest historians of the period. Potter analyzes the break-up of national unity and focuses on the role played by the various political factions.

Ratner, Lorman. POWDER KEG: NORTHERN OPPOSITION TO THE ANTI-SLAVERY MOVEMENT, 1831–1840. New York: Basic Books, 1968. xii, 172 p.

Rawley, James A. RACE AND POLITICS: "BLEEDING KANSAS" AND THE COMING OF THE CIVIL WAR. Philadelphia: J.B. Lippincott Co., 1969. xvi, 304 p.

> An analysis of the controversies that followed the repeal of the Missouri Compromise. The author develops the idea that the issue was not slavery, but race, and asks the question whether the country could tolerate the spread of Negroes, slave or free.

Sewell, Richard H. BALLOTS FOR FREEDOM: ANTISLAVERY POLITICS IN THE UNITED STATES. New York: Oxford University Press, 1976. xvi, 379 p.

Simms, Henry H. A DECADE OF SECTIONAL CONTROVERSY, 1851–1861. Chapel Hill: University of North Carolina Press, 1942. xi, 284 p.

> Although somewhat dry, this work organizes in an effective way the complex events that led to the Civil War.

Smith, Theodore Clarke. THE LIBERTY AND FREE SOIL PARTIES IN THE NORTHWEST. New York: Longmans, Green and Co., 1897. xi, 351 p.

> An early study, still worthwhile, which provides an interesting perspective on American politics between 1830 and 1854.

Sorin, Gerald. THE NEW YORK ABOLITIONISTS: A CASE STUDY OF POLITICAL RADICALISM. Westport, Conn.: Greenwood Press, 1971. xiii, 172 p.

Section 3. STATES AND REGIONS

Adams, William H. THE WHIG PARTY OF LOUISIANA. Lafayette: University of Southwestern Louisiana Press, 1973. vii, 305 p.

    Politics in Louisiana between 1803 and 1865.

Berger, Mark L. THE REVOLUTION IN THE NEW YORK PARTY SYSTEMS, 1840-1860. Port Washington, N.Y.: Kennikat Press, 1973. 172 p.

    Concentrates on the political realignment between 1854 and 1856.

Cole, Arthur C. THE WHIG PARTY IN THE SOUTH. N.p.: American Historical Association, 1914. Reprint. Gloucester, Mass.: Peter Smith, 1962. xii, 392 p. Appendixes.

Donovan, Herbert D. A. THE BARNBURNERS: A STUDY OF THE INTERNAL MOVEMENTS IN THE POLITICAL HISTORY OF NEW YORK STATE AND OF THE RESULTING CHANGES IN POLITICAL AFFILIATION, 1830-1852. New York: New York University Press, 1925. viii, 140 p. Maps.

Eaton, Clement. THE GROWTH OF SOUTHERN CIVILIZATION, 1790-1860. New York: Harper and Row, 1961. xv, 357 p. Illus. Pap.

    A necessary introduction to the understanding of southern political views before the Civil War. The author develops the thesis that the South lacked adequate political leadership because the best minds were shackled by a deep conservatism and a religious orthodoxy.

Evitts, William J. A MATTER OF ALLEGIANCES: MARYLAND FROM 1850 TO 1861. Baltimore: Johns Hopkins University Press, 1974. xii, 212 p.

    The author is concerned with the changing political alignments and the entanglement of social and economic issues with political ones.

Ferguson, Russell J. EARLY WESTERN PENNSYLVANIA POLITICS. Pittsburgh: University of Pittsburgh Press, 1938. vii, 300 p. Illus.

    This volume covers the period from 1775 to 1865.

Formisano, Ronald P. THE BIRTH OF MASS POLITICAL PARTIES: MICHIGAN, 1827-1861. Princeton, N.J.: Princeton University Press, 1971. xii, 356 p. Tables, appendixes.

    Explores the relationship between ethno-religious groupings and party allegiance, with Michigan as a test case.

Franklin, John Hope. THE MILITANT SOUTH, 1800-1861. Cambridge, Mass.: Harvard University Press, 1956. xi, 317 p.

    A most important analysis seen from the perspectives of a famous black historian.

Holt, Edgar Allan. PARTY POLITICS IN OHIO, 1840-1850. Columbus, Ohio: F. J. Heer Printing Co., 1930. 449 p.

Holt, Michael F. FORGING A MAJORITY: THE FORMATION OF THE RE- PUBLICAN PARTY IN PITTSBURGH, 1848-1860. New Haven, Conn.: Yale University Press, 1969. ix, 408 p.

Hugins, Walter E. JACKSONIAN DEMOCRACY AND THE WORKING CLASS: A STUDY OF THE NEW YORK WORKINGMEN'S MOVEMENT, 1829-1837. Stanford, Calif.: Stanford University Press, 1960. vi, 286 p.

An important study of the development of party organization.

Klein, Philip S. PENNSYLVANIA POLITICS, 1817-1832: A GAME WITH- OUT RULES. Philadelphia: Historical Society of Pennsylvania, 1940. viii, 430 p. Appendix.

Mering, John V. THE WHIG PARTY IN MISSOURI. Columbia: University of Missouri Press, 1967. 276 p.

Montgomery, Horace. CRACKER PARTIES. Baton Rouge: Louisiana State Uni- versity Press, 1950. viii, 278 p.

This is a study of Georgia politics in the late antebellum period (1845-61).

Murray, Paul. THE WHIG PARTY IN GEORGIA, 1825-1853. Chapel Hill: University of North Carolina Press, 1948. vii, 219 p.

Overdyke, W. Darrell. THE KNOW-NOTHING PARTY IN THE SOUTH. Bat- on Rouge: Louisiana State University Press, 1950. vi, 322 p. Appendix, illus.

A very useful account of the American party's activities in the 1850s.

Potter, David M. THE SOUTH AND SECTIONAL CONFLICT. Baton Rouge: Louisiana State University Press, 1968. xi, 321 p.

This is an excellent series of essays on the nature of the South and Civil War politics by a distinguished historian.

Rosenberg, Morton M. IOWA ON THE EVE OF THE CIVIL WAR: A DECADE OF FRONTIER POLITICS. Norman: University of Oklahoma Press, 1972. ix, 262 p.

An examination and description of politics in the 1850s.

Simms, Henry H. THE RISE OF THE WHIGS IN VIRGINIA, 1824-1840. Richmond, Va.: William Byrd Press, 1929. ix, 204 p. Illus.

Stevens, Harry R. THE EARLY JACKSON PARTY IN OHIO. Durham, N.C.: Duke University Press, 1957. xi, 187 p. Appendixes.

Sydnor, Charles S. THE DEVELOPMENT OF SOUTHERN SECTIONALISM, 1819-1848. Baton Rouge: Louisiana State University Press, 1948. xii, 400 p. Appendix, illus.

> An excellent study that details the disaffection of the South.

Wooster, Ralph A. THE PEOPLE IN POWER: COURTHOUSE AND STATE-HOUSE IN THE LOWER SOUTH, 1850-1860. Knoxville: University of Tennessee Press, 1969. xi, 189 p.

> An interesting look at local and state politics. This volume and a companion volume on the upper South are very useful to the student of the period.

_____. POLITICIANS, PLANTERS, AND PLAIN FOLK: COURTHOUSE AND STATEHOUSE IN THE UPPER SOUTH, 1850-1860. Knoxville: University of Tennessee Press, 1975. xiii, 204 p.

Section 4. BIOGRAPHY

Abbott, Richard H. COBBLER IN CONGRESS: THE LIFE OF HENRY WILSON, 1812-1875. Lexington: University of Kentucky Press, 1972. xii, 289 p. Illus.

> Elected to the Massachusetts House of Representatives as a Whig, he broke with the Whigs in 1848, briefly backed the Free-Soilers and the Know-Nothings, and finally aligned himself with the Republicans. He at first opposed Johnson's reconstruction policy but later became more conciliatory. Abbott's biography is readable and scholarly.

Ammon, Harry. JAMES MONROE: THE QUEST FOR NATIONAL IDENTITY. New York: McGraw-Hill Book Co., 1971. xi, 706 p.

> A good assessment of Monroe as a political leader.

Bemis, Samuel F. JOHN QUINCY ADAMS AND THE FOUNDATIONS OF AMERICAN FOREIGN POLICY. New York: Alfred A. Knopf, 1949. xix, 588 p. Illus., maps.

> Although the focus of this study is foreign policy, the reader will learn a great deal about American politics in the first several decades of the nineteenth century.

_____. JOHN QUINCY ADAMS AND THE UNION. New York: Alfred A. Knopf, 1956. xv, 546 p.

> Bemis has provided us with an outstanding one-volume biography of our sixth president. One can follow the early political struggles of a young nation to the controversy surrounding slavery and the Mexican War.

Benton, Thomas H. THIRTY YEARS VIEW: OR A HISTORY OF THE WORKING OF THE AMERICAN GOVERNMENT FOR THIRTY YEARS, FROM 1820 TO 1850. 2 vols. New York: D. Appleton and Co., 1897.

> Originally published between 1854-56, Senator Benton's memoirs provide the student of the period with a highly personal, informative, and entertaining look at American politics.

Brown, Norman D. DANIEL WEBSTER AND THE POLITICS OF AVAILABILITY. Athens: University of Georgia Press, 1969. vii, 184 p.

> Although the focus is on Webster, the author provides an interesting account of American politics in the mid-1830s.

Capers, Gerald M. JOHN C. CALHOUN, OPPORTUNIST: A REAPPRAISAL. Gainesville: University of Florida Press, 1960. viii, 275 p. Appendix.

> An excellent political biography that also provides insight into a very complex personality.

_____. STEPHEN A. DOUGLAS: DEFENDER OF THE UNION. Boston: Little, Brown and Co., 1959. x, 239 p.

> A brief but creditable biography of the great Democratic party leader in the 1850s.

Chambers, William N. OLD BULLION BENTON: SENATOR FROM THE NEW WEST. Boston: Little, Brown and Co., 1956. xv, 517 p.

> The author examines in depth the life of Senator Benton, a man of unyielding political convictions and controversial personal traits.

Chitwood, Oliver P. JOHN TYLER: CHAMPION OF THE OLD SOUTH. New York: Appleton-Century Co., 1939. xv, 496 p. Appendixes.

> Virginia legislator and president of the United States who consistently opposed the slave trade but also opposed the legislative efforts to abolish the slave trade. He moved from the Democrats to Whigs because of his states' rights stand, but he fell out with the Whigs during his presidency. Chitwood is sympathetic but generally even-handed in his treatment.

Coit, Margaret L. JOHN C. CALHOUN: AMERICAN PORTRAIT. Boston: Houghton, Mifflin and Co., 1950. ix, 593 p. Illus.

The story of American politics from 1808 to 1850 is related through the career of Calhoun.

Current, Richard N. DANIEL WEBSTER AND THE RISE OF NATIONAL CONSERVATISM. Boston: Little, Brown and Co., 1955. xi, 215 p.

This brief but well-written biography of Webster serves to illustrate a political point of view from 1812 to 1852.

Curtis, James C. THE FOX AT BAY: MARTIN VAN BUREN AND THE PRESIDENCY, 1837-1841. Lexington: University of Kentucky Press, 1970. xi, 234 p.

This study is one of the few works that concentrate on the politics of the Van Buren presidency.

Dalzell, Robert F., Jr. DANIEL WEBSTER AND THE TRIAL OF AMERICAN NATIONALISM, 1843-1852. Boston: Houghton, Mifflin and Co., 1973. xv, 363 p.

A full account of Webster's political career during the last years of his public life.

Dubay, Robert W. JOHN JONES PETTUS, MISSISSIPPI FIRE-EATER: HIS LIFE AND TIMES, 1813-1867. Jackson: University Press of Mississippi, 1974. 234 p.

Although Pettus is little known, his story is useful for understanding southern politics in the pre-Civil War era.

Eaton, Clement. HENRY CLAY AND THE ART OF AMERICAN POLITICS. Boston: Little, Brown and Co., 1957. 209 p.

A brief but well-written biography of Clay.

Foner, Philip S. FREDERICK DOUGLASS. New York: Citadel Press, 1964. 444 p.

A black abolitionist, Douglass led the fight not only for abolition but for woman suffrage and other social reforms.

Fuess, Claude Moore. DANIEL WEBSTER. 2 vols. Boston: Little, Brown and Co., 1930. Illus.

A most thorough study and one generally regarded as a leading example of political biography.

Garraty, John A. SILAS WRIGHT. New York: Columbia University Press, 1949. 426 p.

A nationalist and a Democrat, Wright's political career began in New York State in 1824. He then served in the House of Representatives and the Senate. Shortly before his death he served as governor of New York. Garraty provides the reader with a great deal of information on pre-Civil War politics.

Goebel, Dorothy B. WILLIAM HENRY HARRISON: A POLITICAL BIOGRAPHY. Indianapolis: Indiana Library and Historical Board, 1926. xi, 456 p. Illus.

Although other biographies are available, this one concentrates on politics to a greater degree.

Hamilton, Hollman. ZACHARY TAYLOR: SOLDIER IN THE WHITE HOUSE. Indianapolis: Bobbs-Merrill Co., 1951. 496 p. Illus.

This is the second volume in a two-volume study. The first examines Taylor's role in the opening of the West.

Hendrickson, James E. JOE LANE OF OREGON: MACHINE POLITICS AND THE SECTIONAL CRISIS, 1849-1861. New Haven, Conn.: Yale University Press, 1967. xiii, 274 p. Illus.

Active in Indiana politics in the 1830s, the Mexican War, and Oregon politics in the 1850s. In 1860 he ran for vice-president on the Breckinridge ticket.

Isely, Jeter A. HORACE GREELEY AND THE REPUBLICAN PARTY, 1853-1861: A STUDY OF THE NEW YORK TRIBUNE. Princeton, N.J.: Princeton University Press, 1947. Reprint. New York: Octagon Books, 1965. Illus.

Greeley's influence on the Republican party was considerable.

James, Marquis. ANDREW JACKSON, PORTRAIT OF A PRESIDENT. New York: Garden City Publishing Co., 1940. 627 p.

Although this biography is a little dated, it still is the best introduction to the politics of Jackson.

_____. THE RAVEN: A BIOGRAPHY OF SAM HOUSTON. Indianapolis: Bobbs-Merrill Co., 1929. 489 p. Illus.

James's biography, which is both scholarly and literary, was awarded a Pulitzer prize in 1930.

Johannsen, Robert W. STEPHEN A. DOUGLAS. New York: Oxford University Press, 1973. xii, 993 p. Illus.

A full biography. The author even adds new material not covered by excellent earlier biographies.

Klein, Philip S. PRESIDENT JAMES BUCHANAN: A BIOGRAPHY. University Park: Pennsylvania State University Press, 1962. xviii, 506 p. Illus.

> A thorough biography of one of our less well-known presidents.

Mooney, Chase C. WILLIAM H. CRAWFORD, 1772–1834. Lexington: University of Kentucky Press, 1974. xi, 364 p.

> A definitive treatment of a Georgia politician, diplomat, and cabinet officer.

Morgan, Robert J. A WHIG EMBATTLED. THE PRESIDENCY UNDER JOHN TYLER. Lincoln: University of Nebraska Press, 1954. xiii, 199 p.

> Tyler created political opposition to his presidency in both political parties. Morgan attempts to gauge the extent of Tyler's influence on the political developments of the time.

Nathans, Sydney. DANIEL WEBSTER AND JACKSONIAN DEMOCRACY. Baltimore: Johns Hopkins University Press, 1973. xii, 249 p.

> The author sees Webster as an elitist politician who had to respond to the common man if his opposition to President Jackson was to be effective.

Nichols, Roy F. FRANKLIN PIERCE: YOUNG HICKORY OF THE GRANITE HILLS. Philadelphia: University of Pennsylvania Press, 1931. xvii, 615 p. Illus.

> A complete biography of one of our less highly-rated presidents. His active political career began in 1829 as a loyal Jacksonian Democrat.

Parks, Joseph H. JOHN BELL OF TENNESSEE. Baton Rouge: Louisiana State University Press, 1950. viii, 435 p. Illus.

> Bell's political career began in 1827. He started as a Democrat, became a Whig in 1840. Although the Whig party was dead by 1858, moderates on the slave question and former Whigs supported him for the presidency in 1860. Generally conservative on most issues, he nevertheless was more nationally minded than most southerners in the 1850s.

Penney, Sherry. PATRICIAN IN POLITICS: DANIEL DEWEY BARNARD OF NEW YORK. Port Washington, N.Y.: Kennikat Press, 1974. xv, 206 p.

> An important Whig politician involved in the opposition to Andrew Jackson and the Democrats.

Remini, Robert V. MARTIN VAN BUREN AND THE MAKING OF THE DEMOCRATIC PARTY. New York: Columbia University Press, 1959. viii, 271 p.

The story stops with the election of 1828. New York State and national politics are examined.

Sellers, Charles G., Jr. JAMES K. POLK, CONTINENTALIST: 1843-1846. Princeton, N.J.: Princeton University Press, 1966. x, 513 p. Illus.

Concentrates on the election of 1844 and the first years of Polk's presidency.

_____. JAMES K. POLK, JACKSONIAN: 1795-1843. Princeton, N.J.: Princeton University Press, 1957. xiv, 526 p. Maps, illus.

An examination of Polk's politics before his presidency.

Shenton, James P. ROBERT JOHN WALKER: A POLITICIAN FROM JACK-SON TO LINCOLN. New York: Columbia University Press, 1961. xviii, 288 p.

A leader of the Democratic party in Mississippi, Walker opposed the bank and the protective tariff. He served in the Polk and Buchanan administrations. He was a Unionist during the Civil War. Shenton's study impresses the reader with the continuity in mainstream politics.

Simms, Henry H. LIFE OF JOHN TAYLOR: THE STORY OF A BRILLIANT LEADER IN THE EARLY VIRGINIA STATE RIGHTS SCHOOL. Richmond, Va.: William Byrd Press, 1932. viii, 234 p.

He opposed ratification of the federal Constitution on the grounds that the rights of individuals and states were not adequately pro-tected. He also served several terms in the U.S. Senate. Simms's treatment is sympathetic but fair in the treatment of the issues.

Smith, Elbert B. MAGNIFICENT MISSOURIAN: THE LIFE OF THOMAS HART BENTON. Philadelphia: J. B. Lippincott Co., 1957. 351 p.

Elected to the U.S. Senate in 1820, Benton began a career of thirty years in that body. An extraordinary political figure who maintained his political independence until his death. The author catches the flair of Benton and corrects the myths that surround him.

_____. THE PRESIDENCY OF JAMES BUCHANAN. Lawrence: University Press of Kansas, 1975. xiii, 225 p.

He began his political career as a Federalist but in 1824 changed to the Democratic party. He split the party by recommending the proslavery Lecompton constitution for Kansas during his presidency. Smith's analysis of Buchanan is a useful corrective to some of the earlier studies.

Smith, William E. THE FRANCIS PRESTON BLAIR FAMILY IN POLITICS. 2 vols. New York: Macmillan Co., 1933. Illus.

> The politics of the Blair family encompass the major political developments and personalities of the United States from the 1820s to the 1870s.

Stewart, James B. JOSHUA R. GIDDINGS AND THE TACTICS OF RADICAL POLITICS. Cleveland: Case Western Reserve University Press, 1970. xiv, 318 p.

> A congressman from Ohio who was successively a Whig, Free-Soiler, and Republican.

Tucker, Glenn. ZEB VANCE: CHAMPION OF PERSONAL FREEDOM. Indianapolis: Bobbs-Merrill Co., 1965. viii, 564 p.

> Vance entered politics as a Whig. When Lincoln called for troops, he supported secession and served as a Confederate governor of North Carolina. After Reconstruction he served as governor again.

Van Deusen, Glyndon G. THE LIFE OF HENRY CLAY. Boston: Little, Brown and Co., 1937. viii, 448 p.

> Along with Calhoun, Webster, and Benton, Clay dominated American politics between 1812 and 1850.

_____. THURLOW WEED, WIZARD OF THE LOBBY. Boston: Little, Brown and Co., 1947. xiv, 403 p. Illus.

> A major political influence in the Whig and Republican parties from the 1830s to the mid-1860s.

Ward, John William. ANDREW JACKSON, SYMBOL FOR AN AGE. New York: Oxford University Press, 1955. xii, 274 p.

> More than a biography, this book explores the concept of Jacksonian democracy.

Wiltse, Charles M. JOHN C. CALHOUN. 3 vols. Indianapolis: Bobbs-Merrill Co., 1944-51. Illus.

> A detailed biography of this states' rights champion who attempted to maintain the Union on terms acceptable to the South.

Woodford, Frank B. LEWIS CASS: THE LAST JEFFERSONIAN. New Brunswick, N.J.: Rutgers University Press, 1950. ix, 380 p.

> He served in the Ohio legislature and as a U.S. senator from Michigan before running for the presidency on the Democratic ticket in 1848. This definitive work examines not only the politics of Cass but of the expanding nation prior to the Civil War.

Chapter V
CIVIL WAR AND RECONSTRUCTION, 1860-76

Section 1. SECESSION AND THE CIVIL WAR

Belz, Herman. A NEW BIRTH OF FREEDOM: THE REPUBLICAN PARTY AND FREEDMEN'S RIGHTS, 1861-1866. Westport, Conn.: Greenwood Press, 1976. xv, 200 p.

Catton, Bruce. CENTENNIAL HISTORY OF THE CIVIL WAR. 3 vols. Garden City, N.Y.: Doubleday and Co., 1961-65. Maps.

    A very readable account of the Civil War years.

Craven, Avery O. THE COMING OF THE CIVIL WAR. 2d ed. Chicago: University of Chicago Press, 1957. xi, 491 p.

    Craven views the conflict as an irrepressible one.

Crenshaw, Ollinger. THE SLAVE STATES IN THE PRESIDENTIAL ELECTION OF 1860. Baltimore: Johns Hopkins Press, 1945. Reprint. Gloucester, Mass.: Peter Smith, 1969. 332 p.

Curry, Richard O. A HOUSE DIVIDED: A STUDY OF STATEHOOD POLITICS AND THE COPPERHEAD MOVEMENT IN WEST VIRGINIA. Pittsburgh: University of Pittsburgh Press, 1964. 203 p. Maps.

    West Virginia, created during the Civil War, was to contain within its boundaries the divisions that divided the United States.

Dell, Christopher. LINCOLN AND THE WAR DEMOCRATS: THE GRAND EROSION OF CONSERVATIVE TRADITION. Rutherford, N.J.: Fairleigh Dickinson University Press, 1975. 455 p.

    This book not only analyzes the role of the loyal Democrats but ably connects state and national politics.

Dumond, Dwight L. SECESSION MOVEMENT, 1860-1861. New York: Macmillan Co., 1931. vi, 294 p. Appendixes.

> Although Dumond's study is over forty-five years old, it is still valuable because he carefully limits his field of investigation and focuses on the constitutional questions from April 1860 to April 1861.

Halstead, Murat. THREE AGAINST LINCOLN: MURAT HALSTEAD AND THE CAUCUSES OF 1860. Edited by William B. Hesseltine. Baton Rouge: Louisiana State University Press, 1960. xxi, 321 p.

> Originally published in 1860 under the title CAUCUSES OF 1860.

Hesseltine, William B. LINCOLN AND THE WAR GOVERNORS. New York: Alfred A. Knopf, 1948. x, 405, xxii p.

> The little-known but dramatic story of Lincoln's manipulation of political opinion in the North. Hesseltine believes that the Union was preserved as much by Lincoln's political victories over the Northern governors as by the military victories over the Southern secessionists.

Jones, Robert H. DISRUPTED DECADES: THE CIVIL WAR AND RECONSTRUC-TION YEARS. New York: Charles Scribner's Sons, 1973. xiv, 543 p,

> A good survey of the period.

Klement, Frank L. THE COPPERHEADS IN THE MIDDLE WEST. Chicago: University of Chicago Press, 1960. xiii, 341 p. Illus.

> Klement challenges and substantially revises the traditional interpretation that "Copperheadism" was pro-Southern and treasonable. He also suggests that "Copperheadism" was the forerunner of the postwar Granger and Populist movements.

Luthin, Reinhard H. THE FIRST LINCOLN CAMPAIGN. Cambridge, Mass.: Harvard University Press, 1944. viii, 328 p.

> This book is about the politics of Abraham Lincoln in the 1860 presidential campaign.

Nevins, Allan. ORDEAL OF THE UNION. 2 vols. New York: Charles Scribner's Sons, 1947.

> The author explores the political difficulties faced by the United States between 1847 and 1857.

Stampp, Kenneth M. AND THE WAR CAME: THE NORTH AND THE SECESSION CRISIS, 1860-1861. Baton Rouge: Louisiana State University Press, 1950. viii, 331 p. Illus.

The object of Stampp's analysis is the evaluation of northern public opinion regarding the mounting crisis. He concludes that northern identification of the national interest with sectional self-interest made northern efforts at compromise largely hypocritical.

Williams, T[homas]. Harry. LINCOLN AND THE RADICALS. Madison: University of Wisconsin Press, 1941. 413 p. Illus.

One of the most readable books on the subject.

Wooster, Ralph A. THE SECESSION CONVENTIONS OF THE SOUTH. Princeton, N.J.: Princeton University Press, 1962. viii, 294 p. Tables.

Wright, John S. LINCOLN AND THE POLITICS OF SLAVERY. Reno: University of Nevada Press, 1970. xiii, 215 p.

Zornow, William F. LINCOLN AND THE PARTY DIVIDED. Norman: University of Oklahoma Press, 1954. xi, 264 p. Illus.

The author concentrates on the political divisions in the North during 1864 and how Lincoln's political acumen reunited his party.

Section 2. THE CONFEDERACY

Alexander, Thomas B., and Beringer, Richard E. THE ANATOMY OF THE CONFEDERATE CONGRESS: A STUDY OF THE INFLUENCES OF MEMBER CHARACTERISTICS ON LEGISLATIVE VOTING BEHAVIOR, 1861-1865. Nashville, Tenn.: Vanderbilt University Press, 1972. xi, 435 p. Tables, appendixes.

Coulter, E[llis]. Merton. THE CONFEDERATE STATES OF AMERICA, 1861-1865. Baton Rouge: Louisiana State University Press, 1950. x, 644 p. Illus.

This book focuses on secession and the problems of the Confederate government.

Eaton, Clement. HISTORY OF THE SOUTHERN CONFEDERACY. New York: Macmillan Co., 1954. ix, 351 p.

Eaton's study is wide ranging. In addition to the political questions, he gives attention to the army, civilian population, Negroes, and the personalities of military and civil leaders.

Patrick, Rembert W. JEFFERSON DAVIS AND HIS CABINET. Baton Rouge: Louisiana State University Press, 1944. x, 401 p.

An important work on Confederate politics.

Section 3. RECONSTRUCTION

Benedict, Michael L. A COMPROMISE OF PRINCIPLE: CONGRESSIONAL REPUBLICANS AND RECONSTRUCTION, 1863-1869. New York: W.W. Norton and Co., 1964. 493 p. Illus.

Bowers, Claude G. THE TRAGIC ERA: THE REVOLUTION AFTER LINCOLN. Cambridge, Mass.: Literary Guild of America, 1929. xxii, 567 p. Illus.

> Bowers's account is very partisan and at odds with current scholarship, but his story is very readable.

Brock, William R. AN AMERICAN CRISIS: CONGRESS AND RECONSTRUCTION, 1865-1867. New York: St. Martin's Press, 1963. xii, 312 p.

> Brock, an English scholar, examines the reasons (idealism and political imperatives) for the behavior of American politicians in the process of congressional reconstruction.

Chalmers, David M. HOODED AMERICANISM: THE FIRST CENTURY OF THE KU KLUX KLAN, 1865-1965. Garden City, N.Y.: Doubleday and Co., 1965. xii, 420 p. Illus.

> The author provides not only a history of the Ku Klux Klan but also an analysis of the Klan's political influence.

Coleman, Charles H. THE ELECTION OF 1868: THE DEMOCRATIC EFFORT TO REGAIN CONTROL. New York: Columbia University Press, 1933. 407 p. Appendixes.

Coulter, E[llis]. Merton. THE SOUTH DURING RECONSTRUCTION, 1867-1877. Baton Rouge: Louisiana State University Press, 1947. xii, 426 p. Illus.

> The author focuses on the <u>South</u> during Reconstruction--not <u>Reconstruction</u> in the South.

Cox, La Wanda, and Cox, John H. POLITICS, PRINCIPLE AND PREJUDICE, 1865-1866. New York: Macmillan Co., 1963. xiii, 294 p.

> The authors find that Andrew Johnson was largely responsible for the break between the legislative and executive branches of government in 1866. They also challenge other long-held opinions of the radicals.

Craven, Avery O. RECONSTRUCTION: THE ENDING OF THE CIVIL WAR. New York: Holt, Rinehart and Winston, 1969. vi, 330 p.

Curry, Richard O., ed. RADICALISM, RACISM, AND PARTY REALIGNMENT: THE BORDER STATES DURING RECONSTRUCTION. Baltimore: Johns Hopkins Press, 1969. xxvi, 331 p.

An important introduction to the political problems of the border states.

Donald, David H. THE POLITICS OF RECONSTRUCTION, 1863–1867. Baton Rouge: Louisiana State University Press, 1965. xviii, 105 p. Illus.

Donald's brief survey of Reconstruction politics is a valuable introduction to the subject.

Franklin, John Hope. RECONSTRUCTION: AFTER THE CIVIL WAR. Chicago: University of Chicago Press, 1961. xi, 258 p. Illus.

A lucid study of the subtleties of the period which demonstrates the successes and failures of Reconstruction without the exaggerations which are found in some of the older histories of Reconstruction.

Hesseltine, William B. LINCOLN'S PLAN OF RECONSTRUCTION. Chicago: Quadrangle Books, 1967. 154 p. Pap.

Kutler, Stanley I. JUDICIAL POWER AND RECONSTRUCTION POLITICS. Chicago: University of Chicago Press, 1968. ix, 178 p.

A very important study of the role of the courts and political imperatives.

Mantell, Martin E. JOHNSON, GRANT, AND THE POLITICS OF RECONSTRUCTION. New York: Columbia University Press, 1973. 209 p.

A useful description and analysis of Reconstruction politics and personalities.

Perman, Michael. REUNION WITHOUT COMPROMISE: THE SOUTH AND RECONSTRUCTION, 1865–1868. London: Cambridge University Press, 1973. 376 p. Appendix.

Focuses on events and personalities beyond the radical Congress and President Johnson.

Polakoff, Keith Ian. THE POLITICS OF INERTIA: THE ELECTION OF 1876 AND THE END OF RECONSTRUCTION. Baton Rouge: Louisiana State University Press, 1973. xiv, 343 p.

Details party organization and the techniques employed by the two major parties that led to the compromise of 1877.

Stampp, Kenneth M. THE ERA OF RECONSTRUCTION, 1865-1877. New York: Alfred A. Knopf, 1965. ix, 228, v p.

A brief but realistic political history of Reconstruction. It is Stampp's thesis that many of the traditional views are distorted or untrue.

Stampp, Kenneth M., and Litwack, Leon F., eds. RECONSTRUCTION: AN ANTHOLOGY OF REVISIONIST WRITINGS. Baton Rouge: Louisiana State University Press, 1969. xii, 531 p.

Trefousse, Hans L. IMPEACHMENT OF A PRESIDENT: ANDREW JOHNSON, THE BLACKS, AND RECONSTRUCTION. Knoxville: University of Tennessee Press, 1975. xii, 252 p.

An important analysis of a major political event.

Trelease, Allen W. RECONSTRUCTION: THE GREAT EXPERIMENT. New York: Harper and Row, 1971. 224 p. Illus.

A readable revisionist survey of scholarly efforts on political reconstruction.

_____. WHITE TERROR: THE KU KLUX KLAN CONSPIRACY AND SOUTHERN RECONSTRUCTION. New York: Harper and Row, 1971. xlviii, 557 p. Illus.

Important study on the Democratic party's return to power.

Unger, Irwin. THE GREENBACK ERA: A SOCIAL AND POLITICAL HISTORY OF AMERICAN FINANCE, 1865-1879. Princeton, N.J.: Princeton University Press, 1964. 467 p. Appendixes.

Weinstein, Allen. PRELUDE TO POPULISM: ORIGINS OF THE SILVER ISSUE, 1867-1878. New Haven, Conn.: Yale University Press, 1970. x, 433 p. Appendix, tables.

Woodward, C[omer]. Vann. REUNION AND REACTION: THE COMPROMISE OF 1877 AND THE END OF RECONSTRUCTION. Boston: Little, Brown and Co., 1951. x, 263 p. Illus.

The author completely rewrites the accepted version of the events whereby the disputed election of 1876 was resolved and a renewal of domestic strife averted.

Section 4. STATES AND REGIONS

Alexander, Thomas B. POLITICAL RECONSTRUCTION IN TENNESSEE. Nashville, Tenn.: Vanderbilt University Press, 1950. 292 p.

Baker, Jean H. THE POLITICS OF CONTINUITY: MARYLAND POLITICAL PARTIES FROM 1858 TO 1870. Baltimore: Johns Hopkins Press, 1973. xv, 239 p.

Barney, William L. THE SECESSIONIST IMPULSE: ALABAMA AND MISSISSIPPI IN 1860. Princeton, N.J.: Princeton University Press, 1974. xv, 371 p. Tables, appendixes.

Bonadio, Felice A. NORTH OF RECONSTRUCTION: OHIO POLITICS, 1865–1870. New York: New York University Press, 1970. xi, 204 p.

    Ohio was a key political state in the Reconstruction period. Bonadio notes that radical ideology had little impact on Ohio politics.

Bradley, Erwin S. THE TRIUMPH OF MILITANT REPUBLICANISM: A STUDY OF PENNSYLVANIA AND PRESIDENTIAL POLITICS, 1860-1872. Philadelphia: University of Pennsylvania Press, 1964. 467 p. Appendixes.

    Pennsylvania remained loyal to the Union but the Republican party was not to retain the ideals of the war years. The author's efforts to relate the complexity of political activities are generally successful.

Brummer, Sidney D. POLITICAL HISTORY OF NEW YORK STATE DURING THE CIVIL WAR. Studies in History, Economics and Public Law, vol. 39. New York: Columbia University, 1911. Reprint. New York: AMS Press, 1967. 450 p.

    This reprint of Brummer's study of New York State politics is useful because of his examination of New York newspapers, which provide a wealth of information on the politics of the 1860s.

Knapp, Charles M. NEW JERSEY POLITICS DURING THE PERIOD OF THE CIVIL WAR AND RECONSTRUCTION. Geneva, N.Y.: W. F. Humphrey, 1924. v, 212 p.

Lamson, Peggy. THE GLORIOUS FAILURE: BLACK CONGRESSMAN ROBERT BROWN ELLIOTT AND THE RECONSTRUCTION IN SOUTH CAROLINA. New York: W. W. Norton and Co., 1973. 330 p.

    Elliott also served in the South Carolina legislature.

Mohr, James C. THE RADICAL REPUBLICANS AND REFORM IN NEW YORK DURING RECONSTRUCTION. Ithaca, N.Y.: Cornell University Press, 1973. xv, 300 p.

    This work is a valuable study of Republican state politics in the years 1865-67.

_____, ed. RADICAL REPUBLICANS IN THE NORTH: STATE POLITICS DUR-
ING RECONSTRUCTION. Baltimore: Johns Hopkins University Press, 1976.
xvi, 200 p.

> Nine states are examined. This study is particularly valuable for
> the person interested in a serious treatment of Reconstruction poli-
> tics.

Porter, George H. OHIO POLITICS DURING THE CIVIL WAR. New York:
Columbia University Press, 1911. Reprint. New York: AMS Press, 1968.
255 p.

> Although somewhat dated, this study is useful for its close look at
> state politics during the Civil War.

Smith, Charles P. CHARLES PERRIN SMITH: NEW JERSEY POLITICAL REMI-
NISCENCES, 1828–1882. Edited by Hermann K. Platt. New Brunswick, N.J.:
Rutgers University Press, 1965. vii, 278 p.

Stampp, Kenneth M. INDIANA POLITICS DURING THE CIVIL WAR. Indianapolis: Indiana Historical Bureau, 1949. vii, 278 p.

Taylor, Joe Gray. LOUISIANA RECONSTRUCTED, 1863–1877. Baton Rouge:
Louisiana State University Press, 1975. xii, 552 p.

> The main emphasis is on the political history of the state.

Thompson, Clara M. RECONSTRUCTION IN GEORGIA: ECONOMIC, SO-
CIAL, POLITICAL, 1865–1872. Savannah, Ga.: Beehive Press, 1972. 397 p.
Illus.

> Originally published in 1915, this is one of the better of the early
> studies of Reconstruction politics in the South.

Tredway, G[ilbert]. R. DEMOCRATIC OPPOSITION TO THE LINCOLN AD-
MINISTRATION IN INDIANA. Indianapolis: Indiana Historical Bureau, 1973.
xv, 433 p. Illus.

Williamson, Joel. AFTER SLAVERY: THE NEGRO IN SOUTH CAROLINA
DURING RECONSTRUCTION, 1861–1877. Chapel Hill: University of North
Carolina Press, 1965. ix, 442 p. Pap.

Wright, William C. THE SECESSION MOVEMENT IN THE MIDDLE ATLANTIC
STATES. Rutherford, N.J.: Fairleigh Dickinson University Press, 1973. 274 p.

Section 5. BIOGRAPHY

Bancroft, Frederic. THE LIFE OF WILLIAM H. SEWARD. Vol. 2. New York:
Harper and Brothers, 1900. iv, 576 p.

An outdated but widely distributed account of one of the nation's most important political leaders during the 1860s.

Baringer, William. LINCOLN'S RISE TO POWER. Boston: Little, Brown and Co., 1937. xv, 373 p. Illus.

An analysis of Lincoln's political activities between 1858 and 1860.

Belden, Thomas G., and Belden, Marva R. SO FELL THE ANGELS. Boston: Little, Brown and Co., 1956. 401 p. Illus.

Kate Chase Sprague wished to be the mistress of the White House, but this fascinating woman was never more than a guest. An intensely political woman, she possessed political power even though she did not have the vote. She even played an important role in the election of Hayes over Tilden in the disputed election of 1876.

Brodie, Fawn. THADDEUS STEVENS, SCOURGE OF THE SOUTH. New York: W. W. Norton and Co., 1959. 448 p. Illus.

A psychological study of a fascinating Reconstruction political leader.

Carman, Harry J., and Luthin, Reinhard H. LINCOLN AND THE PATRONAGE. New York: Columbia University Press, 1943. x, 375 p. Illus., appendix.

Cate, Wirt Armistead. LUCIUS Q. C. LAMAR, SECESSION AND REUNION. Chapel Hill: University of North Carolina Press, 1935. xiii, 594 p. Illus.

Lamar represented Mississippi in the two Congresses before the Civil War, and drafted the Mississippi ordinance of secession. His political rise occurred after the war when he served in the House and Senate.

Current, Richard N. OLD THAD STEVENS: A STORY OF AMBITION. Madison: University of Wisconsin Press, 1942. 344 p. Illus.

A leading figure in the Anti-Masonic, Whig, Free-Soil, and Republican parties, Stevens was an outspoken foe of slavery and slaveowners. Independent and enigmatic, he was largely responsible for the destruction of Lincoln's plan for Reconstruction.

Donald, David H. CHARLES SUMNER AND THE COMING OF THE CIVIL WAR. New York: Alfred A. Knopf, 1960. xxii, 388, xxiv p. Illus.

A classic biography by a distinguished scholar, covering the life of the powerful, complex, and almost fanatically dedicated senator from Massachusetts from his birth in 1811 to the firing on Fort Sumter.

_____. LINCOLN RECONSIDERED: ESSAYS ON THE CIVIL WAR ERA. New York: Alfred A. Knopf, 1959. xiii, 200, xiv p.

An important book for those who need an introduction to Lincoln as a man, politician, and president.

Fladeland, Betty L. JAMES GILLESPIE BIRNEY: SLAVEHOLDER TO ABOLI-TIONIST. Ithaca, N.Y.: Cornell University Press, 1955. 323 p.

Birney entered Alabama politics in the early 1820s. In 1830 he joined the American Colonization Society. Opposition to his antislavery activities forced him to move to Ohio. In 1840 and 1844, he was the Liberty party candidate for president.

Harrington, Fred H. FIGHTING POLITICIAN: MAJOR GENERAL N. P. BANKS. Philadelphia: University of Pennsylvania Press, 1948. xi, 301 p. Maps.

General Banks was a Civil War general and a famous Massachusetts political figure.

Hunt, H[arry]. Draper. HANNIBAL HAMLIN OF MAINE: LINCOLN'S FIRST VICE-PRESIDENT. Syracuse, N.Y.: Syracuse University Press, 1969. ix, 292 p.

Initially a Jacksonian Democrat, Hamlin served in the Maine legis-lature, the U.S. House of Representatives, and the U.S. Senate. His antislavery views made him Lincoln's running mate in 1860. He returned to the Senate in 1869.

Jellison, Charles A. FESSENDEN OF MAINE: CIVIL WAR SENATOR. Syra-cuse, N.Y.: Syracuse University Press, 1962. vi, 294 p. Illus.

Originally a Whig, William P. Fessenden joined in the antislavery faction. He served briefly in Lincoln's cabinet. Reelected to the U.S. Senate in 1865, he supported radical Reconstruction but op-posed the radicals at President Johnson's impeachment trial.

Kirwan, Albert D. JOHN J. CRITTENDEN: THE STRUGGLE FOR THE UNION. Lexington: University of Kentucky Press, 1962. xii, 514 p. Illus.

An excellent biography of a major political figure from the ad-ministration of Monroe to that of Lincoln.

Klement, Frank L. THE LIMITS OF DISSENT: CLEMENT L. VALLANDIGHAM AND THE CIVIL WAR. Lexington: University of Kentucky Press, 1970. xii, 351 p. Illus.

The story of one of the most important Copperheads.

McKitrick, Eric L. ANDREW JOHNSON AND RECONSTRUCTION. Chicago: University of Chicago Press, 1960. ix, 534 p.

McKitrick challenges the conventional portrait of Johnson as the misunderstood statesman of Reconstruction and reveals him as a small-minded and vindictive man who delayed the reunion of North and South.

Meade, Robert D. JUDAH P. BENJAMIN: CONFEDERATE STATESMAN. New York: Oxford University Press, 1943. ix, 432 p.

A conservative, Benjamin joined the Whig party and was elected to the U.S. Senate from Louisiana in 1852. In 1856 he became a Democrat and defended southern rights. He served in the Confederate cabinet.

Milton, George Fort. THE AGE OF HATE: ANDREW JOHNSON AND THE RADICALS. New York: Coward-McCann, 1930. xi, 788 p. Appendix.

Milton depicts Johnson and the nation as victims of the radicals.

_____. THE EVE OF THE CONFLICT: STEPHEN A. DOUGLAS AND THE NEEDLESS WAR. Boston: Houghton, Mifflin and Co., 1934. xiii, 608 p. Illus.

A sympathetic but credible study of Douglas.

Nye, Russel B. WILLIAM LLOYD GARRISON AND THE HUMANITARIAN RE-FORMERS. Boston: Little, Brown and Co., 1955. 215 p.

Nye examines Garrison's career as a leader of the antislavery crusade and his politics after the Civil War.

Phillips, Ulrich Bonnell. THE LIFE OF ROBERT TOOMBS. New York: Macmillan Co., 1913. ix, 281 p.

A sympathetic picture of one of Georgia's major political figures prior to the Civil War. A political maverick, Toombs remained outside of politics from 1862 to 1877.

Randall, James G. LINCOLN, THE PRESIDENT. 4 vols. New York: Dodd, Mead and Co., 1944-55. Illus.

A work of immense scholarship.

Roberts, Derrell C. JOSEPH E. BROWN AND THE POLITICS OF RECON-STRUCTION. University: University of Alabama Press, 1973. 159 p. Appendixes.

The author is sympathetic to Brown and sees him as the prototype of the New Southerner. Brown served as governor of Georgia,

1857-65, and was active as a Republican, 1866-71, but reentered the Democratic party and served as U.S. Senator, 1880-91.

Steele, Robert V. [Thomas, Lately]. THE FIRST PRESIDENT JOHNSON: THE THREE LIVES OF THE SEVENTEENTH PRESIDENT OF THE UNITED STATES OF AMERICA. New York: William Morrow and Co., 1968. x, 676 p. Illus.

Strode, Hudson. JEFFERSON DAVIS. 3 vols. New York: Harcourt, Brace and Co., 1955-64. Illus.

A major biography that explores the pre-Civil War political career of Davis in great detail as well as Davis the Confederate president.

Thomas, Benjamin P. ABRAHAM LINCOLN: A BIOGRAPHY. New York: Alfred A. Knopf, 1952. 548, xii p. Illus.

One of the best single-volume biographies of Lincoln.

Thomas, Benjamin P., and Hyman, Harold M. STANTON: THE LIFE AND TIMES OF LINCOLN'S SECRETARY OF WAR. New York: Alfred A. Knopf, 1962. xviii, 643, xiii p.

The biography of a major political figure in the Republican party. A necessary book for the understanding of radical Reconstruction.

Thompson, William Y. ROBERT TOOMBS OF GEORGIA. Baton Rouge: Louisiana State University Press, 1966. xiii, 281 p. Illus.

A new look, based upon more recent scholarship, at this southern politician.

Trefousse, Hans L. BEN BUTLER: THE SOUTH CALLED HIM BEAST. New York: Twayne Publishers, 1957. 365 p. Illus.

Originally a Democrat, at the end of the Civil War Butler was identified with the radical Republicans. He was one of the leaders in the impeachment proceedings against Johnson. Subsequently he deserted the Republicans for the Democrats and third parties.

_____. BENJAMIN FRANKLIN WADE: RADICAL REPUBLICAN FROM OHIO. New York: Twayne Publishers, 1963. 404 p.

Examines a vigorous leader of the antislavery group in the Congress in the 1850s. As a radical Republican, he opposed Lincoln's and Johnson's plans for Reconstruction.

Van Deusen, Glyndon G. HORACE GREELEY: NINETEENTH-CENTURY CRUSADER. Philadelphia: University of Pennsylvania Press, 1953. 445 p. Illus.

An extensive examination of Greeley's politics.

_____. WILLIAM HENRY SEWARD. New York: Oxford University Press, 1967. xi, 666 p. Illus.

A very useful study of politics from 1824 to 1868, although Seward's greatest public service occurred from 1861 to 1868.

Von Abele, Rudolph. ALEXANDER H. STEPHENS: A BIOGRAPHY. New York: Alfred A. Knopf, 1946. xiii, 336, x p. Illus.

Stephens's political career began as a Whig in 1836. Although he opposed secession, he was elected vice-president of the Confederacy. In 1872 Georgia sent him to the U.S. Congress.

Chapter VI
POLITICS IN THE GILDED AGE, 1877-1900

Section 1. GENERAL

Buck, Paul H. THE ROAD TO REUNION, 1865-1900. Boston: Little, Brown and Co., 1937. xi, 320 p.

> This is an important history of how two foes (North and South) overcame their differences in the post-Civil War period.

Clancy, Herbert J. THE PRESIDENTIAL ELECTION OF 1880. Chicago: Loyola University Press, 1958. ix, 294 p.

> The primary object of this study is an analysis of the issues in the presidential election of 1880 rather than a study of the lives of the candidates.

Dearing, Mary R. VETERANS IN POLITICS: THE STORY OF THE G.A.R. Baton Rouge: Louisiana State University Press, 1952. x, 523 p. Illus.

> The power wielded by the Grand Army of the Republic in the post-Civil War period was considerable, and the author examines how this power was used.

De Santis, Vincent P. REPUBLICANS FACE THE SOUTHERN QUESTIONS: THE NEW DEPARTURE YEARS, 1877-1896. Baltimore: Johns Hopkins Press, 1959. 275 p.

Destler, Chester M. AMERICAN RADICALISM, 1865-1901. Chicago: Quadrangle Books, 1966. xii, 276 p. Illus. Pap.

> This book remains one of the better studies of radical political action in this period. It challenges the "robber baron" thesis employed by earlier historians.

Dobson, John M. POLITICS IN THE GILDED AGE: A NEW PERSPECTIVE ON REFORM. New York: Praeger Publishers, 1972. 200 p.

There is a particularly good account of the election of 1884 in this study.

Faulkner, Harold U. POLITICS, REFORM AND EXPANSION, 1890-1900. New York: Harper and Brothers, 1959. xiv, 312 p. Illus.

The author focuses primarily on the politics of the decade, economics, and the reform impulse.

Grantham, Dewey W., Jr. THE DEMOCRATIC SOUTH. Athens: University of Georgia Press, 1963. xii, 109 p.

The author in several interpretative essays explores the origins and development of politics in the post-Civil War South.

Haworth, Paul L. THE HAYES-TILDEN DISPUTED PRESIDENTIAL ELECTION OF 1876. Cleveland: Burrows Brothers Co., 1906. xi, 365 p. Appendix.

This older work has been superseded by more recent scholarship, but it tells the major aspects of the event in considerable detail.

Hirshon, Stanley P. FAREWELL TO THE BLOODY SHIRT: NORTHERN REPUBLICANS AND THE SOUTHERN NEGRO, 1877-1893. Bloomington: Indiana University Press, 1962. 334 p.

A very useful study. The change in direction of the Republican party is carefully analyzed.

Hollingsworth, J. Rogers. THE WHIRLIGIG OF POLITICS: THE DEMOCRACY OF CLEVELAND AND BRYAN. Chicago: University of Chicago Press, 1963. xii, 263 p. Illus.

Well written and full of information on major and minor personalities and events.

Hoogenboom, Ari A. OUTLAWING THE SPOILS: A HISTORY OF THE CIVIL SERVICE REFORM MOVEMENT, 1865-1883. Urbana: University of Illinois Press, 1968. xi, 306 p. Appendixes.

The story of one of the great reform efforts in the latter half of the nineteenth century.

Jensen, Richard. THE WINNING OF THE MIDWEST: SOCIAL AND POLITICAL CONFLICT, 1888-1896. Chicago: University of Chicago Press, 1971. xvii, 357 p. Tables.

This is a study of voting patterns. The author is interested in why the electorate voted as it did.

Jones, Stanley L. THE PRESIDENTIAL ELECTION OF 1896. Madison: University of Wisconsin Press, 1964. x, 436 p. Illus.

Josephson, Matthew. THE POLITICOS, 1865-1896. New York: Harcourt, Brace and Co., 1938. ix, 760 p.

Although the author's prejudice and misinformation mar this study, this is an interesting view of politics in the post-Civil War period.

Kleppner, Paul. THE CROSS OF CULTURE: A SOCIAL ANALYSIS OF MID-WESTERN POLITICS, 1850-1900. New York: Macmillan Co., 1970. x, 402 p. Appendixes.

Kleppner provides the reader with a well-written analysis of the political events and personalities of the late nineteenth century.

Knoles, George H. PRESIDENTIAL CAMPAIGN AND ELECTION OF 1892. Stanford, Calif.: Stanford University Press, 1942. 268 p.

One of the best of the accounts that specifically treat this election.

Kousser, J. Morgan. THE SHAPING OF SOUTHERN POLITICS: SUFFRAGE RESTRICTION AND THE ESTABLISHMENT OF THE ONE-PARTY SOUTH, 1880-1910. New Haven, Conn.: Yale University Press, 1974. xvii, 319 p. Tables.

Kousser's work augments the studies of V. O. Key and C. Vann Woodward.

McFarland, Gerald W. MUGWUMPS, MORALS AND POLITICS, 1884-1920. Amherst: University of Massachusetts Press, 1975. xi, 291 p.

A quantitative approach that is primarily useful in tracing a particular individual's association with reform causes.

McSeveney, Samuel T. THE POLITICS OF DEPRESSION: POLITICAL BEHAVIOR IN THE NORTHEAST, 1893-1896. New York: Oxford University Press, 1972. xvi, 333 p. Tables, appendixes.

Describes the intense amount of political activity and the changes in both major parties caused by the economic changes created by industrialization, urbanization, and immigration.

Marcus, Robert D. GRAND OLD PARTY: POLITICAL STRUCTURE IN THE GILDED AGE, 1880-1896. New York: Oxford University Press, 1971. x, 323 p.

An excellent source for an in-depth examination of the Republican party.

Merrill, Horace S[amuel]. BOURBON DEMOCRACY OF THE MIDDLE WEST, 1865-1896. Seattle: University of Washington Press, 1967. x, 300 p. Illus.

An important work for the study of the post-Civil War Democratic party.

Morgan, H[oward]. Wayne. FROM HAYES TO McKINLEY: NATIONAL PARTY POLITICS, 1877-1896. Syracuse, N.Y.: Syracuse University Press, 1969. x, 618 p. Illus.

An excellent introduction to the political history of the period.

Nugent, Walter T. K. MONEY AND AMERICAN SOCIETY, 1865-1880. New York: Free Press, 1968. xv, 336 p.

An exploration of the effect of the money question on American politics.

Ross, Earle D. THE LIBERAL REPUBLICAN MOVEMENT. New York: Holt, 1919. Reprint. New York: AMS Press, 1971. 267 p.

Rothman, David J. POLITICS AND POWER: THE UNITED STATES SENATE, 1869-1901. Cambridge, Mass.: Harvard University Press, 1966. x, 348 p. Tables, appendixes, illus.

Rothman concludes that the political leaders were far more competent than originally thought. He includes an interesting analysis of state party structures and the "folkways" of political life.

Simkins, F[rancis]. B. THE TILLMAN MOVEMENT IN SOUTH CAROLINA. Durham, N.C.: Duke University Press, 1926. ix, 274 p.

Sproat, John G. "THE BEST MEN": LIBERAL REFORMERS IN THE GILDED AGE. New York: Oxford University Press, 1968. ix, 356 p.

The story of the liberal Republican and mugwump movements. Sproat finds that their influence and goals have been overrated.

Thomas, Harrison Cook. THE RETURN OF THE DEMOCRATIC PARTY TO POWER IN 1884. New York: Columbia University, 1919. 261 p.

Tindall, George B. THE PERSISTENT TRADITION IN NEW SOUTH POLITICS. Baton Rouge: Louisiana State University Press, 1975. xiii, 71 p.

The author notes how tradition is reconciled with innovation by the Bourbons, Populists and Progressives in southern politics.

Woodward, C[omer]. Vann. THE ORIGINS OF THE NEW SOUTH, 1877-1913. Baton Rouge: Louisiana State University Press, 1951. xi, 542 p. Illus.

A very important introduction to southern politics during the latter half of the nineteenth century.

Section 2. THE AGRARIAN CRUSADE

Buck, Solon J. THE AGRARIAN CRUSADE: A CHRONICLE OF THE FARMER
IN POLITICS. New Haven, Conn.: Yale University Press, 1920. xi, 215 p.
Illus.

> A very important study although later scholarship has modified
> some of the author's conclusions.

_____. THE GRANGER MOVEMENT: A STUDY OF AGRICULTURAL OR-
GANIZATION AND ITS POLITICAL, ECONOMIC AND SOCIAL MANIFESTA-
TIONS, 1870–1880. Cambridge, Mass.: Harvard University Press, 1913. Re-
print. Lincoln: University of Nebraska Press, 1963. xi, 384 p. Illus. Pap.

> Originally published in 1913, it remains one of the better studies
> of agrarian politics although some of the author's conclusions re-
> garding the motivation of the farmer have been challenged by a
> few revisionists.

Clanton, O. Gene. KANSAS POPULISM: IDEAS AND MEN. Lawrence:
University Press of Kansas, 1969. xi, 330 p. Illus., appendixes.

> Clanton examines Populist sentiment in the heart of Populist ter-
> ritory.

Clinch, Thomas A. URBAN POPULISM AND FREE SILVER IN MONTANA:
A NARRATIVE OF IDEOLOGY IN POLITICAL ACTION. Missoula: University
of Montana Press, 1970. xiii, 190 p. Illus.

> Although "urban" in the title is somewhat confusing, this book is
> an excellent source for information surrounding the fusion of Popu-
> list reform efforts and free silver.

Durden, Robert F. CLIMAX OF POPULISM: THE ELECTION OF 1896. Lexington: University of Kentucky Press, 1965. xii, 190 p.

> The election of 1896 is seen from a perspective slightly different
> from that in other accounts.

Hicks, John D. THE POPULIST REVOLT: A HISTORY OF THE FARMERS'
ALLIANCE AND THE PEOPLE'S PARTY. Minneapolis: University of Minnesota
Press, 1931. xiii, 473 p. Illus., appendixes.

> The classic study of the Populists. Some of Hicks's conclusions
> have been challenged or modified by other historians.

Nugent, Walter T. K. THE TOLERANT POPULISTS: KANSAS, POPULISM
AND NATIVISM. Chicago: University of Chicago Press, 1963. x, 256 p.

> The author corrects the harsh judgment levied on the Populists.
> He does not find evidence to sustain the indictments that they
> were indecently nativist.

Scott, Roy V. THE AGRARIAN MOVEMENT IN ILLINOIS, 1880-1896. Urbana: University of Illinois Press, 1962. vii, 153 p.

A brief but well-done examination of agrarian interests and politics.

Wright, James E. THE POLITICS OF POPULISM: DISSENT IN COLORADO. New Haven, Conn.: Yale University Press, 1974. xii, 314 p.

A very useful study of the extent of the Populist influence in the Rocky Mountain region.

Section 3. STATE POLITICS

Barr, Alwyn. RECONSTRUCTION TO REFORM: TEXAS POLITICS, 1876-1906. Austin: University of Texas Press, 1971. xiv, 315 p. Illus.

Barr explores a fascinating chapter in Texas's political history, and connects the events in Texas with those in the South and the nation. Also the author includes the role of blacks in Texas politics during this period.

Benson, Lee. MERCHANTS, FARMERS, AND RAILROADS: RAILROAD REGULATION AND NEW YORK POLITICS, 1850-1887. New York: Russell and Russell, 1969. x, 310 p. Illus.

Cooper, William J., Jr. CONSERVATIVE REGIME: SOUTH CAROLINA 1877-1890. Baltimore: Johns Hopkins Press, 1968. 239 p. Illus.

This study is useful to anyone comparing the differences between the Old and New South. Cooper's study reveals that the state did not fit the currently accepted mold. He believes that the political battles arose from a conflict between generations, not classes.

Dilla, Harriette M. POLITICS OF MICHIGAN, 1865-1878. New York: Harriette M. Dilla, 1912. 259 p.

A useful book, but it should be augmented with biographies and more recent state histories.

Edmonds, Helen G. THE NEGRO AND FUSION POLITICS IN NORTH CAROLINA, 1894-1901. Chapel Hill: University of North Carolina Press, 1951. viii, 260 p. Appendix.

A very good analysis of the unsettled conditions troubling southern politics at the end of the nineteenth century.

Evans, Frank B. PENNSYLVANIA POLITICS, 1872-1877: A STUDY IN POLITICAL LEADERSHIP. Harrisburg: Pennsylvania Historical and Museum Commission, 1966. vii, 360 p. Illus.

Evans's description of personalities and events in Pennsylvania augments the general treatment of politics in the period.

Glass, Mary Ellen. SILVER·AND POLITICS IN NEVADA: 1892-1902. Reno: University of Nevada Press, 1969. xi, 242 p.

A thorough examination of one of the major issues of the 1890s.

Going, Allen J. BOURBON DEMOCRACY IN ALABAMA, 1874-1890. University: University of Alabama Press, 1951. ix, 256 p. Appendix.

Hair, William I. BOURBONISM AND AGRARIAN PROTEST: LOUISIANA POLITICS 1877-1900. Baton Rouge: Louisiana State University Press, 1969. vii, 305 p. Appendix, maps, illus.

A very careful study of agrarian protest and Bourbon reaction in a state much affected by the need for change.

Hart, Roger L. REDEEMERS, BOURBONS, AND POPULISTS: TENNESSEE, 1870-1896. Baton Rouge: Louisiana State University Press, 1975. xvi, 290 p.

Maddex, Jack P., Jr. THE VIRGINIA CONSERVATIVES, 1867-1879: A STUDY IN RECONSTRUCTION POLITICS. Chapel Hill: University of North Carolina Press, 1970. xx, 328 p.

Politics in Virginia and how Virginia avoided many of the features of radical reconstruction.

Morton, Richard L. THE NEGRO IN VIRGINIA POLITICS, 1865-1902. Charlottesville: University Press of Virginia, 1919. 199 p.

Although many of Morton's conclusions have been challenged, his work contains information on Virginia politics not available in other works.

Thelen, David P. THE NEW CITIZENSHIP: ORIGINS OF PROGRESSIVISM IN WISCONSIN, 1885-1900. Columbia: University of Missouri Press, 1972. 340 p.

A well-researched examination of political change. Revisionist in its demonstration that all classes stood in the progressive coalition except the business elite.

Wynes, Charles E. RACE RELATIONS IN VIRGINIA, 1870-1902. Charlottesville: University Press of Virginia, 1961. ix, 164 p.

Section 4. SPECIAL INTERESTS

Beisner, Robert L. TWELVE AGAINST EMPIRE: THE ANTI-IMPERIALISTS,

1898-1900. New York: McGraw-Hill Book Co., 1968. xvi, 310 p. Illus.

   A thorough examination of the antiimperialists prior to and after
   the Spanish-American War.

Callow, Alexander B., Jr. THE TWEED RING. New York: Oxford University Press, 1966. xi, 351 p. Illus.

   A well-balanced study of the prototype of all American political
   machines.

Holli, Melvin G. REFORM IN DETROIT: HAZEN S. PINGREE AND URBAN POLITICS. New York: Oxford University Press, 1969. xvi, 269 p.

   Hazen Pingree was a leader in the municipal reform movement before the "official" beginning of progressivism in 1901.

Lynch, Denis Tilden. "BOSS" TWEED: THE STORY OF A GRIM GENERA-TION. New York: Boni and Liveright, 1927. ix, 433 p. Illus.

   An older work but still useful in the study of the Tweed Ring and
   political bossism.

Mandelbaum, Seymour J. BOSS TWEED'S NEW YORK. New York: John Wiley and Sons, 1965. ix, 196 p. Illus.

   Very useful in the study of political machines.

Pratt, Julius W. EXPANSIONISTS OF 1898: THE ACQUISITION OF HAWAII AND THE SPANISH ISLANDS. Baltimore: Johns Hopkins Press, 1936. Reprint. Gloucester, Mass.: Peter Smith, 1959. viii, 393 p.

   Pratt examines the sharp conflict between the expansionists and
   antiexpansionists in the Congress in 1898 and 1899.

Rhodes, Harold V. UTOPIA IN AMERICAN POLITICAL THOUGHT. Tucson: University of Arizona Press, 1967. 115 p.

   The author concentrates on late nineteenth century thought.

Smith, Samuel D. THE NEGRO IN CONGRESS, 1870-1901. Chapel Hill: University of North Carolina Press, 1940. Reprint. Port Washington, N.Y.: Kennikat Press, 1966. xiii, 160 p.

   An early study, originally published in 1940, it contains conclusions that ought to be carefully weighed with more recent studies.

Woodward, C[lomer]. Vann. THE STRANGE CAREER OF JIM CROW. Rev. ed. New York: Oxford University Press, 1957. xix, 183 p.

   A very close and well-written examination of the origin of one-
   party politics in much of the South.

Section 5. BIOGRAPHY

Argersinger, Peter. POPULISM AND POLITICS: 1831-1912, WILLIAM ALFRED PEFFER AND THE PEOPLE'S PARTY OF THE UNITED STATES. Lexington: University of Kentucky Press, 1974. xiii, 337 p.

>As a U.S. Senator from Kansas, 1891-97, he supported the Populist cause. Argersinger also details Peffer's long career in journalism.

Barnard, Harry. "EAGLE FORGOTTEN": THE LIFE OF JOHN PETER ALTGELD. Indianapolis: Bobbs-Merrill Co., 1938. 496 p. Illus.

>An important biography of major political figure in Illinois and the nation in the late nineteenth century.

_____. RUTHERFORD B. HAYES AND HIS AMERICA. Indianapolis: Bobbs-Merrill Co., 1954. 606 p. Illus.

>An excellent biography of one of our less well-known presidents. Barnard emphasizes Hayes's strengths and his sometimes extraordinary political activity.

Beer, Thomas. HANNA. New York: Alfred A. Knopf, 1929. xi, 325 p. Appendix.

>Marcus A. Hanna's association with William McKinley made him an important political leader at the end of the nineteenth century.

Cotner, Robert C. JAMES STEPHEN HOGG: A BIOGRAPHY. Austin: University of Texas Press, 1959. xxvi, 617 p. Illus.

>Although Governor Hogg's name is not well remembered now, he was an important figure in the southwestern United States progressive reform movement.

Croly, Herbert D. MARCUS ALONZO HANNA: HIS LIFE AND WORK. New York: Macmillan Co., 1923. xiii, 495 p. Illus.

>A good biography of an important political leader. Croly views Hanna as the consummate political organizer.

Current, Richard N. PINE LOGS AND POLITICS: A LIFE OF PHILETUS SAWYER, 1816-1900. Madison: State Historical Society of Wisconsin, 1950. 330 p. Illus.

>A major Republican leader in Wisconsin for nearly a half century. He was an opponent of Robert M. LaFollette.

Davenport, Walter. POWER AND GLORY, THE LIFE OF BOIES PENROSE. New York: G. P. Putnam's Sons, 1931. ix, 240 p. Illus.

Although this biography suffers from inadequate research, the main outlines of Penrose's political career as a major political boss and legislator in Pennsylvania are sketched by the author.

Davison, Kenneth E. THE PRESIDENCY OF RUTHERFORD B. HAYES. Contributions in American Studies, no. 3. Westport, Conn.: Greenwood Press, 1972. xvii, 266 p. Illus.

An excellent account of the campaign of 1876 and the presidency of a man whom many historians rank behind Lincoln and Theodore Roosevelt among Republican presidents.

Ellis, Elmer. HENRY MOORE TELLER, DEFENDER OF THE WEST. Caldwell, Idaho: Caxton Printers, 1941. 409 p. Illus.

An important Colorado political leader. Originally a Republican, he became a Democrat at the end of the century and supported a number of reform causes; e.g., woman's suffrage, income taxes, and government regulation of big business.

Flick, Alexander C., and Lobrano, Gustav S. SAMUEL JONES TILDEN: A STUDY IN POLITICAL SAGACITY. New York: Dodd, Mead and Co., 1939. ix, 597 p. Illus.

Tilden was a major figure in the pre-Civil War Democratic party, supporting the Union and the liberal Reconstruction policy. He fought "Boss" Tweed. In 1876 he received the plurality of the popular vote as the Democratic candidate for president but he lost the election in the special electoral commission.

Fuess, Claude Moore. CARL SCHURZ: REFORMER, 1829-1906. New York: Dodd, Mead and Co., 1932. xv, 421 p. Illus.

A German immigrant, Schurz became a major figure in the liberal wing of the Republican party.

Glad, Paul W. McKINLEY, BRYAN, AND THE PEOPLE. Philadelphia: J. B. Lippincott Co., 1964. 222 p.

Glad examines the election of 1896 in great detail. He views both Bryan and McKinley as conservative.

Gosnell, Harold F. BOSS PLATT AND HIS NEW YORK MACHINE: A STUDY OF THE POLITICAL LEADERSHIP OF THOMAS C. PLATT, THEODORE ROOSEVELT AND OTHERS. Chicago, 1924. Reprint. New York: AMS Press, 1969. xxiv, 370 p. Illus.

A fascinating look at one of the major and successful Republican state political machines and its boss.

Grantham, Dewey W., Jr. HOKE SMITH AND THE POLITICS OF THE NEW SOUTH. Baton Rouge: Louisiana State University Press, 1958. 396 p. Illus.

Grantham's study is useful for students of national politics, Georgia, and New South politics.

Howe, George F. CHESTER A. ARTHUR: A QUARTER CENTURY OF MACHINE POLITICS. New York: Dodd, Mead and Co., 1934. xi, 307 p. Illus.

A useful biography that focuses not only on Arthur but also on the politics of the period.

Jordan, David M. ROSCOE CONKLING OF NEW YORK: VOICE IN THE SENATE. Ithaca, N.Y.: Cornell University Press, 1971. xiii, 464 p. Illus.

Politics of the period illuminated by Conkling's hate for his colleagues. Conkling's quarrels with fellow Republicans demonstrate that personality and self-interest often obscure issues.

Katz, Irving. AUGUST BELMONT: A POLITICAL BIOGRAPHY. New York: Columbia University Press, 1968. ix, 296 p. Illus.

A major figure in the conservative wing of the Democratic party.

Lambert, John R. ARTHUR PUE GORMAN. Baton Rouge: Louisiana State University Press, 1953. ix, 397 p. Illus.

A protege of Stephen A. Douglas, Gorman was a major figure in the Democratic party from Maryland.

Lambert, Oscar D. STEPHEN VENTON ELKINS. Pittsburgh: University of Pittsburgh Press, 1955. 336 p. Illus.

A major political figure in West Virginia during the late nineteenth century, although his early political activities took place in New Mexico.

Leech, Margaret. IN THE DAYS OF McKINLEY. New York: Harper and Brothers, 1959. viii, 686 p. Illus.

An able and well-written biography of one of our traditionally underrated presidents.

Lowitt, Richard. GEORGE W. NORRIS: THE MAKING OF A PROGRESSIVE, 1861-1912. Syracuse, N.Y.: Syracuse University Press, 1963. xiv, 341 p. Illus.

A leader in Nebraska politics and in the fight for reform.

Merrill, Horace S[amuel]. BOURBON LEADER: GROVER CLEVELAND AND THE DEMOCRATIC PARTY. Boston: Little, Brown and Co., 1957. viii, 224 p.

> A provocative and dispassionate account of Cleveland and the Democratic party.

Mitchell, Stewart. HORATIO SEYMOUR OF NEW YORK. Cambridge, Mass.: Harvard University Press, 1938. xx, 623 p. Illus.

> A very successful journalist, Seymour was also active in the liberal wing of the Democratic party.

Morgan, H[oward]. Wayne. WILLIAM McKINLEY AND HIS AMERICA. Syracuse, N.Y.: Syracuse University Press, 1963. xi, 595 p. Illus.

> The author focuses not only on McKinley but also on the politics of the latter half of the nineteenth century.

Muzzey, David Saville. JAMES G. BLAINE, A POLITICAL IDOL OF OTHER DAYS. New York: Dodd, Mead and Co., 1934. Reprint. Port Washington, N.Y.: Kennikat Press, 1963. 514 p. Illus.

> Blaine was the acknowledged leader of the Republican party for over a generation.

Neilson, James W. SHELBY M. CULLOM: PRAIRIE STATE REPUBLICAN. Urbana: University of Illinois Press, 1962. vii, 328 p. Pap.

> A major Illinois Republican leader.

Nevins, Allan. GROVER CLEVELAND: A STUDY IN COURAGE. New York: Dodd, Mead and Co., 1933. xiii, 832 p. Illus., appendixes.

> A well-written and complete biography.

_____. HAMILTON FISH: THE INNER HISTORY OF THE GRANT ADMINISTRATION. New York: Dodd, Mead and Co., 1937. xxi, 932 p. Illus.

> A biography of Fish and the Grant administration.

Nixon, Raymond B. HENRY W. GRADY: SPOKESMAN OF THE NEW SOUTH. New York: Alfred A. Knopf, 1943. x, 360, xiv p. Illus.

> As editor of the ATLANTA CONSTITUTION, Grady played an important political role in the development of New South politics.

Reeves, Thomas C. GENTLEMAN BOSS: THE LIFE OF CHESTER ALAN ARTHUR. New York: Alfred A. Knopf, 1975. xvii, 500 xix p.

> A very useful political biography and account of post-Civil War politics.

Ridge, Martin. IGNATIUS DONNELLY: THE PORTRAIT OF A POLITICIAN. Chicago: University of Chicago Press, 1962. x, 427 p. Illus.

An account of a dissenter in late nineteenth century politics. Donnelly played a role in the Populist movement.

Riordon, William L. PLUNKITT OF TAMMANY HALL. New York: E. P. Dutton and Co., 1963. xxv, 98 p.

The author was a New York City newspaperman who recorded the views of one of Tammany Hall's Tigers, George Plunkitt.

Sage, Leland L. WILLIAM BOYD ALLISON: A STUDY IN PRACTICAL POLITICS. Iowa City: State Historical Society of Iowa, 1956. xiv, 401 p. Illus.

A Republican political leader from Iowa.

Sievers, Harry J. BENJAMIN HARRISON. 3 vols. Chicago: Henry Regnery Co., 1952-68. Illus.

A major biography that also explores national Republican and Indiana politics.

Simkins, Francis B. PITCHFORK BEN TILLMAN: SOUTH CAROLINIAN. Baton Rouge: Louisiana State University Press, 1967. xii, 577 p. Pap.

A major political leader in southern politics in the late nineteenth and early twentieth century.

Smith, Theodore Clarke. THE LIFE AND LETTERS OF JAMES ABRAM GARFIELD. 2 vols. New Haven, Conn.: Yale University Press, 1925. Illus.

A sympathetic biography that is helpful in understanding the man and his times.

Spencer, Ivor D. THE VICTOR AND THE SPOILS: A LIFE OF WILLIAM L. MARCY. Providence, R.I.: Brown University Press, 1959. xii, 438 p.

An important pre-Civil War New York political figure who served as secretary of war in the Polk administration and secretary of state in the Pierce administration.

Welch, Richard E., Jr. GEORGE FRISBIE HOAR AND THE HALF-BREED REPUBLICANS. Cambridge, Mass.: Harvard University Press, 1971. 364 p. Illus.

Senator Hoar's politics are a useful illustration of the change in the outlook of the Republican party in the latter half of the nineteenth century.

Woodward, C[omer]. Vann. TOM WATSON: AGRARIAN REBEL. New York: Macmillan Co., 1938. xii, 518 p.

A major southern political figure involved in the Populist movement and racist politics.

Chapter VII

PROGRESSIVISM, 1900-1920

Section 1. GENERAL

Buenker, John D. URBAN LIBERALISM AND PROGRESSIVE REFORM. New
York: Charles Scribner's Sons, 1973. xi, 299 p. Illus.

>   An examination of political activity by different political coalitions
>   in support of various reform efforts. Professor Buenker has extended
>   the examination of urban progressivism begun by J. J. Huthmacher.

Fite, Gilbert C., and Peterson, Horace C. OPPONENTS OF THE WAR, 1917-
1918. Madison: University of Wisconsin Press, 1957. xiii, 399 p. Illus.

>   Included among the opponents of the war were major political
>   figures from the U.S. Senate, such as LaFollette and Norris.

Goldman, Eric F. RENDEZVOUS WITH DESTINY: A HISTORY OF MODERN
AMERICAN REFORM. New York: Alfred A. Knopf, 1952. xiii, 503, xxxvii p.

>   The author is concerned with the origins and development of twen-
>   tieth-century political liberalism.

Gould, Lewis L., ed. THE PROGRESSIVE ERA. Syracuse, N.Y.: Syracuse
University Press, 1974. x, 238 p. Illus.

>   A series of essays that analyze the varieties of progressivism.

Hechler, Kenneth W. INSURGENCY: PERSONALITIES AND POLITICS OF
THE TAFT ERA. New York: Columbia University Press, 1940. 252 p.

>   The attention of the author is directed toward the Republican
>   party and the Taft administration between 1909 and 1913.

Holt, James. CONGRESSIONAL INSURGENTS AND THE PARTY SYSTEM,
1909-1916. Cambridge, Mass.: Harvard University Press, 1967. viii, 188 p.

>   Very useful to the understanding of progressive politics. The weak-

nesses and strengths of the reform politicians in both parties are explored.

Josephson, Matthew. THE PRESIDENT MAKERS: THE CULTURE OF POLITICS AND LEADERSHIP IN AN AGE OF ENLIGHTENMENT, 1896-1919. New York: Harcourt, Brace and Co., 1940. viii, 584 p.

A partisan but well-written account of politics during the progressive era.

Kipnis, Ira. THE AMERICAN SOCIALIST MOVEMENT, 1897-1912. New York: Columbia University Press, 1952. 496 p.

A very important study that explores the successes and failures of one of the leading third-party movements.

Kolko, Gabriel. THE TRIUMPH OF CONSERVATISM: A REINTERPRETATION OF AMERICAN HISTORY, 1900-1916. Chicago: Quadrangle Books, 1967. 344 p. Pap.

The author argues that the "progressive" period was not really liberal, but was conservative. Kolko believes that the leaders of big business supported progressive reforms that enabled giant business to control the economy.

Kuhn, Henry, and Johnson, Olive M. THE SOCIALIST LABOR PARTY DURING FOUR DECADES, 1890-1930. New York: New York Labor News Co., 1931. 126 p.

A partisan account that contains information and conclusions provided by insiders from the radical wing of the Socialist movement.

Link, Arthur S. WOODROW WILSON AND THE PROGRESSIVE ERA, 1910-1917. New York: Harper and Brothers, 1954. xvii, 331 p. Illus.

One of the best surveys of Wilson's participation in the progressive reform fight.

Livermore, Seward W. POLITICS IS ADJOURNED: WOODROW WILSON AND THE WAR CONGRESS, 1916-1918. Middletown, Conn.: Wesleyan University Press, 1966. 324 p.

In spite of the title, politics were an important part of American history during the twenty months of the war.

Merrill, Horace Samuel, and Merrill, Marion G. THE REPUBLICAN COMMAND, 1897-1913. Lexington: University of Kentucky Press, 1971. xi, 360 p.

A conventional history of the Republican party as seen through the eyes of party leaders.

Morgan, H[oward]. Wayne. EUGENE V. DEBS: SOCIALIST FOR PRESIDENT. Syracuse, N.Y.: Syracuse University Press, 1962. 257 p. Illus.

Very useful in exploring Socialist politics as well as the politics of the major parties during the progressive period.

Morlan, Robert L. POLITICAL PRAIRIE FIRE: THE NON-PARTISAN LEAGUE, 1915-1922. Minneapolis: University of Minnesota Press, 1955. 408 p. Illus.

This book examines the complex political and economic problems that created a divergent political movement centered in the upper Great Plains.

Mowry, George E. THEODORE ROOSEVELT AND THE PROGRESSIVE MOVEMENT. Madison: University of Wisconsin Press, 1946. Reprint. New York: Hill and Wang, 1960. viii, 405 p.

A well-written and informative survey of Roosevelt and the Republican progressive movement that culminated in the birth of the Progressive party.

Odegard, Peter H. PRESSURE POLITICS: THE STORY OF THE ANTI-SALOON LEAGUE. New York: Columbia University Press, 1928. Reprint. New York: Octagon Books, 1966. x, 299 p. Appendixes.

An early study of the vital role played by the league in the passage of the Eighteenth Amendment.

O'Neill, William L. THE PROGRESSIVE YEARS: AMERICA COMES OF AGE. New York: Dodd, Mead and Co., 1975. xi, 166 p. Pap.

A good survey that pulls together the new scholarship that is critical of progressivism and the progressive era.

Penick, James L., Jr. PROGRESSIVE POLITICS AND CONSERVATION: THE BALLINGER-PINCHOT AFFAIR. Chicago: University of Chicago Press, 1968. xv, 207 p.

The Richard Ballinger-Gifford Pinchot controversy during the Taft administration was an important factor in the division of the Republican party before 1912.

Pinchot, Amos R. E. HISTORY OF THE PROGRESSIVE PARTY, 1912-1916. Edited by Helene M. Hooker. New York: New York University Press, 1958. xii, 305 p. Appendixes.

Pinchot's account was based on his insider's knowledge of the issues and personalities.

Richardson, Elmo R. POLITICS OF CONSERVATION: CRUSADES AND CONTROVERSIES, 1897-1913. Berkeley and Los Angeles: University of California Press, 1962. ix, 207 p. Pap.

An examination of one of the great progressive causes.

Smith, Frank E. THE POLITICS OF CONSERVATION. New York: Random House, 1966. xii, 338 p.

An excellent introduction to the history of the development of natural resources and the conservation movement in the United States.

Southern, David W. THE MALIGNANT HERITAGE: YANKEE PROGRESSIVES AND THE NEGRO QUESTION, 1901-1914. Chicago: Loyola University Press, 1968. x, 166 p.

One of the greatest failures of the Progressive was the failure to concern himself with civil rights for the American Negro. This study examines the reason why.

Steffens, Joseph Lincoln. THE SHAME OF THE CITIES. New York: McClure, Phillips and Co., 1904. Reprint. New York: Hill and Wang, 1957. ix, 214 p. Pap.

Originally published in 1904, this new edition retains the sense of outrage, legitimate even today, over urban politics.

Stone, Ralph. THE IRRECONCILABLES: THE FIGHT AGAINST THE LEAGUE OF NATIONS. Lexington: University of Kentucky Press, 1970. 208 p. Appendix.

Wilson labeled his opponents in the fight over the Treaty of Versailles a group of "wilfull men." Stone explores the political questions, among others, that created the conflict.

Thelen, David P. ROBERT M. LaFOLLETTE AND THE INSURGENT SPIRIT. Boston: Little, Brown and Co., 1976. ix, 211 p.

A brief but well-written and well-researched political biography.

Timberlake, James H. PROHIBITION AND THE PROGRESSIVE MOVEMENT, 1900-1920. Cambridge, Mass.: Harvard University Press, 1963. 238 p. Illus.

A good survey that describes the aims of Progressives and analyzes the reasons why the United States adopted prohibition.

Wefald, Jon. A VOICE OF PROTEST: NORWEGIANS IN AMERICAN POLITICS, 1890-1917. Northfield, Minn.: Norwegian-American Historical Association, 1971. 94 p.

Useful in trying to gauge the political temper of the recently arrived American.

Weinstein, James. THE DECLINE OF SOCIALISM IN AMERICA, 1912–1925. New York: Monthly Review Press, 1967. xi, 367 p. Tables.

Wilensky, Norman M. CONSERVATIVES IN THE PROGRESSIVE ERA: THE TAFT REPUBLICANS OF 1912. Gainesville: University of Florida Press, 1965. 75 p. Pap.

> Very useful in the unraveling of the complex presidential campaign in 1912.

Section 2. PROGRESSIVES AND THE STATES

Abrams, Richard M. CONSERVATISM IN A PROGRESSIVE ERA: MASSACHU-SETTS POLITICS, 1900–1912. Cambridge, Mass.: Harvard University Press, 1964. xiv, 327 p.

> An excellent study of a "progressive" state that was labeled con-servative. Political leaders from the state on the national level tended to be conservative but the state leaders responded to the demand for reform.

Burts, Robert M. RICHARD IRVINE MANNING AND THE PROGRESSIVE MOVEMENT IN SOUTH CAROLINA. Columbia: University of South Carolina Press, 1974. viii, 259 p.

> Manning, a progressive Democrat, was an opponent of Ben Tillman.

Chrislock, Carl H. THE PROGRESSIVE ERA IN MINNESOTA, 1899–1918. St. Paul: Minnesota Historical Society, 1971. xiii, 242 p. Illus.

> A well-researched examination of progressive politics on the state level.

Flint, Winston A. PROGRESSIVE MOVEMENT IN VERMONT. Washington, D.C.: American Council on Public Affairs, 1941. 110 p.

Flynt, Wayne. DUNCAN UPSHAW FLETCHER: DIXIE'S RELUCTANT PRO-GRESSIVE. Tallahassee: Florida State University Press, 1971. ix, 213 p.

> The political life of an important Florida politician who served in the U.S. Senate from the progressive years to midway in the New Deal years.

Geiger, Louis G. JOSEPH W. FOLK OF MISSOURI. Columbia: Curators of the University of Missouri, 1953. 206 p. Illus.

> One of the major Democratic leaders in the progressive movement. His expose of the link between corrupt business and corrupt poli-tics in St. Louis gained nationwide publicity.

Gould, Lewis L. PROGRESSIVES AND PROHIBITIONISTS: TEXAS DEMO-CRATS IN THE WILSON ERA. Austin: University of Texas Press, 1973. xvi, 339 p. Illus.

> The author relates how state and national concerns had an impact on party affairs.

Hackney, Sheldon. POPULISM TO PROGRESSIVISM IN ALABAMA. Princeton, N.J.: Princeton University Press, 1969. xv, 390 p. Maps.

> An excellent study of the progressive impulse in a deep south state.

Kirby, Jack T. WESTMORELAND DAVIS: VIRGINIA PLANTER-POLITICIAN, 1859-1942. Charlottesville: University Press of Virginia, 1968. viii, 215 p. Illus.

> A Virginia governor, Davis's career illustrates the course of twentieth-century Virginia politics.

LaForte, Robert Sherman. LEADERS OF REFORM: PROGRESSIVE REPUBLICANS IN KANSAS, 1900-1916. Lawrence: University Press of Kansas, 1974. vii, 320 p.

Maxwell, Robert S. LaFOLLETTE AND THE RISE OF PROGRESSIVES IN WISCONSIN. Madison: State Historical Society of Wisconsin, 1956. viii, 271 p. Illus.

> Because Wisconsin was the model for other state reform movements in the early twentieth century, this is an important study.

Mowry, George E. THE CALIFORNIA PROGRESSIVES. Berkeley and Los Angeles: University of California Press, 1951. xi, 349 p. Illus.

> One of the pioneering studies that explored the origins--political, social, and economic--of the progressive leadership. Some of Mowry's conclusions have been challenged by more recent scholarship.

Sageser, A. Bower. JOSEPH L. BRISTOW: KANSAS PROGRESSIVE. Lawrence: University Press of Kansas, 1968. 197 p. Illus.

Warner, Hoyt L. PROGRESSIVISM IN OHIO, 1897-1917. Columbus: Ohio State University Press for the Ohio Historical Society, 1964. xiii, 556 p.

> The study of progressive politics in one of the union's largest states.

Wesser, Robert F. CHARLES EVANS HUGHES: POLITICS AND REFORM IN NEW YORK, 1905-1910. Ithaca, N.Y.: Cornell University Press, 1967. xvi, 366 p. Illus.

This is a penetrating study of Hughes's early political career against the background of New York politics.

Section 3. URBAN POLITICS

Bean, Walton. BOSS RUEF'S SAN FRANCISCO: THE STORY OF THE UNION LABOR PARTY, BIG BUSINESS, AND THE GRAFT PROSECUTION. Berkeley and Los Angeles: University of California Press, 1967. xii, 345 p. Illus.

　　Bean provides a classic study of the political boss, the sources of boss authority, and the movement to reform municipal government. Boss Ruef is Abraham Ruef.

Crooks, James B. POLITICS AND PROGRESS: THE RISE OF URBAN PROGRESSIVISM IN BALTIMORE, 1895 TO 1911. Baton Rouge: Louisiana State University Press, 1968. x, 259 p. Appendix.

　　This is a thorough examination of the municipal reform movement and the politics of the movement in a large American city.

Miller, William D. MEMPHIS DURING THE PROGRESSIVE ERA, 1900-1917. Memphis, Tenn.: Memphis State University Press, 1957. 242 p. Illus.

　　A very helpful study of urban politics in a major upper south city.

Miller, Zane L. BOSS COX'S CINCINNATI: URBAN POLITICS IN THE PROGRESSIVE ERA. New York: Oxford University Press, 1968. xii, 301 p. Maps, tables.

　　Cincinnati was one of America's fastest growing cities. The author believes Cox's machine brought necessary order and that it paved the way for creative reform.

Reynolds, George M. MACHINE POLITICS IN NEW ORLEANS, 1897-1926. New York: Columbia University Press, 1936. 245 p.

Spear, Allan H. BLACK CHICAGO: THE MAKING OF A NEGRO GHETTO, 1890-1920. Chicago: University of Chicago Press, 1967. xvii, 254 p. Tables, illus.

　　Politics played a role in the making of the ghetto.

Tager, Jack. THE INTELLECTUAL AS URBAN REFORMER: BRAND WHITLOCK AND THE PROGRESSIVE MOVEMENT. Cleveland: Press of Case Western Reserve University, 1968. 198 p.

　　Whitlock, writer and diplomat, was also an urban reformer in Toledo, Ohio.

Wachman, Marvin. HISTORY OF THE SOCIAL-DEMOCRATIC PARTY OF MIL-
WAUKEE, 1897-1910. Urbana: University of Illinois Press, 1945. 90 p. Appendixes.

> Milwaukee was one of the few American cities of substantial size
> to create socialist solutions to urban problems.

Wendt, Lloyd, and Kogan, Herman. BOSSES IN LUSTY CHICAGO: THE
STORY OF BATH-HOUSE JOHN AND HINKY DINK. Bloomington: Indiana
University Press, 1967. xv, 384 p.

> Originally published in 1943 under the title LORDS OF THE LE-
> VEE. This is a fascinating account of the development of two
> major political figures.

Section 4. BIOGRAPHY

Bailey, Thomas A. WOODROW WILSON AND THE GREAT BETRAYAL. New
York: Macmillan Co., 1945. xii, 429 p. Illus., maps.

> A study of the politics involved in the U.S. Senate's rejection
> of the Treaty of Versailles.

Baker, Ray Stannard. WOODROW WILSON: LIFE AND LETTERS. 8 vols.
New York: Doubleday, Doran and Co., 1927-39. Illus.

> Although Baker's work has been superseded by Arthur S. Link (see
> below, this section), these volumes are widely available and useful
> for any work except advanced scholarship.

Blum, John M. THE REPUBLICAN ROOSEVELT. Cambridge, Mass.: Harvard
University Press, 1967. xi, 170 p.

> Although this volume is concerned with the political Roosevelt,
> there is much on the man. Blum sees Roosevelt as progressive-
> conservative.

_____. WOODROW WILSON AND THE POLITICS OF MORALITY. Boston:
Little, Brown and Co., 1956. vi, 215 p. Pap.

> Blum's perceptive analysis of Wilson's early career provides an
> interesting view of Wilson's success and failure as a political
> leader.

Bowers, Claude G. BEVERIDGE AND THE PROGRESSIVE ERA. Cambridge,
Mass.: Houghton, Mifflin and Co., 1932. xxiv, 610 p. Illus.

> Bowers's account and scholarship have been surpassed except for
> the detail he provides on the man and on some of his political
> activities.

Braeman, John. ALBERT J. BEVERIDGE: AMERICAN NATIONALIST. Chicago: University of Chicago Press, 1971. x, 370 p.

A well-researched biography on an important early twentieth century politician.

Chessman, G. Wallace. THEODORE ROOSEVELT AND THE POLITICS OF POWER. Boston: Little, Brown and Co., 1969. viii, 214 p. Pap.

A well-researched concise biography.

Coletta, Paolo E. THE PRESIDENCY OF WILLIAM HOWARD TAFT. Lawrence: University Press of Kansas, 1973. ix, 306 p.

A newer biography that does not challenge the older one by Henry F. Pringle (see pp. 86–87).

Garraty, John A. HENRY CABOT LODGE: A BIOGRAPHY. New York: Alfred A. Knopf, 1953. xiii, 433, xvi p. Illus.

A major biography of one of the major Republican leaders in the first two decades of the twentieth century. This volume also includes considerable information on Massachusetts politics and Theodore Roosevelt.

_____. WOODROW WILSON: A GREAT LIFE IN BRIEF. New York: Alfred A. Knopf, 1963. 206, vi p.

Ginger, Ray. THE BENDING CROSS: A BIOGRAPHY OF EUGENE V. DEBS. New Brunswick, N.J.: Rutgers University Press, 1949. x, 516 p.

An excellent biography of the great American Socialist leader.

Glad, Paul W. THE TRUMPET SOUNDETH: WILLIAM JENNINGS BRYAN AND HIS DEMOCRACY, 1896–1912. Lincoln: University of Nebraska Press, 1960. xii, 242 p. Illus.

A major figure in American politics is examined in order to explain the course of Democratic politics in the early twentieth century.

Greenbaum, Fred. ROBERT MARION LaFOLLETTE. Boston: Twayne Publishers, 1975. 275 p.

A short biography for the general reader that makes use of the recently opened LaFollette papers.

Gwinn, William R. UNCLE JOE CANNON, ARCHFOE OF INSURGENCY: A HISTORY OF THE RISE AND FALL OF CANNONISM. New York: Bookman Associates, 1957. vii, 314 p.

Joseph Cannon of Illinois was one of the leaders of the Old Guard faction of the Republican party.

Holmes, William F. THE WHITE CHIEF: JAMES KIMBLE VARDAMAN. Baton Rouge: Louisiana State University Press, 1970. xiii, 418 p.

> Senator Vardaman's career represented the best (reform) and the worst (racism) in southern politics.

Jessup, Philip C. ELIHU ROOT. 2 vols. New York: Dodd, Mead and Co., 1938. Illus.

> A well-researched biography based on Root's papers and the author's interviews with his subject.

Koenig, Louis W. BRYAN: A POLITICAL BIOGRAPHY OF WILLIAM JENNINGS BRYAN. New York: G.P. Putnam's Sons, 1971. 736 p.

> One of the best of the political biographies of Bryan.

LaFollette, Belle Case, and LaFollette, Fola. ROBERT M. LaFOLLETTE, JUNE 14, 1855-JUNE 18, 1925. 2 vols. New York: Macmillan Co., 1953. Illus.

> LaFollette's children provide a sympathetic portrait of their father. Until the LaFollette papers were opened, this was the basic study of this major political leader.

Leopold, Richard W. ELIHU ROOT AND THE CONSERVATIVE TRADITION. Boston: Little, Brown and Co., 1954. x, 222 p. Pap.

> Root's conservative politics are important because he was expressing them during the progressive period at the beginning of the twentieth century.

Link, Arthur S. WILSON. 5 vols. Princeton, N.J.: Princeton University Press, 1947-65. Illus.

> The five volumes completed tell Wilson's story up through the election of 1916.

McKenna, Marian C. BORAH. Ann Arbor: University of Michigan Press, 1961. 450 p. Illus.

> Borah was a very complex politician. He won national prominence as a prosecutor of IWW leader "Big Bill" Haywood and sponsored bills to create the Department of Labor. His most enduring accomplishments came in the progressive period.

Pringle, Henry F. THE LIFE AND TIMES OF WILLIAM HOWARD TAFT. 2 vols. New York: Farrar and Rinehart, 1939. Appendix, illus.

> A moderately critical biography that nevertheless helps to correct the standard view that Taft was an absolute failure as president.

_____. THEODORE ROOSEVELT. New York: Harcourt, Brace and World, 1956. x, 435 p. Pap.

> This paperback is a slightly revised version of the original hardback edition. It is still one of the best one-volume works on Theodore Roosevelt.

Roosevelt, Theodore. THE LETTERS OF THEODORE ROOSEVELT. Edited by Elting E. Morison. 8 vols. Cambridge, Mass.: Harvard University Press, 1951-54.

Schriftgiesser, Karl. THE GENTLEMAN FROM MASSACHUSETTS: HENRY CABOT LODGE. Boston: Little, Brown and Co., 1944. 386 p.

> This is not a sympathetic account.

Steffens, Joseph Lincoln. THE AUTOBIOGRAPHY OF LINCOLN STEFFENS. New York: Harcourt, Brace and Co., 1937. x, 390 p.

> Steffens's associations with and observations of leading political figures of the progressive period are helpful in the understanding of progressive politics.

White, William Allen. THE AUTOBIOGRAPHY OF WILLIAM ALLEN WHITE. New York: Macmillan Co., 1946. 669 p. Illus.

> From the 1890s the editor of the EMPORIA GAZETTE observed the course of American politics in Kansas and the nation.

Whitlock, Brand. FORTY YEARS OF IT. New York: Appleton, 1914. Reprint. Cleveland: Press of Case Western Reserve University, 1970. xxii, 374 p.

> The author relates his association with the reform and progressive movements. His thesis is that democracy's problems must be solved in the city. Also he believes that nonpartisanship and regulation of corporations are necessary for the existence of representative government.

Wilson, Woodrow. THE PUBLIC PAPERS OF WOODROW WILSON. Edited by Ray S[tannard]. Baker and William E. Dodd. 6 vols. New York: Harper and Brothers, 1925-27.

Chapter VIII

THE GOLDEN DECADE AND THE NEW DEAL, 1920-40

Section 1. GENERAL

Bagby, Wesley M. THE ROAD TO NORMALCY: THE PRESIDENTIAL CAM-
PAIGN AND ELECTION OF 1920. Baltimore: Johns Hopkins Press, 1962.
206 p.

> A useful analysis of the candidates, issues, and strategies of the
> campaign.

Baldwin, Sidney. POVERTY AND POLITICS: THE RISE AND DECLINE OF
THE FARM SECURITY ADMINISTRATION. Chapel Hill: University of North
Carolina Press, 1968. xvii, 438 p. Illus.

> A helpful book on the complex story of agricultural politics in
> the 1930s.

Beard, Charles A., and Beard, Mary R. AMERICA IN MIDPASSAGE. Vol. 1.
New York: Macmillan Co., 1939. 500 p.

> The Beards have given us both facts and conclusions about events
> from the mid-1920s through the New Deal. This is a sympathetic
> but critical interpretation of the New Deal.

Bornet, Vaughn D. LABOR POLITICS IN A DEMOCRATIC REPUBLIC: MODERA-
TION, DIVISION, AND DISRUPTION IN THE PRESIDENTIAL ELECTION OF
1928. Washington, D.C.: Spartan Books, 1964. xiii, 376 p. Illus.

> A useful addition to the general studies of the election.

Braeman, John, et al. THE NEW DEAL. 2 vols. Columbus: Ohio State
University Press, 1975.

> The first volume deals with the New Deal and a variety of topics
> of national scope, such as business, agriculture, and blacks. The
> second volume deals with the New Deal and its relationship with
> what is a fair cross section of states and cities.

The Golden Decade & the New Deal

Bunche, Ralph J. THE POLITICAL STATUS OF THE NEGRO IN THE AGE OF FDR. Edited by Dewey W. Grantham, Jr. Chicago: University of Chicago Press, 1973. xxxiii, 682 p. Illus., maps.

> Originally written as a working paper in 1940 for Gunnar Myrdal's AN AMERICAN DILEMMA. Bunche deals largely with the southern Negro.

Buni, Andrew. ROBERT L. VANN OF THE PITTSBURGH COURIER: POLITICS AND BLACK JOURNALISM. Pittsburgh: University of Pittsburgh Press, 1974. xv, 410 p. Illus.

Burner, David. THE POLITICS OF PROVINCIALISM: THE DEMOCRATIC PARTY IN TRANSITION, 1918-1932. New York: Alfred A. Knopf, 1968. xiii, 293, viii p.

> An important study of the reorganization and regeneration of the Democratic party.

Campbell, Christiana M. THE FARM BUREAU AND NEW DEAL: A STUDY OF THE MAKING OF NATIONAL FARM POLICY, 1933-40. Urbana: University of Illinois Press, 1962. viii, 215 p. Tables.

> An excellent source for the examination of agricultural politics and politicians in the New Deal years.

Carter, Paul A. THE DECLINE AND REVIVAL OF SOCIAL GOSPEL: SOCIAL AND POLITICAL LIBERALISM IN AMERICAN PROTESTANT CHURCHES, 1920-1940. Ithaca, N.Y.: Cornell University Press, 1954. x, 265 p.

> Carter examines the upheaval in attitudes and leadership in the Protestant denominations.

Conrad, David E. THE FORGOTTEN FARMERS: THE STORY OF SHARECROPPERS IN THE NEW DEAL. Urbana: University of Illinois Press, 1965. 223 p.

> Although the agricultural community increased its political influence during the 1930s, one segment of agriculture was ignored by the agricultural establishment.

Donahoe, Bernard F. PRIVATE PLANS AND PUBLIC DANGERS: THE STORY OF FDR'S THIRD NOMINATION. Notre Dame, Ind.: University of Notre Dame Press, 1965. x, 256 p.

> This book should attract the interest of those who like a fascinating account of intraparty politics.

Dorsett, Lyle W. THE PENDERGAST MACHINE. New York: Oxford University Press, 1968. xiv, 163 p. Maps.

> An excellent study of a major urban political machine in Kansas City, Missouri.

Ewing, Cortez A. M. PRIMARY ELECTIONS IN THE SOUTH: A STUDY IN UNIPARTY POLITICS. Norman: University of Oklahoma Press, 1953. xii, 112 p. Tables.

> The author concentrates on the period from 1920 to 1948 in the one-party states.

Farley, James A. BEHIND THE BALLOTS: THE PERSONAL HISTORY OF A POLITICIAN. New York: Harcourt, Brace and Co., 1938. 392 p.

> This consummate political technician relates the insider's view of Franklin Roosevelt's political success.

Fausold, Martin L., ed. THE HOOVER PRESIDENCY: A REAPPRAISAL. Albany: State University of New York Press, 1974. vi, 224 p.

> A collection of recent scholarship on the Hoover presidency.

Fite, Gilbert C. GEORGE N. PEEK AND THE FIGHT FOR FARM PARITY. Norman: University of Oklahoma Press, 1954. xiii, 314 p. Illus.

> A useful study of an important figure in agricultural politics during the 1920s and 1930s.

Freidel, Frank B. F.D.R. AND THE SOUTH. Baton Rouge: Louisiana State University Press, 1965. x, 102 p.

> A brief examination of Roosevelt's personal and political connections with the South.

Gosnell, Harold F. CHAMPION CAMPAIGNER: FRANKLIN D. ROOSEVELT. New York: Macmillan Co., 1952. 235 p. Illus.

_____. GRASS ROOTS POLITICS: NATIONAL VOTING BEHAVIOR OF TYPICAL STATES. Washington, D.C.: American Council on Public Affairs, 1942. ix, 195 p. Illus. Tables.

> The typical states selected by the author are Wisconsin, Iowa, California, Illinois, and Louisiana.

Graham, Otis L., Jr. AN ENCORE FOR REFORM: THE OLD PROGRESSIVES AND THE NEW DEAL. New York: Oxford University Press, 1967. viii, 256 p. Appendixes.

> Graham challenges the traditional view that the New Deal was simply a logical extension of the Progressive movement. He finds that the early progressives found the New Deal alien to their concept of reform.

Hicks, John D. REPUBLICAN ASCENDANCY, 1921-1933. New York: Harper and Brothers, 1960. 318 p. Illus.

An excellent survey of the 1920s. The political material serves as a good introduction to major events and personalities.

Holtzman, Abraham. THE TOWNSEND MOVEMENT: A POLITICAL STUDY. New York: Bookman Associates, 1963. 256 p. Tables.

This is an excellent study of an important political movement of the 1930s and its subsequent decline.

Hubbard, Preston J. ORIGINS OF THE TVA: THE MUSCLE SHOALS CON-TROVERSY, 1920-1932. New York: W. W. Norton and Co., 1961. ix, 340 p. Pap.

Very useful in the study of conservation politics and the role of government.

Humphrey, Hubert H. THE POLITICAL PHILOSOPHY OF THE NEW DEAL. Baton Rouge: Louisiana State University Press, 1970. xxiii, 128 p.

This extended essay says as much about Senator Humphrey's political views as it does about the New Deal.

Jackson, Kenneth T. THE KU KLUX KLAN IN THE CITY, 1915-1930. New York: Oxford University Press, 1967. xv, 326 p. Tables.

The author examines the political and other activities of the Klan in Atlanta, Chicago, Dallas, Denver, Detroit, Indianapolis, Knoxville, Memphis, and Portland in detail and more generally in some other cities.

Jonas, Manfred. ISOLATIONISM IN AMERICA, 1935-1941. Ithaca, N.Y.: Cornell University Press, 1966. xi, 315 p.

This analysis of the complex political relationships of the isolationists is very useful to the student of prewar politics.

Kent, Frank R. POLITICAL BEHAVIOR: THE HERETOFORE UNWRITTEN LAWS, CUSTOMS, AND PRINCIPLES OF POLITICS AS PRACTICED IN THE UNITED STATES. New York: William Morrow and Co., 1928. ix, 342 p.

A journalist's look at the foibles of politicians--mainly in the 1920s.

Key, V. O., Jr. POLITICS, PARTIES AND PRESSURE GROUPS. New York: Thomas Y. Crowell Co., 1942. xvii, 814 p. Appendix, tables.

The focus is on the twentieth century and particularly the 1930s.

Leuchtenburg, William E. FLOOD CONTROL POLITICS: THE CONNECTICUT RIVER VALLEY PROBLEM, 1927-1950. Cambridge, Mass.: Harvard University Press, 1953. vi, 339 p. Illus.

McCoy, Donald R. ANGRY VOICES: LEFT-OF-CENTER POLITICS IN THE
NEW DEAL ERA. Lawrence: University Press of Kansas, 1958. viii, 224 p.

> McCoy isolates and explains the numerous groups and personalities
> that made up the "left" in the 1930s.

MacKay, Kenneth C. THE PROGRESSIVE MOVEMENT OF 1924. New York:
Columbia University Press, 1947. Reprint. New York: Octagon Books, 1972.
298 p. Appendix.

> MacKay also provides very useful information for the study of the
> major parties as well as the story of LaFollette's losing presidential
> candidacy.

Mencken, Henry L. A CARNIVAL OF BUNCOMBE. Edited by Malcolm C.
Moos. Baltimore: Johns Hopkins Press, 1956. xix, 370 p.

> The editor has put together some of Mencken's best political essays
> on the behavior of the human animal.

Michelson, Charles. THE GHOST TALKS. New York: G. P. Putnam's Sons,
1944. xvi, 245 p.

> The famous public relations expert hired by the Democratic party
> to discredit President Hoover.

Moore, Edmund A. A CATHOLIC RUNS FOR PRESIDENT: THE CAMPAIGN
OF 1928. New York: Ronald Press, 1956. xv, 220 p. Illus.

> A good account of the 1928 presidential election.

Murray, Robert K. THE 103RD BALLOT: DEMOCRATS AND THE DISASTER IN
MADISON SQUARE GARDEN. New York: Harper and Row, 1976. xiv,
336 p.

> Although Murray focuses on only a moment in recent political his-
> tory, this is excellent political history because he examines the
> troubled state of America in the 1920s.

_____. RED SCARE: A STUDY IN NATIONAL HYSTERIA, 1919-1920. Min-
neapolis: University of Minnesota Press, 1955. 337 p.

> The author has digested the voluminous material on the red scare
> and presents us with a carefully documented study of the politics
> of hysteria after World War I.

Noggle, Burl. INTO THE TWENTIES: THE UNITED STATES FROM ARMISTICE
TO NORMALCY. Urbana: University of Illinois Press, 1974. ix, 233 p.

> A detailed look at the United States, particularly in the year 1919.

_____. TEAPOT DOME: OIL AND POLITICS IN THE 1920'S. Baton Rouge: Louisiana State University Press, 1962. ix, 234 p. Illus.

> The author is concerned with the partisanship that the Teapot Dome affair generated and the character of politics and personalities in the 1920s.

O'Brien, David J. AMERICAN CATHOLICS AND SOCIAL REFORM: THE NEW DEAL YEARS. New York: Oxford University Press, 1968. xi, 287 p.

> This is an interesting study of how American Catholics related the social teachings of the Church to America's political, social, and economic problems in the 1930s.

Parmet, Herbert S., and Hecht, Marie B. NEVER AGAIN: A PRESIDENT RUNS FOR A THIRD TERM. New York: Macmillan Co., 1968. xii, 306 p.

> The 1940 presidential election is explored in great detail.

Patterson, James T. CONGRESSIONAL CONSERVATISM AND THE NEW DEAL: THE GROWTH OF THE CONSERVATIVE COALITION IN CONGRESS, 1933-1939. Lexington: University of Kentucky Press, for the Organization of American Historians, 1967. ix, 369 p. Illus.

> A detailed examination of congressional politics during the 1930s.

Peel, Roy V., and Donnelly, Thomas C. THE 1932 CAMPAIGN: AN ANALYSIS. New York: Farrar and Rinehart, 1935. viii, 242 p.

_____. THE 1928 CAMPAIGN: AN ANALYSIS. New York: R.R. Smith, 1931. xii, 183 p.

> Superseded by later studies but interesting because it does reflect some original views of political observers at the time.

Rauch, Basil. THE HISTORY OF THE NEW DEAL, 1933-1938. New York: Creative Age Press, 1944. xi, 368 p.

> An early and friendly assessment of the politics of the New Deal.

_____. ROOSEVELT FROM MUNICH TO PEARL HARBOR: A STUDY IN THE CREATION OF A FOREIGN POLICY. New York: Creative Age Press, 1950. xiv, 527 p.

> Although the author is primarily concerned with foreign policy, he necessarily deals with the politics of policy development and the nation's politics between 1938 and 1941.

Rice, Arnold S. THE KU KLUX KLAN IN AMERICAN POLITICS. Washington, D.C.: Public Affairs Press, 1962. vi, 150 p.

> The major area covered is Klan involvement in the politics of the 1920s.

Robinson, Edgar E. THEY VOTED FOR ROOSEVELT: THE PRESIDENTIAL VOTE, 1932-1944. Stanford, Calif.: Stanford University Press, 1947. x, 207 p. Illus., tables.

Robinson is critical of Roosevelt's leadership and challenges the liberal view of historians who are friendly to the New Deal.

Romasco, Albert U. POVERTY OF ABUNDANCE: HOOVER, THE NATION, THE DEPRESSION. New York: Oxford University Press, 1965. x, 282 p.

A well-written analysis of relief and recovery politics in the Hoover administration.

Schriftgiesser, Karl. THIS WAS NORMALCY, AN ACCOUNT OF PARTY POLITICS DURING TWELVE REPUBLICAN YEARS, 1920-1932. Boston: Little, Brown and Co., 1948. x, 325 p.

Although only the Republican party is mentioned in the title, the activities of both parties are examined.

Schwarz, Jordan A. THE INTERREGNUM OF DESPAIR: HOOVER, CONGRESS AND THE DEPRESSION. Urbana: University of Illinois Press, 1970. ix, 281 p. Appendix.

A balanced view of the Hoover presidency. Schwarz focuses on the relationship between the Congress and the White House.

Selznick, Philip. TVA AND GRASS ROOTS: A STUDY IN THE SOCIOLOGY OF FORMAL ORGANIZATION. Berkeley and Los Angeles: University of California Press, 1949. Reprint. New York: Harper and Row, 1966. 274 p. Charts.

The author provides a useful analysis of how participatory democracy works in the Tennessee valley.

Shover, John L. CORNBELT REBELLION: THE FARMERS' HOLIDAY ASSOCIATION. Urbana: University of Illinois Press, 1965. vi, 239 p.

Shover explores agrarian discontent that rocked parts of the Midwest in the 1930s. He notes the failure of the Farmers' Holiday Association to achieve little more than piecemeal solutions to vexing problems.

_____, ed. POLITICS OF THE NINETEEN TWENTIES. Waltham, Mass.: Ginn-Blaisdell, 1970. xiii, 210 p.

The series of essays deal with major political questions during the decade.

Simon, Rita J., ed. AS WE SAW THE THIRTIES: ESSAYS ON SOCIAL AND POLITICAL MOVEMENTS OF A DECADE. Urbana: University of Illinois Press, 1967. 253 p.

A series of essays by several radical leaders or observers active in the 1930s.

Wolfskill, George. THE REVOLT OF CONSERVATIVES: A HISTORY OF THE AMERICAN LIBERTY LEAGUE, 1934-1940. Boston: Houghton, Mifflin and Co., 1962. x, 303 p. Illus.

A careful analysis of the major organization of the political Right that challenged the New Deal.

Section 2. STATE AND LOCAL POLITICS

Allswang, John M. A HOUSE FOR ALL PEOPLES: ETHNIC POLITICS IN CHICAGO, 1890-1936. Lexington: University of Kentucky Press, 1971. x, 253 p. Appendix.

Concentrates on period of the 1920s. Uses the quantitative approach.

Burke, Robert E. OLSON'S NEW DEAL FOR CALIFORNIA. Berkeley and Los Angeles: University of California Press, 1953. 279 p.

The Democratic party of California is a very peculiar organization and one of its fascinating members was Culbert L. Olson, governor of California, elected in 1938 and defeated in 1942.

Gosnell, Harold F. MACHINE POLITICS: CHICAGO MODEL. Chicago: University of Chicago Press, 1937. xx, 229 p. Illus., tables.

This study is particularly concerned with the 1920s and 1930s.

Huthmacher, J. Joseph. MASSACHUSETTS PEOPLE AND POLITICS, 1919-1933. Cambridge, Mass.: Harvard University Press, 1959. x, 328 p. Illus., appendix.

Huthmacher notes that politics in Massachusetts may be somewhat different from that in other states, but his focus is on the changes that were taking place in American politics after World War I.

Kane, Harnett T. LOUISIANA HAYRIDE; THE AMERICAN REHEARSAL FOR DICTATORSHIP, 1928-1940. New York: William Morrow and Co., 1941. viii, 471 p. Illus.

Huey Long is the center of the author's attention.

McKean, Dayton David. THE BOSS: THE HAGUE MACHINE IN ACTION. Boston: Houghton, Mifflin and Co., 1940. xviii, 285 p.

An examination of one of the most ruthless and efficient political machines in the country during the 1920s and 1930s. Hague was a major influence in New Jersey politics.

Merriam, Charles Edward. CHICAGO: A MORE INTIMATE VIEW OF URBAN POLITICS. New York: Macmillan Co., 1929. 305 p.

> A reformer's view of Chicago politics in the 1920s.

Milligan, Maurice M. MISSOURI WALTZ: THE INSIDE STORY OF THE PENDERGAST MACHINE BY THE MAN WHO SMASHED IT. New York: Charles Scribner's Sons, 1948. xiii, 281 p.

> The author is no friend of Harry S. Truman or the Pendergast machine.

Mitchell, Franklin D. EMBATTLED DEMOCRACY: MISSOURI DEMOCRATIC POLITICS, 1919-1932. Columbia: University of Missouri Press, 1968. 219 p.

> Another excellent study of state politics during a time of political change.

Morrison, Joseph L. GOVERNOR O. MAX GARDNER: A POWER IN NORTH CAROLINA AND NEW DEAL WASHINGTON. Chapel Hill: University of North Carolina Press, 1971. xii, 323 p. Illus.

> An interesting and successful political leader who represented the moderate Southern view in Washington.

Patterson, James T. THE NEW DEAL AND THE STATES: FEDERALISM IN TRANSITION. Princeton, N.J.: Princeton University Press, 1969. viii, 226 p.

> A useful introduction to state politics and political leaders during the 1930s.

Puryear, Elmer L. DEMOCRATIC PARTY DISSENSION IN NORTH CAROLINA, 1928-1936. Chapel Hill: University of North Carolina Press, 1962. vi, 251 p. Pap.

> A helpful study of Democratic politics in North Carolina and the nation.

Putnam, Jackson K. OLD-AGE POLITICS IN CALIFORNIA: FROM RICHARD-SON TO REAGAN. Stanford, Calif.: Stanford University Press, 1970. 211 p.

> This study concentrates on developments in the 1930s.

Stave, Bruce M. THE NEW DEAL AND THE LAST HURRAH: PITTSBURGH MACHINE POLITICS. Pittsburgh: University of Pittsburgh Press, 1970. x, 262 p. Tables, appendixes.

> An important study of the connection between big city politics and the changes created by the New Deal.

Wooddy, Carroll H. THE CASE OF FRANK L. SMITH: A STUDY IN REPRE-
SENTATIVE GOVERNMENT. Chicago: University of Chicago Press, 1931.
ix, 393 p. Appendixes, illus.

> A fascinating account of corrupt politics and the Illinois Republi-
> can party during the 1920s.

Section 3. BIOGRAPHY

Adams, Samuel Hopkins. INCREDIBLE ERA: THE LIFE AND TIMES OF WAR-
REN G. HARDING. Boston: Houghton, Mifflin and Co., 1939. ix, 457 p.
Illus.

> A sometimes inaccurate but interesting story of Harding's rise and
> his presidency.

Anderson, William. THE WILD MAN FROM SUGAR CREEK: THE POLITICAL
CAREER OF EUGENE TALMADGE. Baton Rouge: Louisiana State University
Press, 1975. xviii, 268 p.

> An important political leader who represented rabid racist views
> and the farming classes in Georgia from a conservative platform.

Ashby, Leroy. THE SPEARLESS LEADER: SENATOR BORAH AND THE PRO-
GRESSIVE MOVEMENT IN THE 1920'S. Urbana: University of Illinois Press,
1972. x, 325 p.

> Eclectic but well-written political biography that focuses on domes-
> tic issues during the 1920s.

Barnard, Harry. INDEPENDENT MAN: THE LIFE OF SENATOR JAMES COUZ-
ENS. New York: Charles Scribner's Sons, 1958. viii, 376 p.

> An interesting biography of a successful businessman and an impor-
> tant political figure from Michigan.

Billington, Monroe L. THOMAS P. GORE: THE BLIND SENATOR FROM
OKLAHOMA. Lawrence: University Press of Kansas, 1967. v, 229 p.

> An active Populist and Democrat, Gore, although blind, served
> as U.S. senator between 1907 and 1920 and 1930 and 1936. Bil-
> lington's book is particularly useful in describing a man that moved
> from radical populism to a conservative political position.

Blackorby, Edward C. PRAIRIE REBEL: THE PUBLIC LIFE OF WILLIAM LEMKE.
Lincoln: University of Nebraska Press, 1963. ix, 339 p.

> Lemke represented the radical viewpoint in upper Great Plains
> politics. In 1936 he was supported for the presidency by Rev.
> Charles Coughlin and Dr. Francis Townsend.

Bryant, Keith L., Jr. ALFALFA BILL MURRAY. Norman: University of Oklahoma Press, 1968. xiii, 287 p. Illus.

William Murray's career as an "agrarian" in American politics is well handled by the author. This volume is essential to any study of agricultural politics.

Burns, James MacGregor. ROOSEVELT: THE LION AND THE FOX. New York: Harcourt, Brace and Co., 1956. xvi, 553 p. Illus.

This is a fascinating political biography of FDR. The author's main interest is how Roosevelt wielded political power in the 1930s.

Connors, Richard J. A CYCLE OF POWER: THE CAREER OF JERSEY CITY MAYOR FRANK HAGUE. Metuchen, N.J.: Scarecrow Press, 1971. 226 p.

A useful account of the rise and fall of a major political machine boss.

Cox, James M. JOURNEY THROUGH MY YEARS. New York: Simon and Schuster, 1946. xi, 463 p.

A progressive governor of Ohio and Democratic candidate for president in 1920.

Davis, Kenneth S. FDR: THE BECKONING OF DESTINY, 1882-1928, A HISTORY. New York: G. P. Putnam's Sons, 1972. 936 p.

Davis combines earlier research on Roosevelt's pregubernatorial years and produces an excellent one-volume study. The scholar as well as the general reader will enjoy this book.

Dinneen, Joseph F. THE PURPLE SHAMROCK: THE HON. JAMES MICHAEL CURLEY OF BOSTON. New York: W. W. Norton and Co., 1949. 331 p. Illus.

Although this volume praises Curley, it is still valuable as a source on the workings of big-city politics.

Downes, Randolph C. THE RISE OF WARREN GAMALIEL HARDING: 1865-1920. Columbus: Ohio State University Press, 1970. x, 734 p.

There is a great deal of material on Harding's early political years and Ohio politics.

Farley, James A. JIM FARLEY'S STORY: THE ROOSEVELT YEARS. New York: McGraw-Hill Book Co., 1948. x, 388 p.

Farley was Roosevelt's political manager in 1932 and 1936. He also served as postmaster general during Roosevelt's first two terms.

Flynn, Edward J. YOU'RE THE BOSS. New York: Viking Press, 1947. x, 244 p.

> The memoirs of an important New York political leader who was associated with Franklin D. Roosevelt.

Freidel, Frank B. FRANKLIN D. ROOSEVELT. 4 vols. to date. Boston: Little, Brown and Co., 1952–73. Illus.

> So far the author has taken his projected multivolume study through the early stages of Roosevelt's first administration.

Fuess, Claude M[oore]. CALVIN COOLIDGE, THE MAN FROM VERMONT. Boston: Little, Brown and Co., 1938. Reprint. Hamden, Conn.: Archon Books, 1965. xii, 522 p. Illus.

> The standard biography.

Gottfried, Alex. BOSS CERMAK OF CHICAGO: A STUDY OF POLITICAL LEADERSHIP. Seattle: University of Washington Press, 1962. xiii, 459 p. Illus.

> Anton Cermak was one of the major political figures in twentieth-century Chicago and Illinois politics.

Green, A. Wigfall. THE MAN BILBO. Baton Rouge: Louisiana State University Press, 1963. xiii, 150 p. Illus.

> This is a brief survey of the career of Theodore Bilbo, a twentieth-century demagogue from Mississippi.

Hamilton, Virginia Van der Veer. HUGO BLACK: THE ALABAMA YEARS. Baton Rouge: Louisiana University State Press, 1972. ix, 330 p. Illus.

> Insight into the politics of Hugo Black and Alabama before 1937.

Handlin, Oscar. AL SMITH AND HIS AMERICA. Boston: Little, Brown and Co., 1958. x, 207 p.

> A brief but well-written biography of one of New York's major political figures who was also the 1928 Democratic presidential nominee. Handlin's portrait is critical but sympathetic.

Henderson, Richard B. MAURY MAVERICK: A POLITICAL BIOGRAPHY: Austin: University of Texas Press, 1970. xxiii, 386 p. Illus.

> A major political figure in Texas and national politics. Henderson's study explores the difficulties in winning political office by a liberal in a conservative state.

Hoover, Herbert C. THE MEMOIRS OF HERBERT HOOVER. 3 vols. New York: Macmillan Co., 1951-52. Illus.

> Somewhat pedestrian, but Hoover explains his views with great care.

Howard, J. Woodford, Jr. MR. JUSTICE MURPHY: A POLITICAL BIOGRAPHY. Princeton, N.J.: Princeton University Press, 1968. x, 578 p. Illus.

> A political leader in Michigan during the 1930s and a Supreme Court justice, appointed by President Franklin Roosevelt, in the 1940s.

Huthmacher, J. Joseph. SENATOR ROBERT F. WAGNER AND URBAN LIBER-ALISM. New York: Atheneum, 1968. xi, 362 p. Illus.

> Wagner represented a new voice in the Democratic party in the 1920s and in the 1930s. He was often moving beyond other Democrats in his concept of the role of government.

Ickes, Harold L. THE SECRET DIARY OF HAROLD L. ICKES. 3 vols. New York: Simon and Schuster, 1953-54.

> Harold Ickes, secretary of the interior in Franklin Roosevelt's administration, has some interesting views on politics and politicians.

Johnson, Roger T. ROBERT M. LaFOLLETTE, JR. AND THE DECLINE OF THE PROGRESSIVE PARTY IN WISCONSIN. Madison: State Historical Society of Wisconsin, 1964. Reprint. Hamden, Conn.: Archon Books, 1970. ix, 195 p.

> The younger LaFollettes continued their father's political odyssey but were unable to cope with the change in outlook by the voters of Wisconsin, who became increasingly conservative.

Keller, Morton. IN DEFENSE OF YESTERDAY: JAMES M. BECK AND THE POLITICS OF CONSERVATISM, 1861-1936. New York: Coward-McCann, 1958. 320 p.

> A member of the Old Guard faction of the Republican party, Beck served as congressman from Pennsylvania from 1927 to 1934.

Levine, Erwin L. THEODORE FRANCIS GREEN: THE RHODE ISLAND YEARS, 1906-1936. Providence, R.I.: Brown University Press, 1963. ix, 222 p.

> A good account of political life in Rhode Island and the development of the modern Democratic party.

Lowitt, Richard. GEORGE W. NORRIS: THE PERSISTENCE OF A PROGRES-SIVE, 1913-1933. Urbana: University of Illinois Press, 1971. xv, 590 p. Illus.

Details of the life of a consummate politician who is credited with originating the Tennessee Valley Authority.

McCoy, Donald R. CALVIN COOLIDGE, THE QUIET PRESIDENT. New York: Macmillan Co., 1967. viii, 472 p. Illus.

McCoy challenges some of the myths that have surrounded the man and his presidency.

_____. LANDON OF KANSAS. Lincoln: University of Nebraska Press, 1966. x, 607 p. Illus.

As governor of Kansas and Republican presidential candidate, Landon was a major political figure in the 1930s.

McFarland, Keith D. HARRY H. WOODRING: A POLITICAL BIOGRAPHY OF FDR'S CONTROVERSIAL SECRETARY OF WAR. Lawrence: University Press of Kansas, 1975. x, 346 p. Illus.

An interesting Kansas politician who was able to win the governorship in a very Republican state. Played an important role in Roosevelt's nomination in 1932.

Malone, Michael P. C. BEN ROSS AND THE NEW DEAL IN IDAHO. Seattle: University of Washington Press, 1970. xii, 191 p.

As governor of Idaho, Ross sometimes took issue with the Roosevelt administration.

Mann, Arthur. LA GUARDIA: A FIGHTER AGAINST HIS TIMES, 1882-1933. Philadelphia: J. B. Lippincott Co., 1959. 384 p. Illus.

A sympathetic portrait of this amazing congressman from New York City.

_____. LA GUARDIA COMES TO POWER, 1933. Philadelphia: J. B. Lippincott Co., 1965. 199 p.

Mann skillfully unravels the complex reasons why La Guardia, nominally a Republican, was able to win the office of New York mayor in 1933.

Marcus, Sheldon. FATHER COUGHLIN: THE TUMULTUOUS LIFE OF THE PRIEST OF THE LITTLE FLOWER. Boston: Little, Brown and Co., 1973. 317 p. Illus.

Rev. Charles Coughlin, a major political figure in the 1930s, was first a supporter of Roosevelt and the New Deal, but by the mid-1930s he was an embittered critic.

Miller, William D. MR. CRUMP OF MEMPHIS. Baton Rouge: Louisiana State University Press, 1964. xiii, 373 p. Illus.

"Boss" Edward Crump controlled politics in Memphis and greatly influenced political decisions in Tennessee from 1909 to 1948.

Mitgang, Herbert. THE MAN WHO RODE THE TIGER: THE LIFE AND TIMES OF JUDGE SAMUEL SEABURY. Philadelphia: J. B. Lippincott Co., 1963. 380 p. Illus.

Judge Seabury's attack on Tammany Hall, New York's Democratic political machine, would enable Fiorello La Guardia to become mayor.

Murray, Robert K. THE HARDING ERA: WARREN G. HARDING AND HIS ADMINISTRATION. Minneapolis: University of Minnesota Press, 1969. ix, 626 p. Illus.

A source for the study of national politics in the early 1920s. Murray demonstrates that Harding was not the bumbling figure many thought he was.

Nevins, Allan. HERBERT H. LEHMAN AND HIS ERA. New York: Charles Scribner's Sons, 1963. 456 p. Illus., appendixes.

Lehman was a major figure in the Democratic party and served as governor of New York after Franklin Roosevelt.

O'Connor, Richard. THE FIRST HURRAH: A BIOGRAPHY OF ALFRED E. SMITH. New York: G. P. Putnam's Sons, 1970. 318 p. Illus.

A popular biography of one of New York's best governors.

O'Keane, Josephine. THOMAS J. WALSH: A SENATOR FROM MONTANA. Francestown, N.H.: M. Jones Co., 1955. 284 p.

A liberal Democratic U.S. senator from Montana, 1913-33, Walsh helped to unravel the sordid story of Teapot Dome and Elk Hills.

Rollins, Alfred B., Jr. ROOSEVELT AND HOWE. New York: Alfred A. Knopf, 1962. 479, xviii p. Illus.

A very good account of the personal and political relationship between these two men. Louis Howe's influence was greatest in the 1920s.

Russell, Francis. THE SHADOW OF BLOOMING GROVE: WARREN G. HARDING IN HIS TIMES. New York: McGraw-Hill Book Co., 1968. xvi, 691 p.

A popular account of Harding's life and politics. Russell incorporates material from the recently discovered Harding love letters.

Schlesinger, Arthur M., Jr. THE AGE OF ROOSEVELT. 3 vols. Boston: Houghton, Mifflin and Co., 1957-60.

So far the author has completed only three volumes in the multi-volume work: THE CRISIS OF THE OLD ORDER, 1919-1933, THE COMING OF THE NEW DEAL, and THE POLITICS OF UP-HEAVAL. Schlesinger is sympathetic to Roosevelt and develops the thesis that the New Deal represents the full flowering of the liberal tradition in American politics.

Sinclair, Andrew. THE AVAILABLE MAN: THE LIFE BEHIND THE MASKS OF WARREN GAMALIEL HARDING. New York: Macmillan Co., 1965. viii, 344 p. Illus.

Sinclair is intrigued by Harding's political availability. He explores the circumstances surrounding Harding's nomination for president.

Stimson, Henry L., and Bundy, McGeorge. ON ACTIVE SERVICE IN PEACE AND WAR. New York: Harper and Brothers, 1948. xxii, 698 p.

There is some valuable political commentary by Stimson, one time secretary of state and secretary of war, on politics in the first half of the twentieth century.

Tompkins, C. David. SENATOR ARTHUR H. VANDENBERG: THE EVOLUTION OF A MODERN REPUBLICAN, 1884-1945. East Lansing: Michigan State University Press, 1970. viii, 312 p.

A major spokesman for isolationist Republicans on the Senate Foreign Relations Committee in the latter half of the 1930s. After Pearl Harbor he helped to create a bipartisan approach to American foreign policy during the 1940s.

Tugwell, Rexford G. THE DEMOCRATIC ROOSEVELT: A BIOGRAPHY OF FRANKLIN D. ROOSEVELT. Garden City, N.Y.: Doubleday and Co., 1957. 712 p. Illus.

Tugwell was a member of Roosevelt's famous brain trust. Although he admires Roosevelt, he does not ignore the president's blind spots and failings.

Tull, Charles J. FATHER COUGHLIN AND THE NEW DEAL. Syracuse, N.Y.: Syracuse University Press, 1965. x, 292 p. Appendixes, illus.

Tull analyzes the tortuous path of Coughlin's politics during the Depression years.

Vadney, Thomas E. THE WAYWARD LIBERAL: A POLITICAL BIOGRAPHY OF DONALD RICHBERG. Lexington: University of Kentucky Press, 1970. xi, 223 p.

Active in the Roosevelt administration, Richberg represented a conservative constituency in the business community while serving on the National Recovery Administration.

Wendt, Lloyd, and Kogan, Herman. BIG BILL OF CHICAGO. Indianapolis: Bobbs-Merrill Co., 1953. 384 p. Illus.

A active during the 1920s, Big Bill Thompson was one of the brassiest political leaders in Chicago's political history.

White, William A[llen]. A PURITAN IN BABYLON: THE STORY OF CALVIN COOLIDGE. New York: Macmillan Co., 1938. Reprint. New York: Capricorn Books, 1965. xvi, 460 p. Pap.

A well-written, witty, and informative biography of Coolidge by a professional observer of American presidents for one-half a century.

Williams, T[homas]. Harry. HUEY LONG. New York: Alfred A. Knopf, 1969. xiv, 884 p. Illus.

A classic biography. Although Williams is sympathetic to some of Long's ambitions and style, he is careful to present Long's record without distortion.

Zinn, Howard. LA GUARDIA IN CONGRESS. Ithaca, N.Y.: Cornell University Press, for the American Historical Association, 1959. xi, 288 p.

A critical examination of La Guardia and American politics and politicians during the 1920s.

Zucker, Norman L. GEORGE W. NORRIS: GENTLE KNIGHT OF AMERICAN DEMOCRACY. Urbana: University of Illinois Press, 1966. 186 p.

This critical evaluation of Norris's political philosophy and legislative achievement relates his famous political deviancy to the national political scene.

Chapter IX

WORLD WAR II AND
THE TRUMAN AND EISENHOWER YEARS, 1940-60

Section 1. GENERAL

Abels, Jules. OUT OF THE JAWS OF VICTORY. New York: Henry Holt, 1959. 336 p. Illus.

A detailed examination of the 1948 election.

Acheson, Dean. A DEMOCRAT LOOKS AT HIS PARTY. New York: Harper and Brothers, 1955. 199 p.

An unconventional Democrat looks at the foibles and ideals of his party. Acheson served as secretary of state in the Truman administration.

Alexander, Charles C. HOLDING THE LINE: THE EISENHOWER ERA, 1952-1961. Bloomington: Indiana University Press, 1975. xviii, 326 p. Pap.

The author focuses on domestic politics as well as other aspects of the Eisenhower presidency.

Altshuler, Alan A., ed. THE POLITICS OF THE FEDERAL BUREAUCRACY. New York: Dodd, Mead and Co., 1968. xi, 452 p.

A series of essays that explore the political power of the federal bureaucracy in the 1950s and 1960s.

Bell, Daniel. END OF IDEOLOGY: ON THE EXHAUSTION OF POLITICAL IDEAS IN THE FIFTIES. Rev. ed. New York: Free Press, 1962. 474 p.

An important analysis of the direction of American politics in the 1950s by one of the country's leading sociologists. The author explores the changes in our society and the effect they have made on our political outlook. His thesis that international events shape our politics has created controversy.

Bell, Jack L. SPLENDID MISERY: THE STORY OF THE PRESIDENCY AND

POWER POLITICS AT CLOSE RANGE. Garden City, N.Y.: Doubleday and
Co., 1960. 474 p.

> Bell is concerned largely with the modern presidency as an insti-
> tution. There are many anecdotes about our recent presidents.

Berelson, Bernard R., et al. VOTING: A STUDY OF OPINION FORMA-
TION IN A PRESIDENTIAL CAMPAIGN. Chicago: University of Chicago
Press, 1954. xix, 395 p. Appendixes.

> The authors minutely examine Elmira, New York, to determine
> why its citizens voted the way they did in the 1948 presidential
> election.

Berman, William C. THE POLITICS OF CIVIL RIGHTS IN THE TRUMAN AD-
MINISTRATION. Columbus: Ohio State University Press, 1970. xi, 261 p.

> Berman carefully explores the postwar civil rights movement and
> particularly concerns himself with the role of President Truman.

Bernstein, Barton J., ed. POLITICS AND POLICIES OF THE TRUMAN AD-
MINISTRATION. Chicago: Quadrangle Books, 1970. 330 p. Pap.

Black, Theodore Milton. DEMOCRATIC PARTY PUBLICITY IN THE 1940 CAM-
PAIGN. New York: Plymouth Publishing Co., 1941. x, 169 p.

> An analysis of how the image of the party was projected in the
> campaign.

Blum, John M. V WAS FOR VICTORY: POLITICS AND CULTURE DURING
WORLD WAR II. New York: Harcourt Brace Jovanovich, 1976. xii, 372 p.

> Blum's observations on wartime politics are as interesting as his
> comments on the political leaders.

Bone, Hugh A. PARTY COMMITTEES AND NATIONAL POLITICS. Seattle:
University of Washington Press, 1958. xv, 256 p. Appendix, illus.

> Although political parties and their leaders have been reluctant to
> have their parties' inner workings made public, the author has
> examined party activities, including such topics as the bureaucracy
> and congressional committees, in the post-World War II period.
> His description and analysis serve the professional and the layman.

Brock, Clifton. AMERICANS FOR DEMOCRATIC ACTION: ITS ROLE IN
NATIONAL POLITICS. Washington, D.C.: Public Affairs Press, 1962. vii,
229 p.

> The objective of the book is to present a descriptive and analyti-
> cal account of the role of the ADA in American politics. Any
> understanding of the Democratic party in the post-World War II

period would be incomplete without knowledge of the activities of the ADA.

Burns, James MacGregor. THE DEADLOCK OF DEMOCRACY: FOUR-PARTY POLITICS IN AMERICA. Englewood, N.J.: Prentice-Hall, 1963. xi, 388 p.

A careful analysis of the sources of political power in the United States to the 1960s.

Calkins, Fay. THE CIO AND THE DEMOCRATIC PARTY. Chicago: University of Chicago Press, 1952. xiii, 162 p. Illus., tables, appendix.

The focus is on the relationship between the CIO and the Democratic party in the 1950 local, state, and congressional elections.

Campbell, Angus, et al. ELECTIONS AND THE POLITICAL ORDER. New York: John Wiley and Sons, 1966. ix, 385 p.

The authors, using data from presidential and congressional elections from 1948 to 1960, seek to analyze voting patterns.

Caridi, Ronald J. THE KOREAN WAR AND AMERICAN POLITICS: THE REPUBLICAN PARTY AS A CASE STUDY. Philadelphia: University of Pennsylvania Press, 1968. 319 p. Appendix.

Darilek, Richard E. A LOYAL OPPOSITION IN TIME OF WAR: THE REPUBLICAN PARTY AND THE POLITICS OF FOREIGN POLICY FROM PEARL HARBOR TO YALTA. Westport, Conn.: Greenwood Press, 1976. xi, 240 p.

This is one of the few works that explore the issues from the perspective of the Republican party. Contrary to the belief of many Americans, politics continued to play an important role in American life even during World War II.

Divine, Robert A. FOREIGN POLICY AND U.S. PRESIDENTIAL ELECTIONS, 1940-1948. New York: New Viewpoints, 1974. xii, 353 p.

Douglas, Paul H. ETHICS IN GOVERNMENT. Cambridge, Mass.: Harvard University Press, 1952. 114 p.

Senator Douglas addresses a problem that is always with us.

Eulau, Heinz. CLASS AND PARTY IN THE EISENHOWER YEARS: CLASS ROLES AND PERSPECTIVES IN THE 1952 AND 1956 ELECTIONS. Glencoe, Ill.: Free Press of Glencoe, 1962. xviii, 162 p. Tables.

A statistical breakdown of the motivation for political decisions by the electorate.

Fenton, John H. THE CATHOLIC VOTE. New Orleans: Hauser Press, 1960. xv, 146 p. Tables.

> An examination of how Roman Catholics voted on certain selected issues in several postwar elections.

Forster, Arnold, and Epstein, Benjamin R. DANGER ON THE RIGHT. New York: Random House, 1964. xviii, 294 p. Appendix.

> The authors identify the organizations and individuals of the radical Right in the 1950s.

Foster, James C. THE UNION POLITIC: THE CIO POLITICAL ACTION COMMITTEE. Columbia: University of Missouri Press, 1975. 224 p.

> Recounts the launching of the CIO/PAC, one of the most important labor initiatives in the political arena, and assesses its specific impact on elections from 1944 to 1954.

Garson, Robert A. THE DEMOCRATIC PARTY AND THE POLITICS OF SECTIONALISM, 1941-1948. Baton Rouge: Louisiana State University Press, 1974. xiii, 353 p.

> The author provides a useful analysis of the role of the States' Rights Democratic Party.

Gerson, Louis L. THE HYPHENATE IN RECENT POLITICS AND DIPLOMACY. Lawrence: University Press of Kansas, 1964. xxvii, 325 p. Illus.

Goldman, Eric F. THE CRUCIAL DECADE: AMERICA, 1945-1955. New York: Alfred A. Knopf, 1956. ix, 298, ix p.

> An excellent survey that evokes the changing moods of the decade.

Griffith, Robert. THE POLITICS OF FEAR: JOSEPH R. McCARTHY AND THE SENATE. Lexington: University of Kentucky Press, for the Organization of American Historians, 1970. xi, 362 p.

> An examination of the red scare hysteria that gripped the nation in the early 1950s.

Gruening, Ernest. THE BATTLE FOR ALASKA STATEHOOD. College: University of Alaska Press, 1967. xi, 122 p. Distributed by the University of Washington Press, Seattle.

> The politics surrounding the admission of Alaska as a state is told by one of the insiders in the fight.

Gunther, John. INSIDE U.S.A. New York: Harper and Brothers, 1947. xvi, 979 p. Maps.

One of Gunther's famous "insider" books. In this one he concentrates on people and politics in the mid-1940s.

Hamby, Alonzo L. BEYOND THE NEW DEAL: HARRY S. TRUMAN AND AMERICAN LIBERALISM. New York: Columbia University Press, 1973. xx, 635 p.

Hamby is critical of the "New Left" interpretation of the Truman years.

Hardin, Charles M. THE POLITICS OF AGRICULTURE: SOIL CONSERVATION AND THE STRUGGLE FOR POWER IN RURAL AMERICA. Glencoe, Ill.: Free Press of Glencoe, 1952. 282 p. Appendix.

Helpful in unraveling the complex story of agricultural politics.

Harper, Alan D. THE POLITICS OF LOYALTY: THE WHITE HOUSE AND THE COMMUNIST ISSUE, 1946-1952. Westport, Conn.: Greenwood Press, 1969. xii, 318 p. Appendixes.

An in-depth exploration of the Truman administration loyalty program and the growing fear of Communist subversion after World War II.

Hart, Jeffrey P. THE AMERICAN DISSENT: A DECADE OF MODERN CONSERVATISM. Garden City, N.Y.: Doubleday and Co., 1966. 262 p.

The author, a well-known conservative, examines conservatism in the post-World War II period.

Hartmann, Susan M. TRUMAN AND THE 80TH CONGRESS. Columbia: University of Missouri Press, 1971. viii, 241 p.

Superbly researched and carefully interpreted account of Truman's relations with the Republican Eightieth Congress.

Hughes, Emmet J. THE ORDEAL OF POWER: A POLITICAL MEMOIR OF THE EISENHOWER YEARS. New York: Dell Publishing Co., 1964. 320 p. Pap.

Although this book has been out of print for some years, it is still one of the best political biographies of Eisenhower's administration.

Johnson, Donald B. THE REPUBLICAN PARTY AND WENDELL WILLKIE. Illinois Studies in the Social Sciences, vol. 46. Urbana: University of Illinois Press, 1960. ix, 354 p.

As a presidential candidate and titular leader of the Republican party, Willkie was sometimes out of step with others in the party.

Larson, Arthur. A REPUBLICAN LOOKS AT HIS PARTY. New York: Harper and Brothers, 1956. 210 p.

Larson, a moderate Republican, attempts to identify the new course of the Republican party and establish a modern ideology for his party.

Lazarsfeld, Paul F., et al. THE PEOPLE'S CHOICE: HOW THE VOTER MAKES UP HIS MIND IN A PRESIDENTIAL CAMPAIGN. 3d ed. New York: Columbia University Press, 1968. xlv, 178 p. Appendix.

The authors focus on the 1940 presidential election.

Lerche, Charles O., Jr. THE UNCERTAIN SOUTH: ITS CHANGING PATTERNS OF POLITICS IN FOREIGN POLICY. Chicago: Quadrangle Books, 1964. 324 p. Appendixes.

This book concentrates on the post-World War II changes in the South's attitudes about American foreign policy.

Lubell, Samuel. THE FUTURE OF AMERICAN POLITICS. New York: Harper and Brothers, 1952. 285 p.

The author seeks to explain the changes in the country's post-World War II political views.

_____. REVOLT OF THE MODERATES. New York: Harper and Brothers, 1956. ix, 308 p. Appendix.

The author evaluates the political effect of the 1952 presidential election.

McCoy, Donald R., and Ruetten, Richard T. QUEST AND RESPONSE: MINORITY RIGHTS AND THE TRUMAN ADMINISTRATION. Lawrence: University Press of Kansas, 1973. ix, 427 p.

Civil rights politics, its ups and downs in the Truman years.

McKean, Dayton D[avid]. PARTY AND PRESSURE POLITICS. Boston: Houghton, Mifflin and Co., 1949. viii, 712 p. Appendix.

This is a textbook approach to the topic, but there is some concentration on the 1948 election.

Markowitz, Norman D. THE RISE AND FALL OF THE PEOPLE'S CENTURY: HENRY A. WALLACE AND AMERICAN LIBERALISM, 1941-1948. New York: Macmillan Co., 1973. xi, 369 p. Appendix.

A provocative account of the politics of the 1940s and Wallace's relation to political change.

Matusow, Allen J. FARM POLICIES AND POLITICS IN THE TRUMAN YEARS. New York: Atheneum, 1970. 267 p. Pap.

A well-written account of a complex subject.

Mayhew, David R. PARTY LOYALTY AMONG CONGRESSMEN: THE DIF-FERENCE BETWEEN DEMOCRATS AND REPUBLICANS, 1947-1962. Cambridge, Mass.: Harvard University Press, 1966. 189 p. Tables.

A brief but useful analysis of partisan differences in the congressional wings of the nation's major parties.

Moore, William H. THE KEFAUVER COMMITTEE AND THE POLITICS OF CRIME, 1950-1952. Columbia: University of Missouri Press, 1974. xii, 269 p.

Brief descriptions of the major figures and a laudable description of congressional politics. Moore focuses on the connections between the gamblers and urban politicians.

Moos, Malcolm C. POLITICS, PRESIDENTS, AND COATTAILS. Baltimore: Johns Hopkins Press, 1952. xxi, 237 p. Appendixes, maps, tables.

The focus is on the twentieth century and particularly on the 1940s.

Moscow, Warren. ROOSEVELT AND WILLKIE. Englewood Cliffs, N.J.: Prentice-Hall, 1968. xi, 210 p.

Moscow examines the reasons for a very curious political relationship in the early 1940s after the 1940 presidential election.

Oshinsky, David M. SENATOR JOSEPH McCARTHY AND THE AMERICAN LABOR MOVEMENT. Columbia: University of Missouri Press, 1975. 216 p.

Relates labor's political actions before and during the McCarthy years to counter the senator's influence, and describes the growth of both the Communist and Democratic organizations in Wisconsin.

Phillips, Cabell. THE TRUMAN PRESIDENCY: THE HISTORY OF A TRIUMPHANT SUCCESSION. New York: Macmillan Co., 1966. xiii, 463 p. Illus.

A friendly but not necessarily uncritical study. Recounts the national political story in some detail.

Potter, Charles E. DAYS OF SHAME. New York: Coward-McCann, 1965. 304 p. Illus.

A useful study on the politics of McCarthyism and the hysteria of the period.

Ross, Irwin. THE LONELIEST CAMPAIGN: THE TRUMAN VICTORY OF 1948. New York: New American Library, 1968. viii, 304 p. Illus.

An exhaustive treatment of one of the recent past's exciting presidential campaigns.

Schmidt, Karl M. HENRY A. WALLACE: QUIXOTIC CRUSADE, 1948. Syracuse, N.Y.: Syracuse University Press, 1960. 362 p. Illus.

Extensive interviews and party documents provide this study of the 1948 Progressive party campaign of Wallace with an inside view of serious third-party politics.

Spanier, John W. THE TRUMAN-MACARTHUR CONTROVERSY AND THE KOREAN WAR. Cambridge, Mass.: Harvard University Press, 1959. xii, 311 p. Illus.

Spanier examines the political upheaval generated by Truman's firing of MacArthur in 1951.

Thomson, Charles A. H., and Shattuck, Francis M. THE 1956 PRESIDENTIAL CAMPAIGN. Washington, D.C.: Brookings Institution, 1960. xv, 382 p.

An in-depth study of the campaign.

Westerfield, H. Bradford. FOREIGN POLICY AND PARTY POLITICS: PEARL HARBOR TO KOREA. New Haven, Conn.: Yale University Press, 1955. 448 p. Appendix.

An excellent source for an analysis of the effect foreign policy has had on American politics.

Wildavsky, Aaron. DIXON-YATES: A STUDY IN POWER POLITICS. New Haven, Conn.: Yale University Press, 1962. xx, 351 p.

A major political clash occurred in the 1950s over public versus private production of electric power.

Wood, Robert C. SUBURBIA: ITS PEOPLE AND THEIR POLITICS. Boston: Houghton, Mifflin and Co., 1958. xi, 340 p.

A good study of the effect of suburbia on American politics.

Yarnell, Allen. DEMOCRATS AND PROGRESSIVES: THE 1948 PRESIDENTIAL ELECTION AS A TEST OF POSTWAR LIBERALISM. Berkeley and Los Angeles: University of California Press, 1974. xii, 155 p.

Young, Roland A. CONGRESSIONAL POLITICS IN THE SECOND WORLD WAR. New York: Columbia University Press, 1956. 281 p. Appendixes.

Section 2. STATE AND LOCAL POLITICS

Barnard, William D. DIXIECRATS AND DEMOCRATS; ALABAMA POLITICS, 1942-1950. University: University of Alabama Press, 1974. viii, 200 p. Appendix.

Barnard analyzes the conservative backlash to New Deal liberalism and how James E. "Big Jim" Folsom upset the conservative resurgence in Alabama. Folsom's power eventually waned, providing the author with the opportunity to delve into the tangled political history of the state.

Bartley, Numan V. FROM THURMOND TO WALLACE: POLITICAL TENDENCIES IN GEORGIA, 1946-1968. Baltimore: Johns Hopkins Press, 1970. viii, 117 p. Tables.

A brief look at the changes in southern politics from the perspective of one state.

Bryan, Frank M. YANKEE POLITICS IN RURAL VERMONT. Hanover, N.H.: University Press of New England, 1974. xviii, 314 p.

Vermont is described as an intensely rural state even in the recent past. The author skillfully examines politics in the post-World War II period.

Derthick, Martha A. CITY POLITICS IN WASHINGTON, D.C. Cambridge: Joint Center for Urban Studies of the Massachusetts Institute of Technology and Harvard University, 1962. 239 p. Maps, tables.

Eisenstein, Louis, and Rosenberg, Elliot. STRIPE OF TAMMANY'S TIGER. New York: Robert Speller and Sons, Publishers, 1966. 300 p.

The authors explore the benefits of a well-run political machine and bemoan the loss of the power of Tammany Hall.

Ely, James W., Jr. THE CRISIS OF CONSERVATIVE VIRGINIA: THE BYRD ORGANIZATION AND THE POLITICS OF MASSIVE RESISTANCE. Knoxville: University of Tennessee Press, 1976. vii, 220 p.

Ely examines the reaction to the federal government's desegregation demands on Virginia, and Harry F. Byrd's political machine in the 1950s and early 1960s.

Epstein, Leon D. POLITICS IN WISCONSIN. Madison: University of Wisconsin Press, 1958. xiv, 218 p. Tables.

Attention is focused on the post-World War II period and on political behavior.

Haas, Edward F. DELESSEPS S. MORRISON AND THE IMAGE OF REFORM: NEW ORLEANS POLITICS, 1946-1961. Baton Rouge: Louisiana State University Press, 1975. xii, 368 p.

Although Morrison aspired to higher political office, he was not able to extend his political power beyond New Orleans. However, his political hold on the city provides useful instruction on big-city politics in the South.

Moscow, Warren. THE LAST OF THE BIG-TIME BOSSES: THE LIFE AND TIMES OF CARMINE DE SAPIO AND THE RISE AND FALL OF TAMMANY HALL. New York: Stein and Day, 1971. 227 p.

De Sapio never exercised the power of a Hague, Curley, or Daley, but this study is important in any attempt to discover the reasons why the big-city machine declined as a force in recent American politics.

_____. POLITICS IN THE EMPIRE STATE. New York: Alfred A. Knopf, 1948. 238, x p.

Price, Hugh D. THE NEGRO AND SOUTHERN POLITICS: A CHAPTER IN FLORIDA HISTORY. New York: New York University Press, 1957. xviii, 133 p.

The author's general observations on the subject are tested by a close look at Negro voting in the 1950s.

Reichley, James. STATES IN CRISIS: POLITICS IN TEN AMERICAN STATES, 1950-1962. Chapel Hill: University of North Carolina Press, 1964. xii, 264 p.

A brief survey of the political conditions in California, Arizona, New York, Massachusetts, Virginia, Ohio, Pennsylvania, Michigan, Texas, and Nebraska by newspaper reporters.

Ruchelman, Leonard I., ed. BIG CITY MAYORS: CRISIS IN URBAN POLITICS. Bloomington: Indiana University Press, 1969. xi, 371 p.

This volume contains a number of essays on urban politics since the 1930s.

Steiner, Gilbert Y., and Gove, Samuel K. LEGISLATIVE POLITICS IN ILLINOIS. Urbana: University of Illinois Press, 1960. x, 208 p.

The focus of the authors is on the politics of the Illinois General Assembly in the 1950s.

Wilkinson, J. Harvie III. HARRY BYRD AND THE CHANGING FACE OF VIRGINIA POLITICS, 1945-1966. Charlottesville: University Press of Virginia, 1968. xvi, 403 p. Appendixes, tables, illus.

The author analyzes the reasons for the diminishing hold of the Byrd machine in Virginia politics.

Wilson, James Q. AMATEUR DEMOCRATS: CLUB POLITICS IN THREE CITIES. Chicago: University of Chicago Press, 1962. xv, 378 p. Tables.

The three cities are New York, Chicago, and Los Angeles. The clubs are California Democratic Council, New York Committee for Democratic Voters, Democratic Federation of Illinois, and Independent Voters of Illinois.

_____. NEGRO POLITICS: THE SEARCH FOR LEADERSHIP. Glencoe, Ill.: Free Press of Glencoe, 1960. x, 342 p.

Wilson examines various organizations and the cities of Chicago and Los Angeles during the 1950s in order to determine the development of political structure and leadership.

Section 3. BIOGRAPHY

Barnard, Ellsworth. WENDELL WILLKIE, FIGHTER FOR FREEDOM. Marquette: Northern Michigan University Press, 1966. xi, 611 p. Illus.

Willkie was the Republican nominee for president in 1940. He represented the liberal and internationalist wing of his party.

Barnes, Joseph. WILLKIE: THE EVENTS HE WAS PART OF, THE IDEAS HE FOUGHT FOR. New York: Simon and Schuster, 1952. 405 p. Illus.

A detailed political biography.

Brown, Stuart G. CONSCIENCE IN POLITICS: ADLAI E. STEVENSON IN THE 1950'S. Syracuse, N.Y.: Syracuse University Press, 1961. xi, 313 p.

This volume is only indirectly concerned with party politics. The author analyzes Stevenson's political beliefs.

Burns, James MacGregor. ROOSEVELT: THE SOLDIER OF FREEDOM. New York: Harcourt Brace Jovanovich, 1970. xiv, 722 p. Illus.

The author culminates his study of FDR, begun in his ROOSEVELT: THE LION AND THE FOX, with Roosevelt's leadership during World War II. A useful volume for the study of politics during the war years.

Caro, Robert A. THE POWER BROKER: ROBERT MOSES AND THE FALL OF NEW YORK. New York: Alfred A. Knopf, 1974. ix, 1,246, xxxiv p.

This is a classic study of appointive political power. Moses dominated politics in New York for several decades.

Cochran, Bert. ADLAI STEVENSON: PATRICIAN AMONG THE POLITICIANS. New York: Funk and Wagnalls, 1969. 424 p. Illus.

A major biography of the Democratic candidate for president in 1952 and 1956.

Davis, Kenneth S. THE POLITICS OF HONOR: A BIOGRAPHY OF ADLAI E. STEVENSON. New York: G.P. Putnam's Sons, 1957. 543 p. Illus.

Although this work has been superseded by more recent efforts, the author's description of the 1952 and 1956 campaigns is very useful.

Douglas, Paul H. IN THE FULLNESS OF TIME: THE MEMOIRS OF PAUL H. DOUGLAS. New York: Harcourt Brace Jovanovich, 1972. xii, 642 p. Illus.

An excellent memoir that explores left-of-center politics at the local level in Illinois (1920s and 1930s) and at the national level when Douglas was elected to the U.S. Senate in 1948.

Gorman, Joseph Bruce. KEFAUVER: A POLITICAL BIOGRAPHY. New York: Oxford University Press, 1971. viii, 434 p. Illus.

Gorman's study examines Kefauver's politics as they affected Tennessee and the nation in the 1940s and 1950s.

Levine, Erwin L. THEODORE FRANCIS GREEN: THE WASHINGTON YEARS, 1937-1960. Providence, R.I.: Brown University Press, 1971. xi, 179 p.

A short biography of an important politician from Rhode Island.

MacNeil, Neil. DIRKSEN: PORTRAIT OF A PUBLIC MAN. New York: World Publishing Co., 1970. xii, 402 p. Illus.

Dirksen was an important political leader from Illinois in the U.S. Senate during the 1950s and 1960s. As Senate minority leader he was one of the most important spokesmen for the Republicans during the Eisenhower and Kennedy years.

Martin, John B. ADLAI STEVENSON OF ILLINOIS: THE LIFE OF ADLAI E. STEVENSON. Garden City, N.Y.: Doubleday and Co., 1976. ix, 828 p. Illus.

This is a solid biography through the 1952 campaign.

Miller, Merle. PLAIN SPEAKING: AN ORAL BIOGRAPHY OF HARRY S. TRUMAN. New York: Berkley Publishing Co., 1974. 448 p. Distributed by G. P. Putnam's Sons, New York.

Details of Truman's political activities. Truman's views on local, state, and national political events and his views of personalities make fascinating reading.

Patterson, James T. MR. REPUBLICAN: A BIOGRAPHY OF ROBERT A. TAFT. Boston: Houghton, Mifflin and Co., 1972. xvi, 749 p. Illus.

A lengthy study of one of the important political leaders in Ohio's and the nation's recent past.

Rovere, Richard H. SENATOR JOE McCARTHY. New York: Harcourt, Brace and Co., 1959. 280 p.

An early and critical assessment of the impact of Senator McCarthy on the United States.

Sawyer, Charles. CONCERNS OF A CONSERVATIVE DEMOCRAT. Carbondale: Southern Illinois University Press, 1968. xv, 399 p. Illus.

An Ohio politician and secretary of commerce in the Truman administration. Sawyer's memoirs provide the reader with an insider's view of Ohio and national politics.

Schaffer, Alan. VITO MARCANTONIO, RADICAL IN CONGRESS. Syracuse, N.Y.: Syracuse University Press, 1966. ix, 256 p. Illus.

An early associate of Fiorello La Guardia, Marcantonio moved toward the Left when liberal politics failed to accommodate his demands for radical solutions to America's foreign and domestic problems.

Schapsmeier, Edward L., and Schapsmeier, Frederick H. EZRA TAFT BENSON AND THE POLITICS OF AGRICULTURE: THE EISENHOWER YEARS, 1953-1961. Danville, Ill.: Interstate Printers and Publishers, 1975. xviii, 374 p.

_____. PROPHET IN POLITICS: HENRY A. WALLACE AND THE WAR YEARS, 1940-1965. Ames: Iowa State University Press, 1970. xv, 268 p. Illus.

An excellent account of Wallace's political thoughts and political activity.

Sherwood, Robert E. ROOSEVELT AND HOPKINS: AN INTIMATE HISTORY. Rev. ed. New York: Grosset and Dunlap, 1950. vi, 1,002 p. Pap.

An excellent dual biography that concentrates on the relationship between the two men during the years between 1940 and 1945.

Truman, Harry S. MEMOIRS. 2 vols. Garden City, N.Y.: Doubleday and Co., 1955-56.

Well worth reading but some care should be taken in accepting Truman's views whole.

White, William S. THE TAFT STORY. New York: Harper and Brothers, 1954. 288 p. Illus.

A friendly but not uncritical look at one of the most powerful Republican party leaders of the 1940s.

Chapter X

POLITICS FROM CAMELOT TO WATERGATE, 1960-76

Section 1. GENERAL

Alsop, Stewart J. O. THE CENTER: PEOPLE AND POWER IN POLITICAL WASHINGTON. New York: Harper and Row, 1968. xiv, 365 p.

> A lively, personal book by a Washington political columnist that explores the nature of politics and politicians during the 1960s.

Baker, Gordon E. THE REAPPORTIONMENT REVOLUTION: REPRESENTATION, POLITICAL POWER AND THE SUPREME COURT. New York: Random House, 1966. xiii, 209 p. Pap.

> A good survey of the effect of Baker v. Carr on American politics.

Bickel, Alexander M. POLITICS AND THE WARREN COURT. New York: Harper and Row, 1965. xii, 299 p. Appendix.

> The theme is the interaction of politics and the Constitution, particularly in the 1960s.

Bolling, Richard W. HOUSE OUT OF ORDER. New York: E. P. Dutton and Co., 1965. 253 p.

> A study by a member of the House of Representatives of the operation and politics of the House.

Cotter, Cornelius P., and Hennessy, Bernard C. POLITICS WITHOUT POWER: THE NATIONAL PARTY COMMITTEES. New York: Atherton Press, 1964. ix, 246 p.

> National party committees are symbols of party government and the authors examine them in order to explain their relationship to our current political concerns.

Davies, J. Clarence III. THE POLITICS OF POLLUTION. New York: Western Publishing Co., 1970. xiii, 231 p.

121

An introduction to a recently discovered issue in American politics.

De Vries, Walter, and Tarrance, V. Lance. THE TICKET-SPLITTER: A NEW
FORCE IN AMERICAN POLITICS. Grand Rapids, Mich.: William B. Erdmans
Publishing Co., 1972. 149 p. Appendixes.

An account of the decline in party loyalty. The authors explore
the difference between the independent voter and the ticket split-
ter.

Donovan, John C. POLITICS OF POVERTY. 2d ed. Indianapolis: Pegasus,
1973. 201 p. Illus.

Dutton, Frederick G. CHANGING SOURCES OF POWER: AMERICAN POLI-
TICS IN THE 1970'S. New York: McGraw-Hill Book Co., 1971. xviii,
263 p.

Garcia, F. Chris, ed. LA CAUSA POLITICA: A CHICANO POLITICS READ-
ER. Notre Dame, Ind.: University of Notre Dame Press, 1974. xi, 444 p.

An examination of Chicano politics: history, individual, and in-
stitutional.

Goldwater, Barry. THE CONSCIENCE OF A CONSERVATIVE. New York:
Hillman Books, 1960. 127 p.

Senator Goldwater's statement of his personal political beliefs.

Heath, Jim F. DECADE OF DISILLUSIONMENT: THE KENNEDY-JOHNSON
YEARS. Bloomington: Indiana University Press, 1976. xvi, 332 p. Pap.

The author focuses on domestic politics as well as other aspects of
the Kennedy-Johnson presidencies.

Huckshorn, Robert J., and Spencer, Robert C. THE POLITICS OF DEFEAT:
CAMPAIGNING FOR CONGRESS. Amherst: University of Massachusetts Press,
1971. xi, 258 p. Appendixes.

The authors have systematically studied the electoral process used
by candidates for election to the U.S. Congress. The focus is
the 1962 congressional election.

Lasch, Christopher. THE AGONY OF THE AMERICAN LEFT. New York:
Alfred A. Knopf, 1969. ix, 212, viii p.

The author is concerned with the reasons why radicalism (of the
Left) has been a failure in America.

Lee, Richard W., ed. POLITICS AND THE PRESS. Washington, D.C.: Acrop-
olis Books, 1970. 191 p.

A collection of lectures that were given at the University of Maryland in 1969 by journalists and scholars of journalism. The collection is a useful commentary on the role of the press in politics in the 1960s.

Lipset, Seymour M., and Schaflander, Gerald M. PASSION AND POLITICS: STUDENT ACTIVISM IN AMERICA. Boston: Little, Brown and Co., 1971. xxiii, 440 p. Illus.

Mailer, Norman. MIAMI AND THE SIEGE OF CHICAGO: AN INFORMAL HISTORY OF THE REPUBLICAN AND DEMOCRATIC CONVENTIONS OF 1968. Cleveland: World Publishing Co., 1968. 223 p.

The famous novelist comments on American politics as he observed their practice at the major party conventions.

Miroff, Bruce. PRAGMATIC ILLUSIONS: THE PRESIDENTIAL POLITICS OF JOHN F. KENNEDY. New York: David McKay Co., 1976. xvii, 334 p. Pap.

A detailed "revisionist" examination of presidential politics. Miroff's reassessment is consistently critical of Kennedy's presidential politics.

Muse, Benjamin. THE AMERICAN NEGRO REVOLUTION: FROM NON-VIOLENCE TO BLACK POWER, 1963-1967. Bloomington: Indiana University Press, 1968. xii, 345 p.

An important study of the changing nature of black politics and style of political leadership in the 1960s.

Novak, Michael. CHOOSING OUR KING: POWERFUL SYMBOLS IN PRESIDENTIAL POLITICS. New York: Macmillan Co., 1974. xviii, 324 p.

A great deal of attention is given to the 1972 presidential election.

O'Neill, William L. COMING APART: AN INFORMAL HISTORY OF AMERICA IN THE 1960'S. New York: Quadrangle Books, 1971. 442, xxvi p. Illus. Pap.

The sections on politics are very readable.

Rather, Dan, and Gates, Gary Paul. THE PALACE GUARD. New York: Harper and Row, 1974. ix, 326 p. Illus.

A behind-the-scenes account of the Nixon administration and the country before Watergate.

Silver, James W. MISSISSIPPI: THE CLOSED SOCIETY. New York: Harcourt, Brace and World, 1963. xxii, 250 p. Appendixes.

> The author shares his observations on the conflict between white supremacy and the civil rights movement during the 1950s and 1960s.

Thayer, George. THE FARTHER SHORE OF POLITICS: THE AMERICAN PO-LITICAL FRINGE TODAY. New York: Simon and Schuster, 1967. 610 p.

> A comprehensive study of extremism on both ends of the political spectrum.

Thernstrom, Stephan. POVERTY AND POLITICS IN BOSTON: ORIGINS OF ABCD. New York: Basic Books, 1969. xiii, 199 p.

> Explores the politics of the Action for Boston Community Development organization in the 1960s.

Walton, Hanes, Jr. BLACK POLITICS: A THEORETICAL AND STRUCTURAL ANALYSIS. Philadelphia: J. B. Lippincott Co., 1972. xvii, 246 p. Illus.

> An examination of black parties and pressure groups. The major area of concern is the 1960s.

White, Theodore H. BREACH OF FAITH: THE FALL OF RICHARD NIXON. New York: Dell Publishing Co., 1975. 476 p. Pap.

> White examines in great detail the political failure of President Nixon. He goes beyond Watergate to examine all of the factors that led to the president's resignation.

Section 2. RECENT PRESIDENTIAL ELECTIONS

Chester, Lewis, et al. AN AMERICAN MELODRAMA: PRESIDENTIAL CAM-PAIGN OF 1968. New York: Viking Press, 1969. xv, 814 p.

> An insider account of the campaign by English journalists.

Cummings, Milton C., Jr., ed. THE NATIONAL ELECTION OF 1964. Washington: Brookings Institution, 1966. xi, 295 p.

> An in-depth examination of the campaign.

David, Paul T., ed. THE PRESIDENTIAL ELECTION AND TRANSITION, 1960-1961. Washington: Brookings Institution, 1961. ix, 353 p.

Kessel, John H. THE GOLDWATER COALITION: REPUBLICAN STRATEGIES IN 1964. Indianapolis: Bobbs-Merrill Co., 1968. ix, 371 p. Tables.

Larner, Jeremy. NOBODY KNOWS: REFLECTIONS ON THE McCARTHY CAMPAIGN OF 1968. New York: Macmillan Co., 1969. 189 p.

The author was a speech writer for Senator Eugene McCarthy in his 1968 presidential campaign.

McGinnis, Joe. THE SELLING OF THE PRESIDENT, 1968. New York: Trident Press, 1969. 253 p.

McGinnis examines the methods employed to advertise Nixon's candidacy.

White, Theodore H. THE MAKING OF THE PRESIDENT, 1960. New York: Atheneum, 1961. viii, 400 p. Appendixes.

The MAKING OF THE PRESIDENT series is very helpful in understanding presidential politics in recent years. See also the entries below.

_____. THE MAKING OF THE PRESIDENT, 1964. New York: Atheneum, 1965. xi, 431 p. Appendixes.

_____. THE MAKING OF THE PRESIDENT, 1968. New York: Atheneum, 1969. xii, 459 p. Appendixes.

_____. THE MAKING OF THE PRESIDENT, 1972. New York: Atheneum, 1973. vi, 391 p. Appendixes.

Section 3. STATE AND LOCAL POLITICS

Banfield, Edward C. BIG CITY POLITICS: A COMPARATIVE GUIDE TO THE POLITICAL SYSTEMS OF NINE AMERICAN CITIES. New York: Random House, 1965. vi, 149 p.

The nine cities are Atlanta, Boston, Detroit, El Paso, Los Angeles, Miami, Philadelphia, St. Louis, and Seattle.

Bollens, John C., and Geyer, Grant B. YORTY: POLITICS OF A CONSTANT CANDIDATE. Pacific Palisades, Calif.: Palisades Publishers, 1973. v, 245 p.

A useful political biography of Samuel W. Yorty, mayor of Los Angeles from 1961 to 1973.

Davidson, Chandler. BIRACIAL POLITICS: CONFLICT AND COALITION IN THE METROPOLITAN SOUTH. Baton Rouge: Louisiana State University Press, 1972. xviii, 301 p. Appendixes.

The author focuses on Houston, Texas, and advances the thesis that change in the political arena is the only sure event.

Hill, Gladwin. DANCING BEAR: AN INSIDE LOOK AT CALIFORNIA POLITICS. Cleveland: World Publishing Co., 1968. 303 p.

Jewell, Malcolm E., and Cunningham, Everett W. KENTUCKY POLITICS. Lexington: University of Kentucky Press, 1968. vi, 278 p. Tables.

> The authors provide a brief historical survey but their attention is on the recent past.

Morlan, Robert L., and Hardy, Leroy C. POLITICS IN CALIFORNIA. Belmont, Calif.: Dickenson Publishing Co., 1968. vi, 122 p.

O'Connor, Len. CLOUT: MAYOR DALEY AND HIS CITY. New York: Avon Books, 1975. xi, 276 p. Pap.

> The author examines the rise of Richard Daley and the methods of political operation in one of America's largest cities.

Royko, Mike. BOSS: RICHARD J. DALEY OF CHICAGO. New York: E. P. Dutton and Co., 1971. 215 p.

> A critical portrait of the most famous of big-city mayors by one of the major newspaper columnists in Chicago.

Sharkansky, Ira. REGIONALISM IN AMERICAN POLITICS. Indianapolis: Bobbs-Merrill Co., 1970. xiv, 194 p. Tables, appendixes.

> An analysis of regional peculiarities in politics and public policies that concentrates on the 1960s.

Sherrill, Robert. GOTHIC POLITICS IN THE DEEP SOUTH: STARS OF THE NEW CONFEDERACY. New York: Grossman Publishers, 1968. 335 p.

> An interesting examination of the varieties of political style of recent political leaders in the South, e.g., Leander Perez, Jim Eastland, and George Wallace.

Weinberg, Kenneth G. BLACK VICTORY: CARL STOKES AND THE WINNING OF CLEVELAND. Chicago: Quadrangle Books, 1968. 250 p. Illus. Pap.

> An important study of black politics in Cleveland, Ohio.

Section 4. BIOGRAPHY

Anson, Robert S. McGOVERN: A BIOGRAPHY. New York: Holt, Rinehart and Winston, 1972. xiii, 303 p. Illus.

> A better-than-average campaign biography.

Bernstein, Carl, and Woodward, Bob. ALL THE PRESIDENT'S MEN. New York: Warner Books, 1975. 382 p.

> One of the important books on the failure of the Nixon presidency.

_____. THE FINAL DAYS. New York: Simon and Schuster, 1976. 476 p. Illus.

A brilliant and controversial account of the tragic events surrounding the fall of the Nixon presidency. The authors' information augments or contradicts the remembrances of many of those in the White House.

Evans, Rowland, and Novak, Robert. LYNDON B. JOHNSON: THE EXERCISE OF POWER. New York: New American Library, 1968. 640 p. Pap.

Evans and Novak analyze the political strategies of a master politician in the Senate and the White House.

_____. NIXON IN THE WHITE HOUSE: THE FRUSTRATION OF POWER. New York: Vintage Books, 1971. 457 p.

An appreciative account of Nixon's skill in political manipulation during his first term. The authors raise the interesting question about Nixon's relationship with the voter, i.e., how far would he go to win their support.

Frady, Marshall. WALLACE. New York: World Publishing Co., 1966. viii, 246 p. Illus.

An examination of Wallace's origin and development as a major political force in the 1960s.

Halberstam, David. THE BEST AND THE BRIGHTEST. New York: Random House, 1972. 688 p.

A fascinating account of the people and decisions made by the people John F. Kennedy relied upon for advice, particularly in the area of foreign policy, and their continued influence after his death. Halberstam is very critical of the decisions that involved the United States in the Vietnam conflict.

_____. THE UNFINISHED ODYSSEY OF ROBERT KENNEDY. New York: Random House, 1968. 211 p.

A sympathetic portrait by an associate and keen observer of the political scene in the 1960s.

Hess, Stephen, and Mazo, Earl. NIXON: A POLITICAL PORTRAIT. New York: Harper and Row, 1968. viii, 326 p.

Hoyt, Edwin P. THE NIXONS: AN AMERICAN FAMILY. New York: Random House, 1972. xii, 307 p. Illus.

A standard campaign piece.

O'Brien, Lawrence F. NO FINAL VICTORIES: A LIFE IN POLITICS, FROM JOHN F. KENNEDY TO WATERGATE. Garden City, N.Y.: Doubleday and Co., 1974. 394 p. Illus.

> An associate of Kennedy, O'Brien became a major force in the apparatus of the Democratic party.

Schlesinger, Arthur M., Jr. A THOUSAND DAYS: JOHN F. KENNEDY IN THE WHITE HOUSE. Boston: Houghton Mifflin Co., 1965. xiv, 1,087 p.

> A major biography of the Kennedy presidency by a participant in the Kennedy administration.

Sorenson, Theodore C. KENNEDY. New York: Harper and Row, 1965. viii, 783 p. Appendixes.

> A sympathetic examination of Kennedy's political career.

Stokes, Carl B. PROMISES OF POWER: A POLITICAL AUTOBIOGRAPHY. New York: Simon and Schuster, 1973. 288 p.

> Although Stokes is reticent about some of the failures of his administration, he does provide an insight into big-city politics, particularly black politics, in the 1960s.

Walton, Hanes, Jr. THE POLITICAL PHILOSOPHY OF MARTIN LUTHER KING, JR. Westport, Conn.: Greenwood Press, 1971. xxxviii, 137 p.

Wicker, Tom. JFK AND LBJ: THE INFLUENCE OF PERSONALITY UPON POLITICS. New York: William Morrow and Co., 1968. 297 p.

> Wicker develops the thesis that personality and circumstance dominate our political life. His examination of the presidencies of two astute politicians includes an in-depth account that notes their failure to achieve their ambitious goals.

Chapter XI
GENERAL

Section 1. REFERENCE WORKS

Adams, James T., ed. DICTIONARY OF AMERICAN HISTORY. 5 vols. New York: Charles Scribner's Sons, 1942.

A mine of information about U.S. history.

Basler, Roy P., et al., eds. A GUIDE TO THE STUDY OF THE UNITED STATES. Washington, D.C.: U.S. Library of Congress, 1960. xv, 1,193 p.

An excellent bibliography that is organized chronologically and topically. Chapter 12 deals with local history, and the titles listed provide directions for the study of state and local politics.

Boehm, Eric H., ed. AMERICA, HISTORY AND LIFE: A GUIDE TO PERIODI-CAL LITERATURE. Santa Barbara, Calif.: ABC–Clio Press, 1964.

A major survey of the periodical literature, much of which covers American politics.

Bradford, Thomas L., ed. THE BIBLIOGRAPHERS MANUAL OF AMERICAN HISTORY. 5 vols. Philadelphia: Stan V. Henkels and Co., 1907-10. Reprint. Detroit: Gale Research Co., 1968.

An exhaustive survey of territorial, state, and local historical literature. If the cited works are available, they should be used with care because the accuracy of the material is not always assured.

Carruth, Gorton, ed. THE ENCYCLOPEDIA OF AMERICAN FACTS AND DATES. 4th ed. New York: Thomas Y. Crowell Co., 1966. vi, 821 p.

Crouch, Milton, and Raum, Hans, eds. DIRECTORY OF STATE AND LOCAL HISTORY PERIODICALS. Chicago: American Library Association, 1977. xi, 124 p. Pap.

A good source for the names of state and local historical periodicals that contain articles, often very well researched, regarding many of the major and minor political events and personalities in our history.

Diamond, Robert A., ed. GUIDE TO U.S. ELECTIONS. Washington, D.C.: Congressional Quarterly, 1975. xvi, 1,103 p. Appendixes.

An excellent source for information on presidential, gubernatorial, and congressional elections.

Dougherty, James J., ed. WRITINGS ON AMERICAN HISTORY. Millwood, N.Y.: Kraus-Thomson Organization, for the American Historical Association, 1974. x, 266 p.

This volume and its predecessors, dating back to 1902, survey periodical literature relating to American history. An excellent reference point for the student seeking sources of information on major political events and personalities.

Freidel, Frank B., ed. HARVARD GUIDE TO AMERICAN HISTORY. 3 vols. Rev. ed. Cambridge, Mass.: Belknap Press of Harvard University Press, 1974.

The 1954 edition contains sections on historical sources not present in this edition. The cutoff date for this edition is June 1970.

Gammons, Ann, ed. WHO'S WHO IN AMERICAN POLITICS. 5th ed. New York: R. R. Bowker Co., 1975. 1,090 p.

This edition and the previous editions are valuable in identifying recent political figures.

Garraty, John A., ed. ENCYCLOPEDIA OF AMERICAN BIOGRAPHY. New York: Harper and Row, 1974. xiv, 1,241 p.

Each of the over one thousand entries contains an objective biographical sketch and a subjective evaluation of the individual's contribution. The average entry is about 850 words.

Garrison, Lloyd B., ed. AMERICAN POLITICS AND ELECTIONS: SELECTED ABSTRACTS OF PERIODICAL LITERATURE, 1964-1968. Santa Barbara, Calif.: ABC-Clio Press, 1968. iii, 45 p.

A must for any serious student of American politics. An excellent source for an annotated index to periodical literature written between 1964 and 1968 on the course of politics in the United States.

Griffin, Appleton P. C., ed. BIBLIOGRAPHY OF AMERICAN HISTORICAL SOCIETIES. An Annual Report of the American Historical Association for the Year 1905. Washington, D.C.: Government Printing Office, 1907. Reprint. Detroit: Gale Research Co., 1966. 1,374 p.

A survey of the publications of historical societies into the year
1905. This volume helps the researcher identify published sources
that contain a wealth of articles on American politics.

Hopkins, Joseph G. E., ed. CONCISE DICTIONARY OF AMERICAN BIOG-
RAPHY. New York: Charles Scribner's Sons, 1964. viii, 1,273 p.

A very useful source for concise information on most major and
many minor figures in American politics who died before December
31, 1940.

Key, V. O., Jr. A PRIMER OF STATISTICS FOR POLITICAL SCIENTISTS.
New York: Thomas Y. Crowell Co., 1959. x, 209 p. Appendixes.

This is a useful explanation of statistical tools in the area of
political analysis.

McCarthy, Eugene J. THE CRESCENT DICTIONARY OF AMERICAN POLITICS.
New York: Macmillan Co., 1962. x, 182 p. Illus.

A brief and useful volume for the novice.

Morris, Dan, and Morris, Inez. WHO WAS WHO IN AMERICAN POLITICS.
New York: Hawthorn Books, 1974. 637 p.

A fairly complete listing except that some of the minor party figures and local leaders are ignored.

Morris, Richard B., ed. ENCYCLOPEDIA OF AMERICAN HISTORY. Rev. ed.
New York: Harper and Brothers, 1961. xiv, 840 p.

A good tool for pinpointing major political events.

Mugridge, Donald H., comp. PRESIDENTS OF THE UNITED STATES 1789-
1962: A SELECTED LIST OF REFERENCES. Washington, D.C.: Library of
Congress, 1963. xviii, 159 p.

A useful bibliography even though it sticks too closely to memoirs
and some of the standard biographies.

Plano, Jack C., and Greenberg, Milton. THE AMERICAN POLITICAL DIC-
TIONARY. 3d ed. New York: Holt, Rinehart and Winston, 1972. viii,
462 p.

Porter, Kirk H., and Johnson, Donald B., eds. NATIONAL PARTY PLATFORMS,
1840-1956. Urbana: University of Illinois Press, 1956. xi, 573 p.

This volume contains the official platforms of the major and important minor parties.

Press, Charles, comp. A BIBLIOGRAPHIC INTRODUCTION TO AMERICAN STATE GOVERNMENT AND POLITICS. East Lansing: Michigan State University, 1964. 34 p.

Reynolds, Clifford P., comp. BIOGRAPHICAL DIRECTORY OF THE AMERICAN CONGRESS, 1774-1961. Washington, D.C.: Government Printing Office, 1961. 1,863 p.

A source of valuable information often not available in convenient form for many minor political figures.

Safire, William. THE NEW LANGUAGE OF POLITICS: A DICTIONARY OF CATCHWORDS, SLOGANS AND POLITICAL USAGE. Rev. ed. New York: Collier Books, 1972. xviii, 782 p. Pap.

One of the most complete dictionaries, particularly on contemporary terms.

Smith, Dwight L., and Garrison, Lloyd W., eds. THE AMERICAN POLITICAL PROCESS: SELECTED ABSTRACTS OF PERIODICAL LITERATURE, 1954-1971. Santa Barbara, Calif.: ABC-Clio Press, 1972. xvi, 630 p.

This volume covers serial publications in this field from 1954 through 1971. It contains 2,274 abstracts of scholarly articles published in the United States and abroad on political parties, American elections, political behavior, and political institutions.

Smith, Edward C., and Zurcher, Arnold J. DICTIONARY OF AMERICAN POLITICS. 2d ed. New York: Barnes and Noble, 1968. vii, 434 p.

Sobel, Robert, ed. THE BIOGRAPHICAL DIRECTORY OF THE GOVERNORS OF THE UNITED STATES, 1789-1978. 4 vols. Westport, Conn.: Meckler Books, 1977.

Although many state governors achieved a national reputation and are the subject of biographies, others were little known outside of their states or time. These volumes contain a mass of information that has been mined from newspapers, archives, and books. Researchers will find this study a convenient and authoritative guide.

_____. BIOGRAPHICAL DIRECTORY OF THE UNITED STATES EXECUTIVE BRANCH, 1774-1977. 2d ed., rev. Westport, Conn.: Greenwood Press, 1977. x, 503 p.

Traces the lives and careers of more than 550 men and women who have served as president, vice-president, and cabinet officers. Each entry includes a short bibliography listing primary and secondary works about the subject's life and role in government.

SOCIAL SCIENCES INDEX. New York: H. W. Wilson Co., 1974.

An index for almost all the journals, other than the major histori-
cal ones, in the social science area. Supersedes the SOCIAL
SCIENCES AND HUMANITIES INDEX and the INTERNATIONAL
INDEX TO PERIODICALS (1907–74).

Sperber, Hans, and Trittschuh, Travis. AMERICAN POLITICAL TERMS: AN
HISTORICAL DICTIONARY. Detroit: Wayne State University Press, 1962. x,
516 p.

In addition to definition of terms, there is a bibliography that re-
fers to many of the older works on American political history.

U.S. Bureau of the Census, comp. THE STATISTICAL HISTORY OF THE UNIT-
ED STATES: FROM COLONIAL TIMES TO THE PRESENT. New York: Basic
Books, 1976. xxix, 1,235 p. Tables.

An excellent source for political statistics and useful information
on sources for additional study.

Wakelyn, Jon L. BIOGRAPHICAL DICTIONARY OF THE CONFEDERACY.
Westport, Conn.: Greenwood Press, 1977. xii, 601 p. Appendixes.

Brief biographical sketches of 651 persons involved with the Confederacy.

Section 2. POLITICAL IDEAS AND PRACTICAL POLITICS

Agar, Herbert. PEOPLE'S CHOICE, FROM WASHINGTON TO HARDING:
A STUDY IN DEMOCRACY. Boston: Houghton, Mifflin and Co., 1933. xxi,
337 p. Illus.

Billington, Monroe L. THE POLITICAL SOUTH IN THE TWENTIETH CENTURY.
New York: Charles Scribner's Sons, 1975. xiii, 205 p.

Billington describes the remarkable transformation in southern politics within the framework of local, state, and regional politics,
referring to the national scene when it is relevant.

Binkley, Wilfred E. AMERICAN POLITICAL PARTIES: THEIR NATURAL HIS-
TORY. 4th ed. New York: Alfred A. Knopf, 1962. xiii, 486, xiv p.

Burdick, Eugene, and Brodbeck, Arthur J., eds. AMERICAN VOTING BE-
HAVIOR. Glencoe, Ill.: Free Press of Glencoe, 1959. 475 p. Illus.

Chambers, William N., and Burnham, Walter, eds. THE AMERICAN PARTY
SYSTEMS: STAGES OF POLITICAL DEVELOPMENT. New York: Oxford University Press, 1967. xi, 321 p.

A collection of essays by historians and political scientists analyzing the development of the American party system and the impact of parties on the recent political scene.

Chute, Marchette. THE FIRST LIBERTY: A HISTORY OF THE RIGHT TO VOTE IN AMERICA, 1619-1850. New York: E. P. Dutton and Co., 1969. xii, 371 p.

David, Paul T. PARTY STRENGTH IN THE UNITED STATES, 1872-1970. Charlottesville: University Press of Virginia, 1972. xiii, 310 p. Tables, appendix.

Excellent statistics.

Ekirch, Arthur A., Jr. THE AMERICAN DEMOCRATIC TRADITION: A HISTORY. New York: Macmillan Co., 1963. 338 p.

An examination of American democracy in terms of social theory as well as of political practice.

Ferguson, Paul. THE AMERICAN PARTY DRAMA. New York: Vantage Press, 1966. 637 p.

Hendrick, Burton J. THE LEES OF VIRGINIA: A BIOGRAPHY OF A FAMILY. Boston: Little, Brown and Co., 1935. xii, 455 p. Illus.

The author begins with Richard Lee (1590?-1663?) and ends with Robert E. Lee (1807-70). This volume is more than biography because Hendrick is concerned with the origins and development of political leadership in America.

Herring, Edward Pendleton. THE POLITICS OF DEMOCRACY: AMERICAN PARTIES IN ACTION. New York: W. W. Norton and Co., 1940. xx, 468 p.

Hess, Stephen. AMERICA'S POLITICAL DYNASTIES FROM ADAMS TO KENNEDY. Garden City, N.Y.: Doubleday and Co., 1966. 736 p. Appendixes, illus.

Hofstadter, Richard. AGE OF REFORM: FROM BRYAN TO F.D.R. New York: Alfred A. Knopf, 1955. 328 p.

A major study of political leadership and political directions in the twentieth century.

Key, V. O., Jr. THE RESPONSIBLE ELECTORATE: RATIONALITY IN PRESIDENTIAL VOTING, 1936-1960. Cambridge, Mass.: Harvard University Press, 1966. xxi, 158 p. Tables.

Ladd, Everett C., Jr. IDEOLOGY IN AMERICA: CHANGE AND RESPONSE IN A CITY, A SUBURB, AND A SMALL TOWN. Ithaca, N.Y.: Cornell University Press, 1969. xiii, 378 p. Tables, illus.

> This study of political ideas and ideology in three American communities focuses on the response and adaption of political ideology in a technological society. The author compares ideational systems in three different settings. The author argues that an ideological orientation still exists in America although it is hardly messianic.

Ladd, Everett C., Jr., with Hadley, Charles D. TRANSFORMATIONS OF THE AMERICAN PARTY SYSTEM: POLITICAL COALITIONS FROM THE NEW DEAL TO THE 1970'S. New York: W. W. Norton and Co., 1975. xxv, 371 p.

> A useful book for understanding the American party system as it relates to the electorate, and the grand coalitions that constitute each major political party.

Luthin, Reinhard H. AMERICAN DEMAGOGUES: TWENTIETH CENTURY. Boston: Beacon Press, 1954. xv, 368 p.

McKay, Robert B. REAPPORTIONMENT: THE LAW AND POLITICS OF EQUAL REPRESENTATION. New York: Simon and Schuster, 1965. xii, 498 p. Appendix. Pap.

> McKay examines the nature of representative government in relation to questions of apportionment and districting.

Madison, Charles A. LEADERS AND LIBERALS IN 20TH CENTURY AMERICA. New York: Frederick Ungar Publishing Co., 1961. xi, 499 p.

> The figures that the author concentrates on are T. Roosevelt, W. Wilson, R. LaFollette, L. Brandeis, F. Roosevelt, G. Norris, H. Black, and H. Truman. They are chosen by Madison to exemplify the struggle for social justice in this century.

Mason, Alpheus T., and Leach, Richard H. IN QUEST OF FREEDOM: AMERICAN POLITICAL THOUGHT AND PRACTICE. Englewood Cliffs, N.J.: Prentice-Hall, 1959. viii, 568 p.

Morison, Samuel E[liot]. THE OXFORD HISTORY OF THE AMERICAN PEOPLE. New York: Oxford University Press, 1965. xxvii, 1153 p. Illus.

> A good one-volume survey with a great deal of information on American political history.

Nichols, Roy F. THE INVENTION OF AMERICAN POLITICAL PARTIES. New York: Macmillan Co., 1967. xii, 416 p. Appendixes.

This is a penetrating analysis of the development of political parties. The author is particularly concerned with the historical
antecedents of the American party system.

Nye, Russel B. MIDWESTERN PROGRESSIVE POLITICS: A HISTORICAL STUDY
OF ITS ORIGINS AND DEVELOPMENT, 1870-1950. East Lansing: Michigan
State College Press, 1951. 422 p.

Porter, Kirk H. A HISTORY OF SUFFRAGE IN THE UNITED STATES. Chicago: University of Chicago Press, 1918. 260 p.

Roseboom, Eugene H. A HISTORY OF PRESIDENTIAL ELECTIONS. 3d ed.
New York: Macmillan Co., 1970. vi, 639 p.

An excellent basic examination of U.S. politics that centers on
the quadrennial battle for the presidency.

Rossiter, Clinton. PARTIES AND POLITICS IN AMERICA. Ithaca, N.Y.:
Cornell University Press, 1960. vii, 205 p.

The author examines some of the variables in twentieth-century
politics.

Shapiro, Martin M. LAW AND POLITICS IN THE SUPREME COURT: NEW
APPROACHES TO POLITICAL JURISPRUDENCE. New York: Free Press, 1964.
xi, 364 p.

Smith, William R. THE RHETORIC OF AMERICAN POLITICS: A STUDY OF
DOCUMENTS. Westport, Conn.: Greenwood Publishing Corp., 1969. xv,
464 p.

A useful analysis of political documents. The author is interested
in the origins and meaning of the politician's vocabulary.

Sorauf, Francis J. PARTY POLITICS IN AMERICA. 2d ed. Boston: Little,
Brown and Co., 1972. x, 445 p.

Stimpson, George W. A BOOK ABOUT AMERICAN POLITICS. New York:
Harper and Brothers, 1952. 554 p.

An interesting feature of this book is the author's concern for the
origin of many political terms, catchwords, phrases, and obscure
political figures and movements.

Sundquist, James L. POLITICS AND POLICY: THE EISENHOWER, KENNEDY,
AND JOHNSON YEARS. Washington, D.C.: Brookings Institution, 1968.
viii, 560 p. Tables.

Williams, T[homas]. Harry. ROMANCE AND REALISM IN SOUTHERN POLI-
TICS. Baton Rouge: Louisiana State University Press, 1966. xii, 84 p.

> Concentrates on the Reconstruction, Populist, and the Huey Long
> periods.

Williamson, Chilton. AMERICAN SUFFRAGE: FROM PROPERTY TO DEMOC-
RACY, 1760-1860. Princeton, N.J.: Princeton University Press, 1960. x,
306 p.

Woodburn, James A. AMERICAN POLITICS: POLITICAL PARTY PROBLEMS
IN THE UNITED STATES: A SKETCH OF AMERICAN PARTY HISTORY AND
OF THE DEVELOPMENT AND OPERATIONS OF PARTY MACHINERY. 3d ed.
New York: G. P. Putnam's Sons, 1916. xiv, 487 p.

Section 3. MAJOR PARTIES

Bailey, Thomas A. DEMOCRATS VS. REPUBLICANS: THE CONTINUING
CLASH. New York: Meredith Press, 1968. xi, 179 p. Charts, tables.

> A brief history of American political parties as seen in successive
> presidential elections.

Chambers, William N. THE DEMOCRATS, 1789-1964: A SHORT HISTORY OF
A POPULAR PARTY. Princeton, N.J.: D. Van Nostrand Co., 1964. 192 p.

Goldman, Ralph M. THE DEMOCRATIC PARTY IN AMERICAN POLITICS.
New York: Macmillan Co., 1966. 152 p.

> A brief survey of the origins and development of the Democratic
> party.

Jones, Charles O. THE REPUBLICAN PARTY IN AMERICAN POLITICS. New
York: Macmillan Co., 1965. 153 p. Pap.

> The author focuses on the Republican party in the 1950s and 1960s.

Kent, Frank R. THE DEMOCRATIC PARTY: A HISTORY. New York: Century Co., 1928. Reprint. New York: Johnson Reprint Corp., 1968. xi,
468 p. Illus., appendixes.

> A popular account by a political reporter examines the history of
> the party prior to the election of 1928.

Mayer, George H. THE REPUBLICAN PARTY, 1854-1964. 2d ed. New York:
Oxford University Press, 1967. xi, 604 p.

Minor, Henry A. THE STORY OF THE DEMOCRATIC PARTY. New York:
Macmillan Co., 1928. x, 501 p.

Moos, Malcolm C. THE REPUBLICANS: A HISTORY OF THEIR PARTY. New York: Random House, 1956. xi, 564 p.

Myers, William S. THE REPUBLICAN PARTY: A HISTORY. New York: Century Co., 1928. xii, 487 p.

Parmet, Herbert S. THE DEMOCRATS: THE YEARS AFTER FDR. New York: Macmillan Co., 1976. xi, 371 p.

Section 4. THIRD PARTIES AND DIVERGENT POLITICS

Bell, Daniel. MARXIAN SOCIALISM IN THE UNITED STATES. Princeton, N.J.: Princeton University Press, 1967. xiii, 212 p. Pap.

> A slim but rewarding study of Marxian socialism in the United States. This essay is from SOCIALISM AND AMERICAN LIFE. Edited by Donald D. Egbert and Stow Persons. Princeton Studies in American Civilization, no. 4. Princeton, N.J.: Princeton University Press, 1952.

_____, ed. THE RADICAL RIGHT. Garden City, N.Y.: Doubleday and Co., 1964. xi, 468 p. Pap.

> This edition is an enlarged and updated version of THE NEW AMERICAN RIGHT, originally published by Criterion Books in 1955.

Degler, Carl N. THE OTHER SOUTH: SOUTHERN DISSENTERS IN THE NINETEENTH CENTURY. New York: Harper and Row, 1974. 392 p.

> A wide-ranging study of the antislavery movements, the Confederacy, and politics in the Old and New South.

Diggins, John P. THE AMERICAN LEFT IN THE TWENTIETH CENTURY. New York: Harcourt Brace Jovanovich, 1973. xii, 210 p. Illus. Pap.

> A brief survey of the political Left, the old and new versions.

Draper, Theodore. ROOTS OF AMERICAN COMMUNISM. New York: Viking Press, 1957. x, 498 p. Illus.

> This survey examines the origin and development of the Communist movement in the United States to 1945.

Egbert, D[onald]. D., and Persons, Stow, eds. SOCIALISM AND AMERICAN LIFE. Princeton Studies in American Civilization, no. 4. 2 vols. Princeton, N.J.: Princeton University Press, 1952.

> Volume 1 contains fifteen essays that explore Socialist thought and development. Volume 2 is a descriptive and critical bibliography.

Fine, Nathan. LABOR AND FARMER PARTIES IN THE UNITED STATES, 1828-1928. New York: Rand School of Social Science, 1928. Reprint. New York: Russell and Russell, 1961. 445 p.

Fleischman, Harry. NORMAN THOMAS: A BIOGRAPHY, 1884-1968. New York: W. W. Norton and Co., 1969. 364 p. Illus.

The author was an associate of Norman Thomas and, like so many others, is sympathetic to one of the twentieth century's great figures.

Foster, William Z. HISTORY OF THE COMMUNIST PARTY OF THE UNITED STATES. New York: International Publishers, 1952. 600 p.

Foster was a major leader in the Communist party in the United States.

Goldberg, Harvey, ed. AMERICAN RADICALS: SOME PROBLEMS AND PERSONALITIES. New York: Monthly Review Press, 1957. x, 308 p.

The essays are mainly concerned with twentieth-century figures who were opposed to the status quo.

Haynes, Fred E. THIRD PARTY MOVEMENTS SINCE THE CIVIL WAR, WITH SPECIAL REFERENCE TO IOWA: A STUDY IN SOCIAL POLITICS. Iowa City: State Historical Society of Iowa, 1918. xii, 564 p.

Hesseltine, William B. THIRD-PARTY MOVEMENTS IN THE UNITED STATES. Princeton, N.J.: D. Van Nostrand Co., 1962. 192 p. Pap.

A brief history is followed by a selection of documents.

Higham, John. STRANGERS IN THE LAND: PATTERNS OF AMERICAN NATIVISM, 1860-1925. New Brunswick, N.J.: Rutgers University Press, 1955. xiv, 431 p. Illus.

This study contains some interesting descriptions and conclusions about many radical leaders and movements.

Hillquit, Morris. HISTORY OF SOCIALISM IN THE UNITED STATES. 5th rev. ed. New York: Funk and Wagnalls, 1910. 389 p.

Hillquit was a major leader in the Socialist party.

Howe, Irving. STEADY WORK: ESSAYS IN THE POLITICS OF DEMOCRATIC RADICALISM, 1953-1966. New York: Harcourt, Brace and World, 1966. xvi, 364 p.

Howe, Irving, and Coser, Lewis. THE AMERICAN COMMUNIST PARTY, A CRITICAL HISTORY, 1919-1957. Boston: Beacon Press, 1957. x, 593 p.

A major history and analysis of the development of the Communist party in the United States.

Lipset, Seymour M., and Raab, Earl. THE POLITICS OF UNREASON: RIGHT WING EXTREMISM, 1790-1970. New York: Harper and Row, 1970. xxiv, 547 p. Tables.

A major history of right-wing political leaders and movements in America.

Madison, Charles A. CRITICS AND CRUSADERS: A CENTURY OF AMERICAN PROTEST. 2d ed. New York: Frederick Ungar Publishing Co., 1959. x, 662 p.

The period covered ranges from the 1840s to the 1940s.

Myers, Gustavus. HISTORY OF BIGOTRY IN THE UNITED STATES. New York: Random House, 1943. viii, 504 p.

A major study of radical leaders and movements in this country.

Nash, Howard P., Jr. THIRD PARTIES IN AMERICAN POLITICS. Washington, D.C.: Public Affairs Press, 1959. ix, 326 p. Illus.

This is a useful survey of the major third parties in American politics.

Quint, Howard H. THE FORGING OF AMERICAN SOCIALISM: ORIGINS OF THE MODERN MOVEMENT. Columbia: University of South Carolina Press, 1953. ix, 409 p.

Saloutos, Theodore, and Hicks, John D. AGRICULTURAL DISCONTENT IN THE MIDDLE WEST, 1900-1939. Madison: University of Wisconsin Press, 1951. viii, 581 p.

This study is an important work on the subject of agricultural politics in the United States, particularly for the third-party groups and radical movements associated with the American farmer.

Shannon, David A. THE SOCIALIST PARTY OF AMERICA: A HISTORY. New York: Macmillan Co., 1955. xi, 320 p.

The major history and analysis of the Socialist party by a professional historian who is not unsympathetic to the goals of the party nor to some of its leaders.

Stedman, Murray S., Jr., and Stedman, Susan W. DISCONTENT AT THE POLLS: A STUDY OF FARMER AND LABOR PARTIES, 1827-1948. New York: Russell and Russell, 1967. x, 190 p. Tables, appendixes.

Thomas, Norman M. A SOCIALIST'S FAITH. New York: W. W. Norton and Co., 1951. x, 326 p.

> Several times the Socialist party candidate for U.S. president, Thomas presents an insider's view of the Socialist prescription for the country's problems.

Weinstein, James. AMBIGUOUS LEGACY: THE LEFT IN AMERICAN POLITICS. New York: Franklin Watts, 1975. xi, 179 p.

> An examination of the three different "Left" movements since 1900.

Young, Alfred F., ed. DISSENT: EXPLORATIONS IN THE HISTORY OF AMERICAN RADICALISM. De Kalb: Northern Illinois University Press, 1968. vi, 388 p.

> A good collection of essays on radicalism in America by traditional and new-Left historians.

Section 5. MECHANICS OF AMERICAN POLITICS

Abels, Jules. THE DEGENERATION OF OUR PRESIDENTIAL ELECTIONS: A HISTORY AND ANALYSIS OF AN AMERICAN INSTITUTION IN TROUBLE. New York: Macmillan Co., 1968. 322 p.

Albright, Spencer D. THE AMERICAN BALLOT. Washington, D.C.: American Council on Public Affairs, 1942. 153 p.

> A technical study on the form of the election ballot in the United States.

Atkins, Chester G. GETTING ELECTED: A GUIDE TO WINNING STATE AND LOCAL OFFICE. Boston: Houghton, Mifflin and Co., 1973. xix, 202 p.

Bain, Richard, and Parris, Judith H. CONVENTION DECISIONS AND VOTING RECORDS. 2d ed. Washington, D.C.: Brookings Institution, 1973. x, 343 p. Appendixes.

> A survey of the major party conventions since 1832. The appendixes provide a useful breakdown of major votes during the conventions.

Bone, Hugh A. PARTY COMMITTEES AND NATIONAL POLITICS. Seattle: University of Washington Press, 1958. xv, 256 p. Appendix, illus.

> An examination of the roles of the Republican and Democratic National Committees during the 1950s.

David, Paul T., et al. THE POLITICS OF NATIONAL PARTY CONVENTIONS. Washington, D.C.: Brookings Institution, 1960. xv, 592 p. Appendixes.

> This is an important book for any student seeking to understand the party convention system.

Eaton, Herbert. PRESIDENTIAL TIMBER: A HISTORY OF NOMINATING CONVENTIONS, 1868-1960. Glencoe, Ill.: Free Press of Glencoe, 1964. 528 p.

Free, Lloyd A., and Cantril, Hadley. THE POLITICAL BELIEFS OF AMERICANS: A STUDY OF PUBLIC OPINION. New York: Simon and Schuster, 1968. xiv, 239 p. Tables, appendixes. Pap.

Gallup, George H. THE GALLUP POLL: PUBLIC OPINION, 1935-1971. 3 vols. New York: Random House, 1972.

> A fantastic treasury of public opinion.

Hess, Stephen, and Moos, Malcolm C. HATS IN THE RING. New York: Random House, 1960. 194 p. Illus.

> A brief look at political conventions and presidential elections.

Joyner, Conrad. THE AMERICAN POLITICIAN. Tucson: University of Arizona Press, 1971. xvi, 231 p.

> This book analyzes how and why the American political process works.

Kelley, Stanley, Jr. PROFESSIONAL PUBLIC RELATIONS AND POLITICAL POWER. Baltimore: Johns Hopkins Press, 1956. 247 p.

Kent, Frank R. THE GREAT GAME OF POLITICS: AN EFFORT TO PRESENT THE ELEMENTARY HUMAN FACTS ABOUT POLITICS, POLITICIANS, AND POLITICAL MACHINES, CANDIDATES AND THEIR WAYS, FOR THE BENEFIT OF THE AVERAGE CITIZEN. Garden City, N.Y.: Doubleday, Doran and Co., 1935. xiv, 354 p.

Lang, Kurt, and Lang, Gladys. POLITICS AND TELEVISION. Chicago: Quadrangle Books, 1968. 315 p.

McKee, Thomas H. THE NATIONAL CONVENTIONS AND PLATFORMS OF ALL POLITICAL PARTIES, 1789-1905. 6th ed. Baltimore: Friedenwald Co., 1906. 418 p. Tables.

MacNeil, Robert. THE PEOPLE MACHINE: THE INFLUENCE OF TELEVISION ON AMERICAN POLITICS. New York: Harper and Row, 1968. xx, 362 p.

Martin, Ralph G. BALLOTS AND BANDWAGONS. Chicago: Rand McNally and Co., 1964. 480 p.

> Martin examines the Republican conventions of 1900, 1912, and 1920 and the Democratic conventions of 1932 and 1956.

Napolitan, Joseph. THE ELECTION GAME AND HOW TO WIN IT. Garden City, N.Y.: Doubleday and Co., 1972. 300 p.

> The author relates his experiences in managing political campaigns.

Nimmo, Dan. THE POLITICAL PERSUADERS: THE TECHNIQUES OF MODERN ELECTION CAMPAIGNS. Englewood Cliffs, N.J.: Prentice-Hall, 1970. x, 214 p. Appendixes.

Peirce, Neal R. THE PEOPLE'S PRESIDENT: THE ELECTORAL COLLEGE IN AMERICAN HISTORY AND THE DIRECT-VOTE ALTERNATIVE. New York: Simon and Schuster, 1968. 400 p. Appendixes.

> A brief but worthwhile history of the electoral college is included.

Pomper, Gerald. NOMINATING THE PRESIDENT: THE POLITICS OF CON-VENTION CHOICE, WITH A NEW POSTSCRIPT ON 1964. Evanston, Ill.: Northwestern University Press, 1966. xii, 304 p. Tables, appendix.

Rogers, Lindsay. THE POLLSTERS: PUBLIC OPINION, POLITICS, AND DEMOCRATIC LEADERSHIP. New York: Alfred A. Knopf, 1949. xi, 239 p.

> An examination of the methods, strengths, and weaknesses of po-litical poll taking.

Rosenbloom, David L. THE ELECTION MEN: PROFESSIONAL CAMPAIGN MANAGERS AND AMERICAN DEMOCRACY. New York: Quadrangle Books, 1973. ix, 182 p.

> A detailed examination of the professional organizers in politics that focuses on the period between 1968 and 1972.

_____, ed. THE POLITICAL MARKET PLACE. New York: Quadrangle Books, 1972. xix, 944 p.

> A compendium of campaign information and election services for the 1972 presidential campaign.

Sayre, Wallace S., and Parris, Judith H. VOTING FOR PRESIDENT: THE ELECTORAL COLLEGE AND THE AMERICAN POLITICAL SYSTEM. Washington, D.C.: Brookings Institution, 1970. xii, 169 p. Appendix.

> A brief historical treatment supplements a close examination of the institution as it exists today.

Scammon, Richard, comp. AMERICA AT THE POLLS: A HANDBOOK OF AMERICAN PRESIDENTIAL ELECTION STATISTICS, 1920-1964. Pittsburgh: University of Pittsburgh Press, 1965. 521 p. Tables.

A statistical history of American presidential elections in the years since the end of World War I. The information notes our country's voting behavior in twelve presidential elections, starting with the national enfranchisement of women and the election of President Warren Harding and ending with the election of President Lyndon Johnson in 1964.

Schwartzman, Edward. CAMPAIGN CRAFTSMANSHIP: A PROFESSIONAL'S GUIDE TO CAMPAIGNING FOR ELECTIVE OFFICE. New York: Universe Books, 1973. 272 p. Appendix.

A good introduction to the methods used in running a modern political campaign.

Stoddard, Henry L. PRESIDENTIAL SWEEPSTAKES: THE STORY OF POLITICAL CONVENTIONS AND CAMPAIGNS. New York: G. P. Putnam's Sons, 1948. 224 p. Illus.

Theis, Paul A., and Steponkus, William A. ALL ABOUT POLITICS: QUESTIONS AND ANSWERS ON THE U.S. POLITICAL PROCESS. New York: R. R. Bowker Co., 1972. xii, 228 p. Illus.

Two political pros ask and then answer four hundred of the most important questions on the American political process.

Wilmerding, Lucius, Jr. THE ELECTORAL COLLEGE. New Brunswick, N.J.: Rutgers University Press, 1958. xiii, 224 p. Appendix.

A brief historical summary is followed by an extensive examination of the various proposals for change.

Section 6. PRESIDENT AND CONGRESS

Bean, Louis H. BALLOT BEHAVIOR: A STUDY OF PRESIDENTIAL ELECTIONS. Washington, D.C.: American Council on Public Affairs, 1940. 102 p. Tables.

A survey of forty years of presidential election results (1896-1936).

Binkley, Wilfred E. THE MAN IN THE WHITE HOUSE: HIS POWERS AND DUTIES. Baltimore: Johns Hopkins Press, 1958. 310 p.

An examination of the politics of the presidency in its many guises.

Brown, Stuart G. THE AMERICAN PRESIDENCY: LEADERSHIP, PARTISANSHIP, AND POPULARITY. New York: Macmillan Co., 1966. viii, 279 p.

Although the history of the presidency is incidental to Brown's purpose, he manages to illuminate certain aspects of presidential politics.

Burnham, W. Dean. PRESIDENTIAL BALLOTS, 1836-1892. Baltimore: Johns Hopkins Press, 1955. xix, 956 p. Tables, appendix.

A compilation of presidential ballots cast by counties is preceded by the compilers' conclusions about changing political preference.

Burns, James MacGregor. PRESIDENTIAL GOVERNMENT: THE CRUCIBLE OF LEADERSHIP. Boston: Houghton, Mifflin and Co., 1966. xvii, 366 p.

A historical examination of the presidency.

Cornwell, Elmer E., Jr. PRESIDENTIAL LEADERSHIP OF PUBLIC OPINION. Bloomington: Indiana University Press, 1965. x, 370 p. Tables, illus.

Cornwell is concerned with the twentieth-century president.

Cummings, Milton C., Jr. CONGRESSMEN AND THE ELECTORATE: ELECTIONS FOR THE U.S. HOUSE AND THE PRESIDENT, 1920-1964. New York: Free Press, 1966. xvii, 233 p. Tables.

Davis, James W. PRESIDENTIAL PRIMARIES: ROAD TO THE WHITE HOUSE. New York: Thomas Y. Crowell Co., 1967. xii, 324 p. Appendix. Pap.

The focus of this study is on recent presidential primaries.

Ewing, Cortez A. M. CONGRESSIONAL ELECTIONS, 1896-1944: THE SECTIONAL BASIS OF POLITICAL DEMOCRACY IN THE HOUSE OF REPRESENTATIVES. Norman: University of Oklahoma Press, 1947. xiii, 110 p. Graphs, tables.

_____. PRESIDENTIAL ELECTIONS FROM ABRAHAM LINCOLN TO FRANKLIN D. ROOSEVELT. Norman: University of Oklahoma Press, 1940. xiii, 226 p. Tables.

Hargrove, Erwin C. PRESIDENTIAL LEADERSHIP AND POLITICAL STYLE. New York: Macmillan Co., 1966. v, 153 p.

An interesting examination of the presidents of action and restraint in the twentieth century.

James, Dorothy B. THE CONTEMPORARY PRESIDENCY. New York: Pegasus, 1969. xviii, 187 p. Pap.

A study of the structure, uses, and expansion of presidential power from the Roosevelt era to the late 1960s. Chapter 1 is particularly valuable because in it James examines the primary features of the American political system within which the president must operate.

Johnson, Walter. 1600 PENNSYLVANIA AVENUE: PRESIDENTS AND THE PEOPLE, 1929-1959. Boston: Little, Brown and Co., 1960. 390 p.

Laski, Harold. THE AMERICAN PRESIDENCY: AN INTERPRETATION. New York: Harper and Brothers, 1940. viii, 278 p.

A classic analysis of the politics of the presidency.

Lorant, Stefan. THE GLORIOUS BURDEN: THE AMERICAN PRESIDENCY. New York: Harper and Row, 1968. 959 p. Illus.

A concise, lavishly illustrated political history of the United States in terms of our presidents and presidential elections.

Matthews, Donald R., ed. PERSPECTIVES ON PRESIDENTIAL SELECTION. Washington, D.C.: Brookings Institution, 1973. xii, 246 p. Illus.

Mooney, Booth. MR. SPEAKER: FOUR MEN WHO SHAPED THE UNITED STATES HOUSE OF REPRESENTATIVES. Chicago: Follett Publishing Co., 1964. xi, 226 p.

The four speakers are Henry Clay, Thomas B. Reed, Joseph G. Cannon, and Sam Rayburn. A delightfully chatty book about a few of our political leaders.

Neustadt, Richard E. PRESIDENTIAL POWER: THE POLITICS OF LEADER-SHIP. New York: John Wiley and Sons, 1960. 244 p.

An examination of the presidency and the expansion of the president's political power after World War II.

Overacker, Louise. THE PRESIDENTIAL PRIMARY. New York: Macmillan Co., 1926. ix, 308 p. Tables.

Petersen, Svend. A STATISTICAL HISTORY OF PRESIDENTIAL ELECTIONS. Rev. ed. New York: Frederick Ungar Publishing Co., 1963. xxiii, 247 p. Tables.

Robinson, Edgar E. THE PRESIDENTIAL VOTE, 1896-1932. Stanford, Calif.: Stanford University Press, 1934. ix, 403 p. Illus.

Runyon, John H., et al., comps. SOURCE BOOK OF AMERICAN PRESIDEN-TIAL CAMPAIGN AND ELECTION STATISTICS, 1948-1968. New York: Frederick Ungar Publishing Co., 1971. xiv, 380 p. Tables.

A very useful collection of statistics that covers the primaries, conventions, staff, itineraries, expenditures, media, polls, results, and minor party voting.

Schlesinger, Arthur M., Jr. THE IMPERIAL PRESIDENCY. Boston: Houghton, Mifflin and Co., 1973. x, 505 p.

Schlesinger traces the escalation of presidential power and considers what the Congress and the people can do about it. He believes the office has become a mighty political machine that must be held in check by the Congress, the courts, and the ballot box.

Schlesinger, Arthur M., Jr., and Israel, Fred L., eds. HISTORY OF AMERI-CAN PRESIDENTIAL ELECTIONS, 1789-1968. 4 vols. New York: Chelsea House Publishers in association with McGraw-Hill Book Co., 1971.

Although these volumes contain a few statistics, their real value lies in the documents and commentaries on all the presidential elections through 1968.

Stone, Irving. THEY ALSO RAN: THE STORY OF THE MEN WHO WERE DEFEATED FOR THE PRESIDENCY. Garden City, N.Y.: Doubleday, Doran and Co., 1943. xi, 389 p. Illus.

Warren, Sidney. BATTLE FOR THE PRESIDENCY. Philadelphia: J. B. Lippin-cott Co., 1968. viii, 426 p.

Ten presidential elections are reviewed.

Section 7. ANALYSES OF AMERICAN POLITICS

Auerbach, M. Morton. THE CONSERVATIVE ILLUSION. New York: Colum-bia University Press, 1959. xii, 359 p.

An examination of the conservative political outlook and its re-lationship to American society.

Bazelon, David T. POWER IN AMERICA: THE POLITICS OF THE NEW CLASS. New York: New American Library, 1971. xxiv, 407 p. Pap.

The author focuses on the new force, the larger academic commu-nity, that is shaping America. He suggests that the old political coalition is being usurped by a new class.

Beard, Charles A. THE ECONOMIC BASIS OF POLITICS. 3d ed. New York: Alfred A. Knopf, 1945. 114 p.

The main body of this book consists of four lectures given in 1916.

Beitzinger, Alfons J. A HISTORY OF AMERICAN POLITICAL THOUGHT. New York: Dodd, Mead and Co., 1972. xii, 628 p.

Boorstin, Daniel. THE GENIUS OF AMERICAN POLITICS. Chicago: University of Chicago Press, 1953. ix, 202 p.

Brogan, Denis W. POLITICS IN AMERICA. New York: Harper and Brothers, 1954. vii, 467 p.

Bunzel, John H. ANTI-POLITICS IN AMERICA: REFLECTIONS ON THE ANTI-POLITICAL TEMPER AND ITS DISTORTIONS OF THE DEMOCRATIC PROCESS. New York: Alfred A. Knopf, 1967. xi, 291, x p.

> An examination of American politics outside of the framework of the two-party system. Bunzel analyzes recent antipolitical attitudes that run the political gamut from Left to Right.

Charles, Joseph. THE ORIGINS OF THE AMERICAN PARTY SYSTEM: THREE ESSAYS. Williamsburg, Va.: Institute of Early American History and Culture, 1956. 147 p.

Dalfiume, Richard M., ed. AMERICAN POLITICS SINCE 1945. Chicago: Quadrangle Books, 1969. 247 p. Pap.

> A good collection of essays by some of the country's best political commentators.

Ekirch, Arthur A., Jr. THE DECLINE OF AMERICAN LIBERALISM. New York: Longmans, Green and Co., 1955. xiii, 401 p.

Guttmann, Allen. THE CONSERVATIVE TRADITION IN AMERICA. New York: Oxford University Press, 1967. viii, 214 p.

Handlin, Oscar, and Handlin, Mary. THE DIMENSIONS OF LIBERTY. Cambridge, Mass.: Harvard University Press, 1961. 204 p.

> The authors are concerned with the meaning and use of political power in the United States.

Hartz, Louis. THE LIBERAL TRADITION IN AMERICA: AN INTERPRETATION OF AMERICAN POLITICAL THOUGHT SINCE THE REVOLUTION. New York: Harcourt, Brace and World, 1955. ix, 329 p.

> Hartz's view is that America was a nonfeudal society and as a result this nation has escaped a revolutionary tradition. Because we are nonrevolutionary, our politics have remained liberal and not radical.

Hofstadter, Richard. THE AMERICAN POLITICAL TRADITION AND THE MEN
WHO MADE IT. New York: Alfred A. Knopf, 1948. xi, 378 p. xviii.

Hofstadter interprets the lives and ideas of twelve major political
figures from the founding fathers to Franklin D. Roosevelt. He
believes that we, all too often, allow tradition to overwhelm the
necessity of systematic innovation.

_____. THE PARANOID STYLE IN AMERICAN POLITICS AND OTHER ES-
SAYS. New York: Alfred A. Knopf, 1965. xiv, 315, xii p.

The essays are concerned with the milieu of our politics rather
than organizations.

Holcombe, Arthur N. THE MIDDLE CLASSES IN AMERICAN POLITICS. Cambridge, Mass.: Harvard University Press, 1940. vi, 304 p.

Kaufman, Arnold S. RADICAL LIBERAL: NEW MAN IN AMERICAN POLITICS.
New York: Atherton Press, 1968. xv, 175 p.

The author develops the thesis that a historic liberal base is necessary in order to find solutions to contemporary problems; however,
liberalism must continually confront the status quo rather than accept it.

Lasch, Christopher. THE NEW RADICALISM IN AMERICA, 1889-1963: THE
INTELLECTUAL AS A SOCIAL TYPE. New York: Alfred A. Knopf, 1965.
xviii, 349, ix p.

Lipset, Seymour M. POLITICAL MAN: THE SOCIAL BASES OF POLITICS.
Garden City, N.Y.: Doubleday and Co., 1960. 432 p. Illus.

A wide-ranging study by an eminent social scientist. Chapters 9,
10, and 11 focus on what the author suggests are unique features
of American political behavior.

Morgenthau, Hans J. THE DECLINE OF DEMOCRATIC POLITICS. Chicago:
University of Chicago Press, 1962. xii, 431 p.

_____. THE PURPOSE OF AMERICAN POLITICS. New York: Alfred A.
Knopf, 1962. xi, 359, viii p. Appendixes.

The author concentrates on the twentieth century.

Odegard, Peter H., and Helms, Elva A. AMERICAN POLITICS: A STUDY IN
POLITICAL DYNAMICS. 2d ed. New York: Harper and Brothers, 1947.
xiii, 896 p. Illus.

Rossiter, Clinton. CONSERVATISM IN AMERICA. New York: Alfred A.
Knopf, 1956. 327, xii p.

A survey of conservative thought and politics in American history.

Tourtellot, Arthur B. AN ANATOMY OF AMERICAN POLITICS: INNOVA-TION VERSUS CONSERVATION. Indianapolis: Bobbs-Merrill Co., 1950. 349 p.

Wiltse, Charles M. THE JEFFERSONIAN TRADITION IN AMERICAN DEMOC-RACY. Chapel Hill: University of North Carolina Press, 1935. xii, 273 p.

Section 8. NEGRO POLITICS

Brooks, Maxwell R. THE NEGRO PRESS RE-EXAMINED: POLITICAL CON-TENT OF LEADING NEGRO NEWSPAPERS. Boston: Christopher Publishing House, 1959. 125 p. Appendixes.

Although this book is a survey of the Negro press in the United States, it also contains some useful information and opinions on the politics of the Negro press.

Buni, Andrew. THE NEGRO IN VIRGINIA POLITICS, 1902-1965. Charlottes-ville: University Press of Virginia, 1967. ix, 296 p.

The Negro role in Virginia politics between 1902 and 1965. Based on documents, newspapers, and interviews (primarily with the par-ticipants).

Callcott, Margaret L. THE NEGRO IN MARYLAND POLITICS, 1870-1912. Baltimore: Johns Hopkins Press, 1969. xv, 199 p. Appendixes, tables.

An examination of the Negro's political activity in post-Civil War politics in Maryland. Callcott analyzes the political base of the major parties and explores the Negro's relationship to them. A coalition of white and Negro politicians frustrated the Demo-crats' attempt to create the one-party politics that occurred in other southern states.

Carmichael, Stokely, and Hamilton, Charles V. BLACK POWER: THE POLI-TICS OF LIBERATION IN AMERICA. New York: Random House, 1967. xii, 198 p.

A statement by two black activist leaders on the necessity of black political organization.

Franklin, John Hope. FROM SLAVERY TO FREEDOM: A HISTORY OF NEGRO AMERICANS. New York: Random House, 1969. xii, 686, xliii p. Illus. Pap.

An excellent survey of the Negro politics in addition to other as-pects of the Negroes' life in America.

Gosnell, Harold F. NEGRO POLITICIANS: THE RISE OF NEGRO POLITICS IN CHICAGO. Chicago: University of Chicago Press, 1935. xxxi, 404 p. Illus.

A classic study that is also useful as an examination of urban politics.

Hickey, Neil, and Edwin, Ed. ADAM CLAYTON POWELL AND THE POLITICS OF RACE. New York: Fleet Publishing Corp., 1965. 308 p. Illus.

Powell was a major black political leader from New York in the 1950s.

Klingman, Peter D. JOSIAH WELLS: FLORIDA'S BLACK CONGRESSMAN OF RECONSTRUCTION. Gainesville: University Presses of Florida, 1976. xi, 157 p.

A concise, well-written biography and account of Reconstruction politics in addition to an examination of the Negro's political activity in Florida following the Civil War.

Ladd, Everett C., Jr. NEGRO POLITICAL LEADERSHIP IN THE SOUTH. New York: Atheneum, 1969. 348 p. Illus.

An important study of developing black political leadership in southern politics.

Lewinson, Edwin R. BLACK POLITICS IN NEW YORK CITY. New York: Twayne Publishers, 1974. 232 p.

The primary focus from the revolutionary period is on black political leaders rather than the electorate. Also the author is descriptive rather than analytical.

Lewinson, Paul. RACE, CLASS, AND PARTY: A HISTORY OF NEGRO SUFFRAGE AND WHITE POLITICS IN THE SOUTH. New York: Grosset and Dunlap, 1965. xxiv, 302 p.

A good analysis and history of the role of the black in the political process.

Nowlin, William F. THE NEGRO IN AMERICAN NATIONAL POLITICS. Boston: Stratford Co., 1931. 148 p.

Rice, Lawrence D. THE NEGRO IN TEXAS, 1874-1900. Baton Rouge: Louisiana State University Press, 1971. ix, 309 p.

During Reconstruction Negroes attained substantial power in the state. In the post-Reconstruction period Negroes continued to wield some political power until 1902, when the poll tax almost completely eliminated the black vote.

Sherman, Richard B. THE REPUBLICAN PARTY AND BLACK AMERICA: FROM MCKINLEY TO HOOVER, 1896-1933. Charlottesville: University Press of Virginia, 1973. viii, 274 p. Appendixes.

Smith, Frank E. CONGRESSMAN FROM MISSISSIPPI. New York: Capricorn Books, 1964. ix, 338 p. Pap.

  A southern moderate's honest and revealing account of the politics of race, 1950-62.

Stone, Chuck. BLACK POLITICAL POWER IN AMERICA. New York: Dell Publishing Co., 1970. 303 p. Pap.

  Stone explores the background of black political power in America and the activities of major political figures like Adam Clayton Powell, William L. Dawson, and J. Raymond Jones.

Strong, Donald S. NEGROES, BALLOTS, AND JUDGES: NATIONAL VOTING RIGHTS LEGISLATION IN THE FEDERAL COURTS. University: University of Alabama Press, 1968. vii, 100 p.

Tatum, Elbert L. THE CHANGED POLITICAL THOUGHT OF THE NEGRO, 1915-1940. New York: Exposition Press, 1951. 205 p.

Vincent, Charles. BLACK LEGISLATORS IN LOUISIANA DURING RECON-STRUCTION. Baton Rouge: Louisiana State University Press, 1976. xv, 262 p. Appendixes, illus.

  Vincent finds that black legislators acted with intelligence and vigor in support of programs for universal education, prison reform, and fiscal controls.

Walton, Hanes, Jr. BLACK POLITICAL PARTIES: AN HISTORICAL AND PO-LITICAL ANALYSIS. New York: Free Press, 1972. xi, 276 p.

  A survey of black political activity based on secondary sources.

_____. THE NEGRO IN THIRD PARTY POLITICS. Philadelphia: Dorrance, 1969. 123 p.

_____. THE STUDY AND ANALYSIS OF BLACK POLITICS: A BIBLIOGRAPHY. Metuchen, N.J.: Scarecrow Press, 1973. xviii, 161 p.

Watters, Pat, and Cleghorn, Reese. CLIMBING JACOB'S LADDER: THE AR-RIVAL OF NEGROES IN SOUTHERN POLITICS. New York: Harcourt, Brace and World, 1967. xvi, 389 p.

Young, Richard P. ROOTS OF REBELLION: THE EVOLUTION OF BLACK POLITICS AND PROTEST SINCE WORLD WAR II. New York: Harper and Row, 1970. xii, 482 p. Pap.

A good collection of essays.

Section 9. CARTOONS

Becker, Stephen. COMIC ART IN AMERICA: A SOCIAL HISTORY OF THE FUNNIES, THE POLITICAL CARTOONS, MAGAZINE HUMOR, SPORTING CARTOONS AND ANIMATED CARTOONS. New York: Simon and Schuster, 1959. xi, 387 p. Illus.

Block, Herbert. THE HERBLOCK BOOK. Boston: Beacon Press, 1952. 244 p. Illus.

Block's political cartoons have had substantial impact on American politics since the late 1940s.

_____. THE HERBLOCK GALLERY. New York: Simon and Schuster, 1968. 224 p. Illus.

_____. HERBLOCK SPECIAL REPORT. New York: W. W. Norton and Co., 1974. 255 p. Illus.

Craven, Thomas, ed. CARTOON CAVALCADE. New York: Simon and Schuster, 1943. vi, 456 p. Illus.

This volume focuses on twentieth-century cartoons, including some political ones.

Fitzpatrick, Daniel R. AS I SAW IT: A REVIEW OF OUR TIMES WITH 311 CARTOONS AND NOTES. New York: Simon and Schuster, 1953. xvi, 238 p. Illus.

Many of the cartoons have a political theme.

Hess, Stephen, and Kaplan, Milton. THE UNGENTLEMANLY ART: A HISTORY OF AMERICAN POLITICAL CARTOONS. New York: Macmillan Co., 1968. 252 p. Illus.

A magnificent collection of political cartoons and the effect they have had on our politics.

Keller, Morton. THE ART AND POLITICS OF THOMAS NAST. New York: Oxford University Press, 1968. ix, 353 p. Illus.

A collection of Nast cartoons that illustrate his greatness and bigotry.

Lurie, Ranan R. NIXON RATED CARTOONS. New York: Quadrangle Books, 1973. 320 p. Illus.

A biting political commentary.

Murrell, William. A HISTORY OF AMERICAN HUMOR. 2 vols. New York: Macmillan Co., for the Whitney Museum of American Art, 1933-38. Illus.

Many of the cartoons are political in nature and the period covered extends from 1747 to 1938.

Nevins, Allan, and Weitenkampf, Frank. A CENTURY OF POLITICAL CAR-TOONS: CARICATURE IN THE UNITED STATES FROM 1800 TO 1900. New York: Charles Scribner's Sons, 1944. 190 p. Illus.

Trudeau, Gary B. BUT THIS WAR HAD SUCH PROMISE. New York: Holt, Rinehart and Winston, 1973. Illus.

A Doonesbury book. Trudeau's political cartoons are savage.
In this work he focuses on the political nonsense that accompanied our involvement in Vietnam.

Vinson, J. Chal. THOMAS NAST: POLITICAL CARTOONIST. Athens: University of Georgia Press, 1967. x, 46 p. Illus.

A magnificent collection of some of Nast's best work.

Weitenkampf, Frank, comp. POLITICAL CARICATURE IN UNITED STATES IN SEPARATELY PUBLISHED CARTOONS: AN ANNOTATED LIST. 1953. Reprint. New York: New York Public Library and Arno Press, 1971. 184 p. Illus.

Section 10. MONEY AND INFLUENCE

Adamany, David. FINANCING POLITICS: RECENT WISCONSIN ELECTIONS. Madison: University of Wisconsin Press, 1969. xv, 302 p. Tables.

Alexander, Herbert E. MONEY IN POLITICS. Washington, D.C.: Public Affairs Press, 1972. ix, 353 p. Appendixes.

An examination of the troublesome question whether too much or too little money is spent on politics. The author successfully demolishes the myth that money can buy major elections. He also notes that expenditures are rising.

Crawford, Kenneth G. THE PRESSURE BOYS: THE INSIDE STORY OF LOB-BYING IN AMERICA. New York: Messner, 1939. 308 p.

The author includes, in addition to the description and nature of lobbying activities, several case studies.

Garrigues, Charles H. YOU'RE PAYING FOR IT! A GUIDE TO GRAFT. New York: Funk and Wagnalls, 1936. 254 p.

Overacker, Louise. PRESIDENTIAL CAMPAIGN FUNDS. Boston: Boston University Press, 1946. vii, 76 p.

Schriftgiesser, Karl. THE LOBBYISTS: THE ART AND BUSINESS OF INFLUENCING LAWMAKERS. Boston: Little, Brown and Co., 1951. xiv, 297 p. Appendixes.

A history of lobbying from the Boston Tea Party to 1951.

Shannon, Jasper B. MONEY AND POLITICS. New York: Random House, 1959. 126 p. Pap.

Thayer, George. WHO SHAKES THE MONEY TREE? AMERICAN CAMPAIGN FINANCING PRACTICES FROM 1789 TO THE PRESENT. New York: Simon and Schuster, 1973. 320 p.

A major study of the topic.

Section 11. STATE AND LOCAL POLITICS

Casdorph, Paul. A HISTORY OF THE REPUBLICAN PARTY IN TEXAS, 1865-1965. Austin, Tex.: Pemberton Press, 1965. 315 p. Appendix.

Childs, Richard S. CIVIC VICTORIES: THE STORY OF AN UNFINISHED REVOLUTION. New York: Harper and Brothers, 1952. xvii, 350 p.

The author examines and comments on the political process particularly as it relates to local and state governments. He notes that at the state and local levels there has been great progress toward the establishment of truly effective democratic institutions but that the effort is still unfinished.

Church, Charles A. HISTORY OF THE REPUBLICAN PARTY IN ILLINOIS, 1854-1912. Rockford, Ill.: Wilson Brothers Co., 1912. xiii, 248 p. Illus.

The student of Illinois politics will find this volume helpful in providing information unavailable elsewhere.

Costikyan, Edward N. BEHIND CLOSED DOORS: POLITICS IN PUBLIC INTERESTS. New York: Harcourt Brace and World, 1966. xi, 369 p. Illus.

The author is mainly concerned with New York City.

Fenton, John H. POLITICS IN THE BORDER STATES: A STUDY OF THE PATTERNS OF POLITICAL ORGANIZATION AND POLITICAL CHANGE COMMON

TO THE BORDER STATES. New Orleans: Hauser Press, 1957. vi, 230 p.
Tables.

> The states are Maryland, West Virginia, Kentucky, and Missouri.
> Fenton focuses on the period from 1850 to 1950 with particular
> attention to the later period.

Ferguson, Walter K. GEOLOGY AND POLITICS IN FRONTIER TEXAS, 1845-
1909. Austin: University of Texas Press, 1969. xii, 233 p. Appendixes.

Fesler, James W., et al. THE 50 STATES AND THEIR LOCAL GOVERNMENTS.
New York: Alfred A. Knopf, 1967. xviii, 603, xi p. Tables.

> A good survey that also provides a historical introduction to each
> state's politics and government.

Franklin, Jimmie L. BORN SOBER: PROHIBITION IN OKLAHOMA, 1907-
1959. Norman: University of Oklahoma Press, 1971. xvii, 212 p.

> Although the focus is on Prohibition, there is considerable informa-
> tion on Oklahoma politics and politicians from statehood to 1959.

Hohnes, Jack E. POLITICS IN NEW MEXICO. Albuquerque: University of
New Mexico Press, 1967. ii, 335 p. Illus.

> A study of politics and political shifts between 1900 and 1965.

Howard, Perry H. POLITICAL TENDENCIES IN LOUISIANA, 1812-1952.
Rev. ed. Baton Rouge: Louisiana State University Press, 1971. xxxvi, 476 p.
Tables, maps, appendixes.

Isaac, Paul E. PROHIBITION AND POLITICS: TURBULENT DECADES IN
TENNESSEE, 1885-1920. Knoxville: University of Tennessee Press, 1965.
xi, 301 p.

> A major study that examines and analyzes the impact of an impor-
> tant issue in American politics.

Jacob, Herbert, and Vines, K. N. POLITICS IN THE AMERICAN STATES:
A COMPARATIVE ANALYSIS. 2d ed. Boston: Little, Brown and Co., 1971.
xxvi, 627 p. Tables, appendixes.

> This book is a useful text. The authors analyze the political pro-
> cess involved in our political institutions and in several policies
> and programs.

Kaufman, Herbert. POLITICS AND POLICIES IN STATE AND LOCAL GOV-
ERNMENTS. Englewood Cliffs, N.J.: Prentice-Hall, 1963. viii, 120 p.
Tables.

Key, V. O., Jr. AMERICAN STATE POLITICS: AN INTRODUCTION. New York: Alfred A. Knopf, 1956. xviii, 289, ix p. Tables.

The author concentrates on the period between 1920 and 1952.

_____. SOUTHERN POLITICS: IN STATE AND NATION. New York: Alfred A. Knopf, 1950. xxvi, 675, xiv p. Tables, illus.

The author concentrates on the first half of the twentieth century.

Kirwan, Albert D. REVOLT OF THE REDNECKS: MISSISSIPPI POLITICS, 1876-1925. Lexington: University of Kentucky Press, 1951. viii, 330 p. Reprint. New York: Harper and Row, 1965.

A major contribution to the literature on the lower South's political history. Kirwan's thesis is that racism gave the farmer the opportunity to take undisputed control of the state government for nearly two decades.

LeBlanc, Hugh L., and Allensworth, D. Trudeau. THE POLITICS OF STATES AND URBAN COMMUNITIES. New York: Harper and Row, 1971. vii, 469 p.

One of the many good surveys on the subject.

Lowi, Theodore J. AT THE PLEASURE OF THE MAYOR: PATRONAGE AND POWER IN NEW YORK CITY, 1898-1958. New York: Macmillan Co., 1964. xvi, 272 p. Appendix.

Lubove, Roy. TWENTIETH-CENTURY PITTSBURGH: GOVERNMENT, BUSINESS, AND ENVIRONMENTAL CHANGE. New York: John Wiley and Sons, 1969. x, 189 p. Illus.

McLoughlin, William G. NEW ENGLAND DISSENT, 1630-1833: THE BAPTISTS AND THE SEPARATION OF CHURCH AND STATE. 2 vols. Cambridge, Mass.: Harvard University Press, 1971.

Moger, Allen W. VIRGINIA: BOURBONISM TO BYRD, 1870-1925. Charlottesville: University Press of Virginia, 1968. ix, 397 p. Appendix, illus.

An important study that connects with major political events in the upper South and the nation.

Moscow, Warren. WHAT HAVE YOU DONE FOR ME LATELY? THE INS AND OUTS OF NEW YORK CITY POLITICS. Englewood Cliffs, N.J.: Prentice-Hall, 1967. xii, 241 p.

An interesting look at politics in "Gotham" in the first half of the twentieth century.

Mushkat, Jerome. TAMMANY: THE EVOLUTION OF A POLITICAL MA-
CHINE, 1789-1865. Syracuse, N.Y.: Syracuse University Press, 1971. xii,
476 p. Illus.

> Mushkat ties the major political events in New York City to the
> national scene when the connection is appropriate.

Ostrander, Gilman M. NEVADA: THE GREAT ROTTEN BOROUGH, 1859-
1964. New York: Alfred A. Knopf, 1966. xii, 247, viii p.

_____. THE PROHIBITION MOVEMENT IN CALIFORNIA, 1848-1933. Berke-
ley and Los Angeles: University of California Press, 1957. vi, 241 p.

Parrish, William E. DAVID RICE ATCHISON OF MISSOURI: BORDER POLI-
TICIAN. Columbia: University of Missouri Press, 1961. 271 p. Illus.

> A Democrat in the proslavery faction and an opponent of Thomas
> Hart Benton.

Peel, Roy V. THE POLITICAL CLUBS OF NEW YORK CITY. New York:
G. P. Putnam's Sons, 1935. xii, 360 p. Illus.

Peirce, Neal R. THE BORDER SOUTH STATES: PEOPLE, POLITICS, AND
POWER IN THE FIVE BORDER SOUTH STATES. New York: W. W. Norton
and Co., 1975. 415 p.

> A useful introduction to the contemporary scene. In this work and
> the others listed below, Peirce takes a look at the politics and per-
> sonalities in the individual states. The states covered in this vol-
> ume are Virginia, North Carolina, West Virginia, Kentucky, and
> Tennessee. Also includes a chapter on the TVA.

_____. THE DEEP SOUTH STATES OF AMERICA: PEOPLE, POLITICS AND
POWER IN THE SEVEN DEEP SOUTH STATES. New York: W. W. Norton
and Co., 1974. 528 p.

> The states are Alabama, Arkansas, Florida, Georgia, Louisiana,
> Mississippi, and South Carolina. The student is advised to look
> for other volumes that the author and publisher have projected
> but not yet published on the Great Lakes' states and the New En-
> gland states.

_____. THE GREAT PLAINS STATES OF AMERICA: PEOPLE, POLITICS, AND
POWER IN THE NINE GREAT PLAINS STATES. New York: W. W. Norton
and Co., 1973. 402 p.

> The states are Missouri, Iowa, Minnesota, North Dakota, South
> Dakota, Nebraska, Kansas, Oklahoma, and Texas. This and the
> other volumes by the same author contain useful bibliographies on
> state and regional history and politics.

_____. THE MEGASTATES OF AMERICA: PEOPLE, POLITICS, AND POWER IN THE TEN GREAT STATES. New York: W. W. Norton and Co., 1972. 745 p.

The states are Massachusetts, New Jersey, New York, Pennsylvania, Ohio, Illinois, Michigan, Florida, Texas, and California.

_____. THE MOUNTAIN STATES OF AMERICA: PEOPLE, POLITICS, AND POWER IN THE EIGHT ROCKY MOUNTAIN STATES. New York: W. W. Norton and Co., 1972. 317 p.

The states are Colorado, Wyoming, Montana, Idaho, Nevada, Utah, Arizona, and New Mexico.

_____. THE PACIFIC STATES OF AMERICA: PEOPLE, POLITICS, AND POWER IN THE FIVE PACIFIC BASIN STATES. New York: W. W. Norton and Co., 1972. 387 p.

The states are California, Oregon, Washington, Alaska, and Hawaii.

Pratt, John W. RELIGION, POLITICS, AND DIVERSITY: THE CHURCH-STATE THEME IN NEW YORK HISTORY. Ithaca, N.Y.: Cornell University Press, 1967. xi, 327 p.

The author is mainly concerned with the topic before the twentieth century.

Press, Charles. MAIN STREET POLITICS: POLICY MAKING AT THE LOCAL LEVEL: A SURVEY OF THE PERIODICAL LITERATURE SINCE 1950. East Lansing: Michigan State University, 1962. xii, 150 p.

Pulley, Raymond H. OLD VIRGINIA RESTORED: AN INTERPRETATION OF THE PROGRESSIVE IMPULSE, 1870-1930. Charlottesville: University Press of Virginia, 1968. x, 207 p. Illus.

Riker, Dorothy L., and Thornbrough, Gayle, comps. INDIANA ELECTION RETURNS, 1816-1851. Indianapolis: Indiana Historical Bureau, 1960. xxv, 493 p. Tables.

Rogin, Michael Paul, and Shover, John L. POLITICAL CHANGE IN CALIFORNIA: CRITICAL ELECTIONS AND SOCIAL MOVEMENTS, 1890-1966. Westport, Conn.: Greenwood Press, 1970. xx, 231 p.

Although the study is limited to California, it challenges traditional interpretations of recent American politics.

Sarasohn, Stephen B., and Sarasohn, Vera H. POLITICAL PARTY PATTERNS IN MICHIGAN. Detroit: Wayne State University Press, 1957. x, 76 p. Appendixes.

Schlesinger, Joseph A. HOW THEY BECAME GOVERNOR: COMPARATIVE STATE POLITICS, 1870-1950. East Lansing: Governmental Research Bureau, Michigan State University, 1957. 103 p. Tables.

Sindler, Allan P. HUEY LONG'S LOUISIANA: STATE POLITICS, 1920-1952. Baltimore: Johns Hopkins Press, 1956. xv, 316 p. Tables.

Sorauf, Francis J. PARTY AND REPRESENTATION, LEGISLATIVE POLITICS IN PENNSYLVANIA. New York: Atherton Press, 1963. 173 p.

Steinberg, Alfred. THE BOSSES. New York: New American Library, 1972. 378 p. Pap.

A very readable account of a few of the most successful political bosses in the first half of the twentieth century: Frank Hague, James Curley, Ed Crump, Huey Long, Gene Talmadge, and Tom Pendergast.

Straetz, Ralph A. PR POLITICS IN CINCINNATI: THIRTY-TWO YEARS OF CITY GOVERNMENT THROUGH PROPORTIONAL REPRESENTATION. New York: New York University Press, 1958. 312 p.

Tarr, Joel Arthur. A STUDY IN BOSS POLITICS: WILLIAM LORIMER OF CHICAGO. Urbana: University of Illinois Press, 1971. xi, 376 p. Appendixes.

An important political leader in Chicago early in the twentieth century. Explores the importance of the ethnic coalition in big-city politics.

Throne, Mildred. CYRUS CLAY CARPENTER AND IOWA POLITICS, 1854-1898. Iowa City: State Historical Society of Iowa, 1974. xi, 302 p.

Townsend, Walter A. ILLINOIS DEMOCRACY: A HISTORY OF THE PARTY AND ITS REPRESENTATIVE MEMBERS--PAST AND PRESENT. 4 vols. Springfield, Ill.: Democratic Historical Association, 1935. Illus.

Even though this study lauds the party, it contains information not available elsewhere.

Zink, Harold. CITY BOSSES IN THE UNITED STATES: A STUDY OF TWENTY MUNICIPAL BOSSES. Durham, N.C.: Duke University Press, 1930. Reprint. New York: AMS Press, 1968. xi, 371 p.

A classic study of big-city bosses of the late nineteenth and early twentieth centuries.

Section 12. SPECIALIZED WORKS

Bickel, Alexander M. THE LEAST DANGEROUS BRANCH: THE SUPREME
COURT AT THE BAR OF POLITICS. Indianapolis: Bobbs-Merrill Co., 1962.
viii, 303 p.

> Bickel analyzes the role of the Court and its limits in American
> politics. He believes, contrary to what many Americans believe,
> the Supreme Court cannot and should not attempt to solve a great
> many of our political problems.

Chafe, William H. THE AMERICAN WOMAN: HER CHANGING SOCIAL,
ECONOMIC, AND POLITICAL ROLE, 1920-1970. New York: Oxford University Press, 1972. xiii, 351 p. Pap.

Chamberlin, Hope. A MINORITY OF MEMBERS: WOMEN IN THE U.S.
CONGRESS. New York: New American Library, 1974. xiii, 391 p. Appendix. Pap.

> Brief biographical accounts of the women who have served in the
> U.S. Congress since 1917.

Clark, Norman H. DELIVER US FROM EVIL: AN INTERPRETATION OF
AMERICAN PROHIBITION. New York: W. W. Norton and Co., 1976. 246 p.
Pap.

> This analysis of the Prohibition movement also contains a great
> deal of information on prohibition politics.

Fowler, Dorothy G. CABINET POLITICIAN: THE POSTMASTERS GENERAL,
1829-1909. New York: Columbia University Press, 1943. Reprint. New
York: AMS Press, 1967. x, 344 p. Appendix.

Goodman, Walter. ALL HONORABLE MEN: CORRUPTION AND COMPRO-
MISE IN AMERICAN LIFE. Boston: Little, Brown and Co., 1963. 342 p.

> Goodman focuses on the present, but he artfully develops the his-
> torical setting of his subject.

Graham, George A. MORALITY IN AMERICAN POLITICS. New York: Random House, 1952. 337 p.

> An examination of attitudes of morality in the profession of poli-
> tics.

Gusfield, Joseph R. SYMBOLIC CRUSADE: STATUS POLITICS AND THE
TEMPERANCE MOVEMENT. Urbana: University of Illinois Press, 1966. viii,
198 p. Pap.

Lamson, Peggy. FEW ARE CHOSEN: AMERICAN WOMEN IN POLITICAL LIFE TODAY. Boston: Houghton, Mifflin and Co., 1968. xxxii, 240 p.

Penick, James L., Jr., et al., eds. POLITICS OF AMERICAN SCIENCE. Rev. ed. Cambridge: MIT Press, 1972. 453 p.

Sorauf, Francis J. THE WALL OF SEPARATION: THE CONSTITUTIONAL POLITICS OF CHURCH AND STATE. Princeton, N.J.: Princeton University Press, 1976. xiii, 394 p.

Stanton, Elizabeth C., et al. HISTORY OF WOMAN SUFFRAGE. 6 vols. 1922. Reprint. New York: Arno Press, 1969. Illus.

   A classic study of the suffrage movement by one of the early
   leaders of the movement.

Stedman, Murray S., Jr. RELIGION AND POLITICS IN AMERICA. New York: Harcourt, Brace and World, 1964. vi, 168 p. Pap.

Vale, Vivian. LABOUR IN AMERICAN POLITICS. New York: Barnes and Noble, 1971. 172 p.

   A clear, precise survey of the subject.

Wiesner, Jerome B. WHERE SCIENCE AND POLITICS MEET. New York: McGraw-Hill Book Co., 1965. viii, 302 p.

Wilson, John F., ed. CHURCH AND STATE IN AMERICAN HISTORY. Boston: D. C. Heath and Co., 1965. xxiii, 227 p.

AUTHOR INDEX

This index is alphabetized letter by letter. Numbers refer to page numbers. In addition to authors, this index includes all editors and compilers cited in the text.

A

Abbot, William W. 3
Abbott, Richard H. 42
Abbott, Wilbur C. 11
Abels, Jules 107, 141
Abernethy, Thomas P. 23, 28
Abrams, Richard M. 81
Acheson, Dean 107
Adamany, David 154
Adams, James T. 3, 129
Adams, R.G. 11
Adams, Samuel Hopkins 98
Adams, William H. 39
Agar, Herbert 133
Albright, Spencer D. 141
Alden, John R. 8
Aldridge, Alfred O. 19
Alexander, Charles C. 107
Alexander, Herbert E. 154
Alexander, Thomas B. 35, 51, 54
Allan, Herbert S. 19
Allensworth, D. Trudeau 157
Allswang, John M. 96
Alsop, Stewart J.O. 121
Altshuler, Alan A. 107
Ames, William E. 35
Ammerman, David 11
Ammon, Harry 42
Anderson, William 98

Andrews, Charles M. 1
Anson, Robert S. 126
Aptheker, Herbert 15
Argersinger, Peter 71
Ashby, Leroy 98
Atkins, Chester G. 141
Auerbach, M. Morton 147

B

Bagby, Wesley M. 89
Bailey, Thomas A. 84, 137
Bailyn, Bernard 1, 11, 19
Bain, Richard 141
Bakeless, John E. 15
Baker, Gordon E. 121
Baker, Jean H. 55
Baker, Ray Stannard 84, 87
Baldwin, Leland D. 28
Baldwin, Sidney 89
Bancroft, Frederic 56
Banfield, Edward C. 125
Banner, James M., Jr. 28
Barck, Oscar T. 1
Baringer, William 57
Barnard, Ellsworth 117
Barnard, Harry 71, 98
Barnard, William D. 114-15
Barnes, Gilbert Hobbs 38
Barnes, Joseph 117

Author Index

C

Calhoon, Robert M. 16
Calkins, Fay 109
Callcott, Margaret L. 150
Callow, Alexander B., Jr. 70
Campbell, Angus 109
Campbell, Christiana M. 90
Cantril, Hadley 142
Capers, Gerald M. 43
Caridi, Ronald J. 109
Carman, Harry J. 57
Carmichael, Stokely 150
Caro, Robert A. 117
Carr, Lois G. 4
Carroll, E. Malcom 35
Carruth, Gorton 129
Carter, Paul A. 90
Cary, John 19
Casdorph, Paul 155
Cate, Wirt Armistead 57
Catton, Bruce 49
Chafe, William H. 161
Chalmers, David M. 52
Chamberlin, Hope 161
Chambers, William N. 23, 43, 133, 137
Clark, Norman H. 161
Charles, Joseph 28, 148
Chase, James S. 23
Chessman, G. Wallace 85
Chester, Lewis 124
Childs, Richard S. 155
Chitwood, Oliver P. 43
Chrislock, Carl H. 81
Church, Charles A. 155
Chute, Marchette 134
Clancy, Herbert J. 63
Clanton, O. Gene 67
Cleghorn, Reese 152
Clinch, Thomas A. 67
Cochran, Bert 117
Cochran, Thomas C. 25
Coit, Margaret L. 44
Cole, Arthur C. 40
Coleman, Charles H. 52
Coleman, John M. 19
Coleman, Kenneth 16
Coles, Harry L. 29
Coletta, Paolo E. 85

Conner, Paul W. 20
Connors, Richard J. 99
Conrad, David E. 90
Cooper, William J., Jr. 68
Cornwell, Elmer E., Jr. 145
Coser, Lewis 139
Costikyan, Edward N. 155
Cotner, Robert C. 71
Cotter, Cornelius P. 121
Coulter, Ellis Merton 51, 52
Cox, James M. 99
Cox, John H. 52
Cox, La Wanda 52
Crane, Verner W. 20
Craven, Avery O. 49, 52
Craven, Thomas 153
Craven, Wesley F. 1, 4
Crawford, Kenneth G. 154
Crenshaw, Ollinger 49
Croly, Herbert D. 71
Crooks, James B. 83
Crouch, Milton 129
Cummings, Milton C., Jr. 124, 145
Cunliffe, Marcus 23-24
Cunningham, Everett W. 126
Cunningham, Noble E., Jr. 29
Current, Richard N. 44, 57, 71
Curry, Richard O. 49, 53
Curtis, James C. 44

D

Dalfiume, Richard M. 148
Dalzell, Robert F., Jr. 44
Dangerfield, George 20, 36
Daniell, Jere R. 12
Darilek, Richard E. 109
Darling, Arthur B. 24
Dauer, Manning J. 29
Davenport, Walter 71
David, Paul T. 124, 134, 142
Davidson, Chandler 125
Davies, J. Clarence III 121
Davis, James W. 145
Davis, Kenneth S. 99, 118
Davison, Kenneth E. 72
Dearing, Mary R. 63
Degler, Carl N. 138
Dell, Christopher 49
DeMond, Robert O. 16

Author Index

DePauw, Linda G. 26
Derthick, Martha A. 115
De Santis, Vincent P. 63
Destler, Chester M. 32, 63
De Vries, Walter 122
Diamond, Robert A. 130
Dickerson, Oliver M. 12
Diggins, John P. 138
Dilla, Harriette M. 68
Dillon, Dorothy R. 8
Dillon, Merton L. 38
Dinneen, Joseph F. 99
Divine, Robert A. 109
Dobson, John M. 63
Dodd, William E. 87
Donahoe, Bernard F. 90
Donald, David H. 53, 57-58
Donnelly, Thomas C. 94
Donoughue, Vernard 12
Donovan, Herbert D. A. 40
Donovan, John C. 122
Dorsett, Lyle W. 90
Dougherty, James J. 130
Douglas, Paul H. 109, 118
Douglass, Elisha P. 16
Downes, Randolph C. 99
Draper, Theodore 138
Dubay, Robert W. 44
Dumond, Dwight L. 38, 50
Dunn, Mary Maples 8
Dunn, Richard S. 8
Durden, Robert F. 67
Dutton, Frederick G. 122

E

Eaton, Clement 44, 51
Eaton, Herbert 142
Edmonds, Helen G. 68
Edwin, Ed 151
Egbert, Donald D. 138
Egerton, Hugh E. 12
Eisenstein, Louis 115
Ekirch, Arthur A., Jr. 134, 148
Ellis, Elmer 72
Ely, James W., Jr. 115
Epstein, Benjamin R. 110
Epstein, Leon D. 115
Ernst, Joseph A. 12
Ernst, Robert 32

Eulau, Heinz 109
Evans, Frank B. 68-69
Evans, Rowland 127
Evitts, William J. 40
Ewing, Cortez A.M. 91, 145

F

Farley, James A. 91, 99
Farrand, Max 26
Faulkner, Harold U. 64
Fausold, Martin L. 91
Fehrenbacher, Don E. 39
Fenton, John H. 110, 155
Ferguson, Elmer J. 17
Ferguson, Paul 134
Ferguson, Russell J. 40
Ferguson, Walter K. 156
Fesler, James W. 156
Filler, Louis 38
Fine, Nathan 139
Fischer, David H. 29
Fite, Gilbert C. 77, 91
Fitzpatrick, Daniel R. 153
Fladeland, Betty L. 58
Fleischman, Harry 139
Flick, Alexander C. 72
Flint, Winston A. 81
Flynn, Edward J. 100
Flynt, Wayne 81
Foner, Eric 38
Foner, Philip S. 44
Formisano, Ronald P. 40
Forster, Arnold 110
Foster, James C. 110
Foster, William Z. 139
Fowler, Dorothy G. 161
Frady, Marshall 127
Franklin, Jimmie L. 156
Franklin, John Hope 40, 53, 150
Free, Lloyd A. 142
Freeman, Douglas Southall 20
Freidel, Frank B. 91, 100, 130
Fuess, Claude Moore 44, 72, 100

G

Gallup, George H. 142
Gammon, Samuel R., Jr. 36
Gammons, Ann 130

Author Index

Hofstadter, Richard 24, 134, 149
Hohnes, Jack E. 156
Holcombe, Arthur N. 149
Holli, Melvin G. 70
Hollingsworth, J. Rogers 64
Holmes, William F. 86
Holt, Edgar Allan 41
Holt, James 77
Holt, Michael F. 41
Holtzman, Abraham 92
Hoogenboom, Ari A. 64
Hooker, Helene M. 79
Hooker, Richard J. 13
Hoover, Herbert C. 101
Hopkins, Joseph G.E. 131
Howard, J. Woodford, Jr. 101
Howard, Perry H. 156
Howe, George F. 73
Howe, Irving 139
Howe, John R., Jr. 20
Hoyt, Edwin P. 127
Hubbard, Preston J. 92
Huckshorn, Robert J. 122
Hughes, Emmet J. 111
Hugins, Walter E. 41
Humphrey, Hubert H. 92
Hunt, Harry Draper 58
Huthmacher, J. Joseph 96, 101
Hutson, James H. 5
Hyman, Harold M. 60

I

Ickes, Harold L. 101
Illick, Joseph E. 8
Isaac, Paul E. 156
Isely, Jeter A. 45
Israel, Fred L. 147

J

Jackson, Kenneth T. 92
Jacob, Herbert 156
James, Dorothy B. 145
James, Marquis 45
Jellison, Charles A. 58
Jensen, Merrill 13, 26
Jensen, Richard 64
Jessup, Philip C. 86
Jewell, Malcolm E. 126

Johannsen, Robert W. 45
Johnson, Donald B. 111, 131
Johnson, Olive M. 78
Johnson, Roger T. 101
Johnson, Walter 146
Jonas, Manfred 92
Jones, Charles O. 137
Jones, Robert H. 50
Jones, Stanley L. 64
Jordan, David W. 4, 73
Josephson, Matthew 65, 78
Joyner, Conrad 142

K

Kammen, Michael 2, 13
Kane, Harnett T. 96
Kaplan, Milton 153
Kass, Alvin 24
Katz, Irving 73
Katz, Stanley N. 5
Kaufman, Arnold S. 149
Kaufman, Herbert 156
Keller, Morton 101, 153
Kelley, Stanley, Jr. 142
Kent, Frank R. 92, 137, 142
Kerber, Linda K. 29
Kessel, John H. 124
Ketcham, Ralph 33
Key, V.O., Jr. 92, 131, 134, 157
Kipnis, Ira 78
Kirby, Jack T. 82
Kirk, Russell 33
Kirwan, Albert D. 58, 157
Klein, Philip S. 41, 46
Klement, Frank L. 50, 58
Kleppner, Paul 65
Klingman, Peter D. 151
Knapp, Charles M. 55
Knoles, George H. 65
Knollenberg, Bernhard 8, 13
Koch, Adrienne 33
Koenig, Louis W. 86
Kogan, Herman 84, 105
Kolko, Gabriel 78
Kousser, J. Morgan 65
Kuhn, Henry 78
Kurtz, Stephen G. 30
Kutler, Stanley I. 53

Author Index

Author Index

S

Safire, William 132
Sage, Leland L. 75
Sageser, A. Bower 82
Saloutos, Theodore 140
Sarasohn, Stephen B. 159
Sarasohn, Vera H. 159
Sawyer, Charles 119
Sayre, Wallace S. 143
Scammon, Richard 144
Schachner, Nathan 34
Schaffer, Alan 119
Schaflander, Gerald M. 123
Schapsmeier, Edward L. 119
Schapsmeier, Frederick H. 119
Schlesinger, Arthur Meier 15
Schlesinger, Arthur M., Jr. 6, 37,
   104, 128, 147
Schlesinger, Joseph A. 160
Schmidt, Karl M. 114
Schriftgiesser, Karl 87, 95, 155
Schwartzman, Edward 144
Schwarz, Jordan A. 95
Scott, Roy V. 68
Sellers, Charles G., Jr. 47
Selznick, Philip 95
Sewell, Richard H. 39
Shannon, David A. 140
Shannon, Jasper B. 155
Shapiro, Martin M. 136
Sharkansky, Ira 126
Sharp, James Roger 37
Shattuck, Francis M. 114
Shenton, James P. 47
Sherman, Richard B. 152
Sherrill, Robert 126
Sherwood, Foster H. 36
Sherwood, Robert E. 119
Shover, John L. 95, 159
Sievers, Harry J. 75
Silver, James W. 123
Simkins, Francis B. 66, 75
Simms, Henry H. 39, 42, 47
Simon, Rita J. 95
Sinclair, Andrew 104
Sindler, Allan P. 160
Sirmans, M. Eugene 6
Smelser, Marshall 31
Smith, Charles P. 56

Smith, Dwight L. 132
Smith, Edward C. 132
Smith, Elbert B. 47
Smith, Frank E. 80, 152
Smith, James M. 31
Smith, Page 34
Smith, Samuel D. 70
Smith, Theodore Clarke 39, 75
Smith, William E. 48
Smith, William R. 136
Sobel, Robert 132
Sorauf, Francis J. 136, 160, 162
Sorenson, Theodore C. 128
Sorin, Gerald 39
Sosin, Jack M. 6, 15
Southern, David W. 80
Spanier, John W. 114
Spaulding, Ernest 27
Spear, Allan H. 83
Spencer, Ivor D. 75
Spencer, Robert C. 122
Sperber, Hans 133
Sproat, John G. 66
Stampp, Kenneth M. 50-51, 54,
   56
Stanton, Elizabeth C. 162
Stave, Bruce M. 97
Stedman, Murray S., Jr. 140, 162
Stedman, Susan M. 140
Steele, Robert V. [Thomas, Lately]
   60
Steffens, Joseph Lincoln 80, 87
Steinberg, Alfred 160
Steiner, Gilbert Y. 116
Steponkus, William A. 144
Stevens, Harry R. 42
Stewart, James B. 48
Stimpson, George W. 136
Stimson, Henry L. 104
Stoddard, Henry L. 144
Stokes, Carl B. 128
Stone, Chuck 152
Stone, Irving 147
Stone, Ralph 80
Straetz, Ralph A. 160
Strode, Hudson 60
Strong, Donald S. 152
Sundquist, James L. 136
Sydnor, Charles S. 6, 42

Author Index

Wilson, John F. 162
Wilson, Woodrow 87
Wiltse, Charles M. 25, 48, 150
Winslow, Ola E. 10
Wolfskill, George 96
Wood, Robert C. 114
Woodburn, James A. 137
Wooddy, Carroll H. 98
Woodford, Frank B. 48
Woodward, Bob 126-27
Woodward, Comer Vann 54, 66, 70, 76
Wooster, Ralph A. 42, 51
Wright, Esmond 18
Wright, James E. 68
Wright, John S. 51
Wright, William C. 56
Wynes, Charles E. 69

Y

Yarnell, Allen 114
Young, Alfred F. 18, 141
Young, Richard P. 153
Young, Roland A. 114

Z

Zahniser, Marvin R. 34
Zeichner, Oscar 15
Zemsky, Robert 3
Zink, Harold 160
Zinn, Howard 105
Zornow, William F. 51
Zucker, Norman L. 105
Zurcher, Arnold J. 132

TITLE INDEX

This index is alphabetized letter by letter. Numbers refer to page numbers. All titles of books cited in the text are listed. In some instances, lengthy titles have been shortened.

A

Aaron Burr 34
Aaron Burr Conspiracy, The 30
Abolitionists, The 38
Abraham Lincoln 60
Adam Clayton Powell and the Politics of Race 151
Adams Federalists, The 29
Adlai Stevenson 117
Adlai Stevenson of Illinois 118
After Slavery 56
Agents and Merchants 15
Age of Hate, The 59
Age of Jackson, The 37
Age of Reform 134
Age of Roosevelt, The 104
Agony of the American Left, The 122
Agrarian Crusade, The 67
Agrarian Movement in Illinois, 1880-1896, The 68
Agricultural Discontent in the Middle West, 1900-1939 140
Albert Gallatin 34
Albert J. Beveridge 85
Alexander Hamilton 34
Alexander Hamilton: Youth to Maturity 20
Alexander Hamilton in the American

Tradition 32
Alexander H. Stephens 61
Alfalfa Bill Murray 99
All About Politics 144
All Honorable Men 161
All the President's Men 126
Al Smith and His America 100
Amateur Democrats 117
Ambiguous Legacy 141
America at the Polls 144
America, History and Life 129
America in Midpassage 89
American Ballot, The 141
American Catholics and Social Reform 94
American Communist Party, a Critical History, 1919-1957, The 139
American Crisis, An 52
American Demagogues 135
American Democratic Tradition, The 134
American Dilemma, An 90
American Dissent, The 111
American Left in the Twentieth Century, The 138
American Loyalist 20
American Melodrama, An 124
American Negro Revolution, The 123
American Party Drama, The 134

Title Index

Title Index

Title Index

Title Index

Title Index

R

Title Index

SUBJECT INDEX

This index is alphabetized letter by letter. Underlined page numbers refer to main areas within the subject.

Subject Index

Subject Index

Indiana
  Civil War and Reconstruction
    (1860-1876) 56
  Democratic Party in 56
  early national period (1815-1860) 45
  election returns for 159
  Republican Party of the late nineteenth century 75
Indianapolis, Ku Klux Klan in (1915-1930) 92
Industrialization, politics and 65
Industrial Workers of the World (IWW) 86
Ingersoll, Jared 20
Iowa 160
  early national period (1815-1860) 41
  Republican Party of the late nineteenth century 75
  third parties in 139
  voting patterns in (1920-1940) 91
Isolationism 92, 104. See also Expansionism

J

Jackson, Andrew (Jacksonian democracy) 35, 37, 45, 46, 48
  working class and 41
Jay, John 33
Jefferson, Thomas (Jeffersonian democracy) 25, 28, 29, 30, 31, 32, 33, 34, 150
Jersey City, N.J., political machine of (1920-1940) 99
Johnson, Andrew 42, 52, 53, 54, 58, 59, 60
Johnson, Lyndon Baines 122, 127, 128, 136
Jones, J. Raymond 152
Judicial branch. See Courts; U.S. Supreme Court
Justice. See Social justice
Justices of the peace. See Magistrate

K

Kansas 158
  Lecompton Constitution (1857-1858) 47

political parties of (1920-1940) 102
Populism in 67, 71
progressive era (1900-1920) 82, 87
  Republican Party in 82
Kansas City, Mo., machine politics in (1920-1940) 90
Kefauver, Estes 113, 118
Kennedy, John F. 118, 122, 123, 127, 128, 136
Kennedy, Robert 127
Kentucky 156, 158
  federal period (1783-1815) 25
  present day politics of 126
Key, V.O. 65
King, Martin Luther 128
King, Rufus 32
Know-Nothing Party. See American Party
Knoxville, Ku Klux Klan in (1915-1930) 92
Korean War 109, 114
Ku Klux Klan 52, 54, 92, 95. See also individual cities

L

Labor and laboring classes 162
  during the McCarthy years 113
  political parties of 139, 140
LaFollette, Robert Marion 71, 77, 80, 82, 85, 86, 93, 135
LaFollette, Robert Marion, Jr. 101
La Guardia, Fiorello 102, 103, 105
Lamar, Lucius Q.C. 57
Landon, Alfred M. 102
Lane, Joe 45
Leadership
  George III's lack of 13
  in the pre-Civil War south 40
League of Nations 80
Lecompton Constitution 47
Lee family (Virginia) 134
Legislatures. See Assemblies, colonial; Councils, colonial; U.S. Congress
Lehman, Herbert H. 103
Leisler's rebellion (1688) 9
Lemke, William 98
Liberalism 148, 149

Subject Index

U.S. Farm Security Administration 89
U.S. National Recovery Administration 105
U.S. Supreme Court 136
  Jackson's appointments to 36
  reapportionment (1962) and 121
  role of in politics 161
  Warren Court (1960s) 121
  World War II years 101
U.S. Tennessee Valley Authority 92, 95, 102, 158
Upper classes
  interests of in the Constitution 25
  in the Revolutionary War 14
Urban politics 157, 160
  1893–1896 65
  1950–1952 113
  progressive era (1900–1920) 80, 83–84, 87
  See also Local politics; names of cities
Utah 159

V

Vallandigham, Clement L. 58
Van Buren, Martin 44, 46–47
Vance, Zeb 48
Vandenberg, Arthur H. 104
Vann, Robert L. 90
Vardaman, James Kimble 86
Vermont
  post-World War II 115
  progressive era (1900–1920) 81
Vice-Admiralty Courts 15
Vietnamese conflict 127
  cartoons of 154
Virginia 157, 158, 159
  blacks in 150
  colonial period (1607–1763) 6–7, 9
    county government in 6
    democracy in 4
    House of Burgesses in 5, 7
  early national period (1815–1860)
    states' rights in 47
    Whigs in 42
  gilded age (1877–1900) 69
  progressive era (1900–1920) 82
  recent politics of 115, 116

Revolutionary War era (1763–1783) 20, 33
  See also Bacon's Rebellion (1676)
Voting patterns and behavior 122, 130
  1888–1896 64
  golden decade and the New Deal (1920–1940) 91
  from World War II through Eisenhower (1940–1960) 109, 112
  of blacks 116
  of Catholics 110
  in the 1948 presidential election 108

W

Wade, Benjamin Franklin 60
Wagner, Robert F. 101
Walker, Robert John 47
Wallace, George 126, 127
Wallace, Henry A. 112, 114, 119
Walsh, Thomas J. 103
War of 1812 29
  causes of 31
Warren, Joseph 19
War with Mexico. See Mexican War (1845–1848)
Washington 159
Washington, D.C., recent politics of 115
Washington, George 9, 20, 28, 30
Watergate Affair 124, 126–27, 128
Watson, Tom 76
Wealth, political power and competition for 5
Webster, Daniel 43, 44, 46
Weed, Thurlow 48
Weld, Theodore 38
Wells, Josiah 151
West Virginia 156, 158
  Civil War and Reconstruction (1860–1876) 49
Whig Party 43, 57, 61
  in Louisiana 39–40, 59
  loyalty to the Crown by 16
  in Maine 58
  in Missouri 41
  in New York 46
  in North Carolina 48
  in Ohio 48

212